UNEXPLORED PARIS

Photographs of cover *(top to bottom, left to right)* : Loo's House, 8th; Square Jean-Paul-II, 4th; Villa de l'Adour, 19th; Clown Bar, 11th; Hameau Boileau, 16th; Cité Daviel, 13th; caryatid, 3th; Turncock's house, 14th; ***flap 1***: Pitié-Salpêtrière Hospital, 13th; Castel Béranger, 16th; ***flap 2***: Square de Montsouris, 14th; 39, Rue Réaumur, 3th; ***Outside back cover:*** telescoping street lights on Pont du Carrousel, 1st; staircase, 48, Rue de Valois, 1st; Buttes-Chaumont Park, 19th.

UNEXPLORED
PARIS

RODOLPHE TROUILLEUX

PHOTOGRAPHS BY
JACQUES LEBAR

TRANSLATED BY
PATRICIA ABBOU and DAVID W. COX

PARIGRAMME

With special thanks to:

Daniel Catan,

Alexandre Gady,

Pierre-Émile Renard,

Danièle Rousseau-Aicardi,

Pierre Cavillon,

Pierre Housieaux, of the Association for the Preservation and Enhancement of Historical Paris,

Paul Bonno, Director, the Wine Museum,

Georges-Olivier Châteaureynaud, General Secretary of the Literary Society and Cristina Campodonico, Public Relations Officer,

Mr. Roland-Gosselin, chairman of the Charity Bazaar Memorial,

We also extend our thanks to: The Paris-Nature Section of the City of Paris Parks, Gardens and Green Space Department,

the staff at Montmartre Museum,

and to all those who gave us friendly advice and support during these long walks.

Add three letters to Paris...
and it's Paradise

JULES RENARD

SERENDIPITY IN THE STREETS OF PARIS

Unexplored Paris... Secretive Paris... France's capital still has many surprises in store for visitors already familiar with the more renowned historical landmarks of the city. Yes, you can still find numerous "villages" locked within the city limits, verdant dead-end streets that seemingly ignore the surrounding urban environment. These are the discreet and fragile testimonies of both modern and historic Paris. These places are charming, moving, and fascinating, and yet, far from familiar to many residents of Paris. City life is not conducive to making such new discoveries. City dwellers are rarely strollers because strolling is time consuming. It takes time to learn suddenly to stop, to look up, or to dare to get lost. Strolling is practically a profession, requiring skill and knowing the tricks of the trade.

The rewards, however, are manifold. Surprises, rare finds, and odd treasures can only be chanced upon by those on the lookout for them. A fleeting glimpse of an unusual building, a secluded garden, a picturesque view, through a half-open door or down a side street, is usually enough to whet the appetite! Guidebooks often highlight certain sites and note "worth the travel time".

For Paris, however, such advice is practically superfluous, as these lesser-known sites are almost all in close proximity to better-known places. Taking time out in this case is more a question of deciding whether to make a short detour, or turn down one street in preference over another for the sake of exploring. Those who have taken the extra time for the simple pleasures of making a new discovery will understand.

The delight taken in building up a personal museum collection of historic relics depends on two factors: an open mind and a passion for history in all its forms. Strollers, whose curiosity is aroused and who allow themselves to be guided by their whims and temperament, will collect their finds like bees gathering nectar. They will come upon secluded culs-de-sac, cloisters, manor houses, artists' ateliers, inscriptions, greenery, old shop signs, all with one thing in common: the incalculable power to enchant lovers of Paris wishing to become more intimately acquainted with the city's history. Whether they notice the melody in underground halts, or soak up the open-air concerts, amateurs of this urban music always find plenty to feed their passion for Paris.

Our aim has been to compile a book supplying information on sites rarely mentioned in tourist guides, and yet easily accessible. We have had to leave out many charming spots, which are under lock and key to keep out the general public. Our list is neither exhaustive nor final. Quite the contrary! The content of our list requires updates and changes owing to the constantly changing face of Paris, and, unfortunately, fine specimens are frequently "struck" off the list. Nevertheless, we are all free to contribute our own precious discoveries to this catalogue of fragile relics.

Straying from the beaten track and looking at Paris from another angle, as one might scrutinize the reverse side of a garment to see how it is made, is a delightful way of becoming even better acquainted with the city, but on certain conditions. "Fragile, handle with care!" is the password. The appeal of these sites stems mainly from the fact that they are readily accessible and "unmapped". This means, of course, that each one of us is, to a certain extent, responsible for their upkeep, and care must be taken not to upset the already precarious equilibrium of the capital's "endangered species" – precious, often unprotected, relics of the city's past.

An attentive visitor is the contrary of a predator. Visitors interested in history do not set out to despoil the city landscape, rather, they absorb the sights, smells and sounds, in order to bear witness to it, and, if necessary, protect it. For this, they will be richly rewarded, as they will have the infinite joy of taking home the nectar they have gathered down previously unexplored alleys and courtyards of Paris, and transforming it into honey by sharing it with their families and friends.

Absolutely "ox-some!"

STEELY DETERMINATION

TELESCOPING STREET LIGHTS

PONT DU CARROUSEL / 1st

METRO: PALAIS-ROYAL-MUSÉE-DU-LOUVRE

The first Pont du Carrousel was an iron and wood bridge built in 1833 by Antoine-Rémy Polonceau. Although a marvel of engineering, it was not high enough to accommodate barges.
It was replaced by a new, more classic, stone bridge in 1936. Four statues by Louis Petitot from the old bridge were added, representing the Seine, the City of Paris, Abundance, and Industry.
For the lighting, the Corps of Bridges and Roads called upon Raymond Subes, a talented ironworker who actively contributed to the revival of the subtle art of ironworking. The proximity of the Louvre complicated the task of designing street lights, as the design could be neither too modern, nor exceed the 13-meter height of the palace's roofline. Furthermore, the required light coverage of the lamps was 20 meters so as to avoid inconveniencing automobilists with glare and to light up the whole of the bridge and the embankments below. Subes' solution, telescopic street lights, was novel, to say the least.
Construction was halted when the war broke out in 1939. Subes resumed construction a year later, however. As all the copper stocks had been reported to the occupying authorities, Subes continued working in secret, and, at great risk, hid his finished street lamps in the bridge's underground sections. There, the twenty tons of copper and forty tons of steel were flooded more than once. When the war was over, he restored them and set them up on the bridge.
The four steel street lights still light up the bridge, housed in their bronze casings, ever ready to offer passersby a creaking light and sound show.

NO FLEUR-DE-LIS FOR THE REPUBLIC

VESTIGES OF THE FLEUR-DE-LIS

COMÉDIE-FRANÇAISE, 2 BIS PLACE ANDRÉ-MALRAUX / 1st

METRO: PALAIS-ROYAL-MUSÉE-DU-LOUVRE

The fleurs-de-lis over the colonnade at the Comédie-Française, though now only a faint outline remains, were probably chipped away in the French Revolution as they were visible symbols of the monarchy. The Duke of Chartres, Louis-Philippe d'Orléans, the owner of the Palais-Royal, commissioned architect Victor Louis to erect a theater to house the prince's opera troupe. The Théâtre des Variétés Amusantes was inaugurated on May 15, 1790. The name was later changed to Théâtre de la Liberté et de l'Égalité, then to Théâtre de la République. The great actor François-Joseph Talma, surrounded by a troupe that espoused new ideas, gave shows in the so-called Roman style, then quite fashionable. The hall fell into neglect for numerous years before being restored to house the Société des Comédiens-Français, which moved in on May 30, 1799, or on the 11th Prairial of the year VII, according to the Revolutionary calendar.

Since then, the neighborhood has changed greatly. When it was built, there was no Avenue de l'Opéra and no Place André-Malraux. This colonnade only had eleven bays, as opposed to its present fifteen, and it only overlooked Rue de Richelieu.

On the same side of this street, on the right, the demolished buildings that ringed the courtyard of the sheds vacated ample space for the creation of today's Place Colette. Enlargement of the theater began in 1860 and the Victor Louis's façade was extended at a right angle. Fire ravaged the theatre on March 8, 1900. A careful restoration was carried out, leaving us with mere shadows of the fleurs-de-lis as a reminder of the prince who first commissioned the theater.

THE FORMER BŒUF À LA MODE RESTAURANT

8 RUE DE VALOIS / 1st
METRO: PALAIS-ROYAL-MUSÉE-DU-LOUVRE

While the *Grand Véfour* is the most famous old restaurant in the Palais-Royal area, the Bœuf à la Mode must be the most unheard of. Patrons used to go there in droves, but today all that remains are the façade and the sign. The restaurant was first called *Méot* when it opened in 1796, and then *Le Bœuf à la mode* [the fashion-conscious ox]. It got its name both from the sign representing an ox and from a statuette in the dining area. The latter's style of dress depended on Paris fashions in vogue at the time. During the French Directory, government of the First Republic of France [1795-99], a certain Mr. Tissot dressed the ox up as a fashionable *Directoire coquette*. During the Restoration of the Bourbons [1830], it wore a dress and shawl, complete with feathered hat and pendant earrings. Good, plain cooking was served in the small dining room, and there were reception and private dining rooms on the mezzanine below. However, the restaurant went out of fashion, and ended up as a small bar. It had several owners, including the famous Prosper Montagné. It finally closed in 1936. A gallery specializing in animal art took over the premises.

The inconspicuous sign remains in place but few passers by ever notice. And yet, what could be more "ox-some" than this beast all dolled up in grandma's clothes!

TOWERING AND SPIRALING

DOUBLE SPIRAL STAIRCASE
48 RUE DE VALOIS / 1st
METRO: PALAIS-ROYAL-MUSÉE-DU-LOUVRE

This rather austere structure located at the start of Rue de Beaujolais astonished many 18th-century Parisians as its nine stories towered over the city. It was the highest building in Paris then. While this granddaddy of modern-day high-rise apartment buildings, designed by François Guireaud de Talairac in 1781, blends in fine with today's neighboring buildings, its staircase remains exceptional. Imagine two screws stacked on the same axis but each serving different landings, and you will have a rough idea of how ingenious this construction is. The passage that it crossed, now closed to the public, led to Rue Radziwill. Although this street now dead-ends, it used to be the start of Rue Neuve-des-Bons-Enfants which ran all the way to Rue Saint-Honoré. Neighboring

the Palais-Royal, Passage Radziwill, with its rather unique layout, afforded hucksters and wheelers-and-dealers ideal terrain. Dark and narrow, it lent itself perfectly to trickery and dissembling. It was thronged by the idle and the curious who gathered here to engage in veritable organized crime. Paid lookouts were posted in the stairwells and on the steps. Their job was to sound the alarm or to beat up recalcitrant victims ensnared in their clandestine gaming houses.

Once "a grand hostelry of human passions," today, the Palais-Royal is a serene garden setting where one can safely climb the remarkably restored staircase.

THE ASTROLOGER'S TOWER

COLONNE MÉDICIS
RUE DE VIARMES / 1st
METRO: CHÂTELET OR LOUVRE-RIVOLI
Open to public on Heritage Site Days

Right next to the Bourse de Commerce stands a tall column, which looks somewhat out of place in the Paris cityscape. It is one of the monuments of Paris most surrounded by mystery.
At the base, an inscription in Latin states that it is the sole relic of the manor house built in 1572 by Catherine de Médicis (Queen of France, wife of Henry II) on the site of one of Louis d'Orléans' residences. She had the 31-meter-high tower built for her astrologer, Cosimo Ruggieri, who had considerable influence over her. This "handsome, somber-looking man, who had a way with instruments, sometimes clad in trunk hose, always dressed in black", regularly climbed to the top of the tower with his patron, in order to mutter magic formulae and read the future in the stars.
A spiral staircase of 147 steps leads up to this chamber which was once entirely encased in glass skylights. All that remains is a metal skeleton, buffeted by the wind. Nobody knows what the building was used for, although the cardinal points are marked on the corners of the capital of the tower.
After Ruggieri's death in 1615, the column fell into disuse. The manor house became a shady gambling establishment where card games such as *lansquenet* were played.
In 1748, the building was demolished in order to settle the debts of its last owner, Amédée de Savoie. The column narrowly escaped demolition and, in 1750, was sold to the Paris City Council which installed a fountain – now dry – and a sundial.
In view of the upheavals that this district has gone through over time, the tower would appear to be protected by some sort of magic spell. Legend has it that on stormy nights, a tall, black silhouette appears in the metal cage at the top of the column as lightning dances across the sky.

A REMINDER OF WORLD POVERTY

SAINT-GERMAIN-L'AUXERROIS CHURCH
PLACE DU LOUVRE / 1st
METRO: LOUVRE-RIVOLI

Not many people know that, to the left of Saint-Germain-l'Auxerrois Church, there is a collection of mythical, medieval animals carved in stone. To admire them, enter the courtyard located between the city hall building and the church, behind the incongruous-looking bell-tower marking the dividing line between republic and religion, then gaze up at the gargoyles. Underneath you will see some very strange representations of animals. The most unusual of these – a multitude of rats gnawing away at a globe – can be seen under the middle gargoyle, right next to a scene of suckling animals.

The sculptor's intention was to represent the world (the globe) gradually being destroyed by poverty (the rats), perhaps to remind passersby of the harsh realities of life... On close inspection, just above the rats, you can see a rather diabolical figure of a cat watching the rodents at work. There are other "rats-on-the-globe" sculptures in France, notably on Le Mans Cathedral and the other on Saint-Siffrein-de-Carpentras Church, but with one notable difference: the rats here are gnawing their way in, whereas in Paris they are gnawing their way out.

A STAR IS BORN

COMMEMORATIVE PLAQUE AND BUST OF MOLIÈRE
96 RUE SAUVAL AND 31 RUE DU PONT-NEUF / 1st
METRO: PALAIS-ROYAL-MUSÉE-DU-LOUVRE

Until 1802, on the corner of Rue Saint-Honoré and Rue de la Croix-du-Trahoir (now Rue Sauval), there was a remarkable, carved wooden corner post that reached several stories in height. Because of it, the house became known as the *pavillon des singes* (the monkey house). These animals, a total of seven, seem to stand in the branches of an apple tree. While the younger, more agile and audacious ones reach out to grab ripe fruit, the ripest apples fall at the feet of their elders on the ground who effortlessly pick them up. It was beneath this sign of both prodigality and wisdom, that France's greatest playwright, Jean-Baptiste Poquelin (Molière for his stage name), son of tapestry-maker Jean Poquelin and Marie Cressé, was born on January 1622. A commemorative plaque

on the front of the building tells us so. As for the house at 31 Rue du Pont-Neuf with its plaque stating the house was built upon Molière's birthplace "in the year 1620 [sic]" that is another story which we owe to Alexandre Lenoir. In 1799, the curator of the Musée des Monuments Français ordered a bust of the playwright to be placed there as, at that time, the address was then believed to be great man's place of birth. Here, in his rounded niche, Molière seems equally at home as his other bust surveying the entrance to the Comédie Française.

CHARNEL HOUSES AND SMALL SHOPS

THE FORMER INNOCENTS CEMETERY
RUE DES INNOCENTS AND RUE DE LA FERRONNERIE / 1st
RER: LES HALLES

Square des Innocents was the site of the largest cemetery in Paris from the 12th and 18th centuries. When Innocents Cemetery was demolished in 1780, more than two million bodies had been buried in the communal graves! This was due to the fact that it received the dead from parishes without cemeteries, the city morgue, and the Hôtel-Dieu hospital.

The cemetery became overcrowded, and to make room for more graves, charnel houses in the form of arcades were built around it. Bones were disinterred and deposited under the roofs. This did not deter those still in the land of the living! Small shops, public letter-writers, prostitutes, and crooks all prospered under the arcades. Despite this bustling activity, the charnel houses were destroyed during the second half of the 18th century. In 1786, the bones from the cemetery were transferred to disused quarries, which later became the Denfert-Rochereau Catacombs.

Nothing remains of the charnel houses today. The present building has arcades and shops, thus continuing the pursuits of centuries ago, albeit in less macabre surroundings than those of the Ancien Régime (social and political system before the French Revolution).

The passageway through the building in Rue des Innocents leads to Rue de la Ferronnerie. An engraving amid the cobblestones indicates the site where King Henry IV's carriage stood on May 14th, 1610, the day Ravaillac, a religious fanatic, plunged his knife into the heart of the King of France (who had obtained toleration for the Huguenots with the Edict of Nantes in 1598).

SIGNS
OF OLD PARIS

RUE MONTORGUEIL
RER: LES HALLES / 1st AND 2nd
METRO: SENTIER

Between the 13th and 19th centuries, wholesale fish merchants from the ports of Normandy, delivering fish and oysters to Les Halles, went down Rue Montorgueil every day. Owing to the intense activity of the huge market nearby, this street was, and still is, very busy, with its many taverns, inns and shops.
Some of the shop signs, still on view today, bear witness to the thriving trades of the past.
At no. 9, near Saint-Eustache Church, there is the *Au Croissant* sign of the cabaret with its crescent moon pointing its tips to the sky.
At no. 38, on the other side of the street, stands the *Escargot d'Or* (Golden Snail), one of the oldest restaurants in Paris, founded in 1832. The painted ceiling in the entrance hall was taken from actress Sarah Bernhardt's manor house, and is visible from the street. A brief foray into Rue Tiquetonne on your right, after crossing Rue Étienne-Marcel, is a must in order to admire the 18th-century *À l'arbre-à-liège* (Cork Oak) sign at no. 10.
The architect's tools in the fanlight at 51 Rue Montorgueil advertise the profession of Rohault de Fleury, who designed the greenhouses in Le Jardin des Plantes in 1830. The renowned confectioner's, Stohrer, with its wall paintings under glass, is just nearby.

A PEARL OF A RESTAURANT

AU ROCHER DE CANCALE RESTAURANT
78 RUE MONTORGUEIL / 2nd
METRO: SENTIER

Located at the corner of Rue Montorgueil and Rue Greneta, this historic restaurant is hard for passersby to miss. The wooden and plaster molding on the façade and the old sign incorporated in the corner at eye-level is highly original. The carving represents an oyster- and mussel-encrusted rock.
For two centuries, Rue Montorgueil was the capital's oyster park, with record annual sales. In the mid-19th century, up to six million dozens of the shellfish were sold. In 1846, a certain Pécune took over the famous operation widely frequented by celebrities in the arts and in literature, which had closed the previous year. The first *Rocher* was located right across the street at no. 59-61. It was known for its quality oysters. The Caveau literary society met there and several scenes depicted in Balzac's *Human Comedy* took place there.

After a hiatus of many years, the famed establishment has only recently returned to its initial gastronomic vocation. The sole survivors of the grand era are the five little scenes painted directly on the plaster on the second floor depicting restaurant regulars – the dining guest, the gourmet, etc., all in amusing postures accompanied by lovely still lifes in charming, cheerful colors. Nothing remains of the woodwork that framed these delightful pieces, credited by some to the talented brush of Gavarni, a respected lithographer and a Romantic who painted demimondaines.

A PRISON TOWER FOR SAFETY

JEAN SANS PEUR TOWER
20 RUE ÉTIENNE-MARCEL / 2nd
METRO: ÉTIENNE-MARCEL
Tel: 01 40 26 20 28
www.tourjeansanspeur.com
Open 1:30 PM to 6 PM, Wednesday to Sunday (April to October), Wednesday, Saturday, and Sunday (November to Mars)

Jean sans Peur Tower is a rare example of architectural design in feudal times in Paris. In the early 15th century, Jean sans Peur, the Duke of Burgundy, inherited the Hôtel d'Artois, on the site of Philip Augustus' enclosure. He shut himself away there after he had had Louis d'Orléans (brother of Charles VI, known as Charles the Foolish, whose daughter Catherine of Valois married Henry V of England) assassinated on November 23rd, 1407, thus sparking the civil war between the Armagnac and Burgundy factions.
Fearing revenge from the Armagnac faction, he built a fortified, rectangular tower, 23 meters high, onto the house. At the top were two high-security chambers, one above the other. This closely guarded residence was protected by machicolations, still there today, and crenellations.
An empty, 10-foot-high chamber was built under the two security chambers, to prevent assault and any attempts to set fire to the floorboards. Double-locked metal gates and guards completed the defense system. The tympanum over the front door bears Jean sans Peur's coat of arms, a level crossed with a plumb line. A plane at each end of the level symbolizes the harm to be done to the bludgeon, emblem of Louis d'Orléans.

THE VIDOCQ STAIRCASE

GALERIE VIVIENNE
4 RUE DES PETITS-CHAMPS / 6 RUE VIVIENNE / 2nd
METRO: BOURSE

In 1823, on the site of three manor houses, notary public Marchoux had architect F. J. Delannoy build the arcade, which was first named after the notary, and then called Galerie Vivienne two years later. Its elegant features were one of the reasons for its instant success. Another was its proximity to Palais-Royal, a very busy district until Louis Philippe, known as the Citizen King, became established there. His "cleaning up" of the area and the arcade led to its depopulation.
At no. 13, there is staircase, with a wrought-iron balustrade, which the famous François Vidocq, former convict who became founder and head of a crime squad, used to climb. While he lived here in 1840, he set up a private police force for the protection of shopkeepers. He also defended many artists and writers, including personalities such as Victor Hugo and actress Juliette Drouet.
A friend of Alexandre Dumas, the adventurer was described by Balzac, an expert on human nature, as a "great saver of souls".

THE PHOTOGRAPHER WHO SAW RED

THE FORMER STUDIOS OF NADAR THE PHOTOGRAPHER
35 BOULEVARD DES CAPUCINES / 2nd
METRO: OPÉRA

During the Second Empire when Napoleon III ruled as emperor, many photographers such as Disderi, Bisson, Le Gray, Mayer, to name but a few, set up business along the busy Grands Boulevards where clients were legion.
Félix Tournachon, known as Nadar, was one such photographer who, already very experienced, opened his studio at 35 Boulevard des Capucines in 1860.
The building had only one story, and Nadar converted it into a veritable glass palace with the help of new metal construction work technology. His most recent photographic works were presented in the shop on the ground floor. The floor above had luxuriously-appointed reception rooms. An upper floor housed his studio, air-conditioned by means of water continuously flowing down the glass walls. Everything was painted in red – the photographer had an obsession for red – and he always wore a crimson frock coat.
Nadar was the first to install a neon sign – on the balcony and still there today – made by a craftsman called Antoine Lumière, a name of the future, as, some years later, he presented his sons' invention, a motion-picture camera, at the *Grand Café* on the other side of the boulevard.
In 1872, Nadar left Boulevard des Capucines for less ostentatious premises in Rue d'Anjou because of debts incurred by his passion for aerostation.
In 1993, promoters demolished Nadar's studios, showing total disregard for its distinguished past. However, they did spare the glass façade and the front door.

EMBELLISHMENTS FOR THE TENANTS

BAS-RELIEFS
75 RUE RÉAUMUR / 2nd
METRO: SENTIER

The only noteworthy feature of this building is the silhouette of a swan carved above the old carriage door. Its two rectangular bas-reliefs over the doorway can only be viewed by stepping into the staircase vestibule.
Crafted by sculptor Martin Van den Bogaert (also known as Desjardins), the plaster pieces may have been the originals for the bronze bas-reliefs placed on the base of the old statue of the Sun King located on Place des Victoires which represented two major events in the reign of Louis XIV, namely France's prerogative as recognized by Spain and the Treaties of Peace of Nijmegen. Although the statue was destroyed in 1792, the bas-reliefs as well as the medallions and the impressive statues of chained captives placed around the equestrian statue were conserved. Today, they are on display in the Cour Puget at the Louvre Museum.
In 1674, Martin Desjardins, the owner of the plot of land, ordered the construction of rental property on the corner of what was then called Rue Thévenot, part of which has survived on the odd side of today's Rue Réaumur and on Rue Dussoubs.
As a discerning decorator, the sculptor of these two works of art placed them over the entrance where they continue to offer tenants and passersby precious testimony of a rich and exuberant baroque period.

PLACE DU CAIRE AND ITS BIG NOSE

PASSAGE DU CAIRE
237-239 RUE SAINT-DENIS, 2 PLACE DU CAIRE / 2nd
METRO: RÉAUMUR-SÉBASTOPOL

Passage du Caire, just off Rue Saint-Denis, is the longest alley in Paris, and the result of a vast building operation carried out on land belonging to the Filles-Dieu Convent. In 1798, the company in charge called the new district, *The Cairo Fair*, as Napoleon Bonaparte, future Emperor of France, was about to embark on his Egyptian Campaign.
Unlike numerous other projects of this type, deliberate efforts were made to keep the decoration simple and the rents attractive so as to encourage businesses to move in at low cost. However, opinions on this differed greatly, as shown by Amédée de Kermel's comment in his book entitled *Le Livre des Cent et Un* (The Hundred and One Book), published in 1831: "I can see nothing of the treasures of Egypt, its perfumes, its children, the magnificence of its monuments. Cairo in this corridor! Sacrilege, sheer sacrilege!"
Egypt's splendor is more clearly evoked by the building overlooking Place du Caire, a pastiche of Egyptian and neo-gothic styles. If you look carefully, you will see a strange profile, with an enormous nose, in the cornice. It is the portrait of Bouginier, a painter who often visited the atelier run by Antoine Gros (former pupil of David, Napoleon Bonaparte's official painter), and whose extraordinary nose was often caricatured by his friends on the walls of Paris.

BENEATH THE RAMPARTS OF CHARLES V

PASSAGE SAINTE-FOY AND RUE SAINTE-FOY, RUE D'ABOUKIR, RUE DE CLÉRY / 2nd
METRO: STRASBOURG-SAINT-DENIS

In the mid-14th century, the city wall was extended to include the urban development spilling over the ramparts built by Philip Augustus, ramparts which in any case no longer offered much resistance to the new instruments of warfare. Charles V, King of France, known as Charles the Wise, had the new wall built on the right bank, in a curve from the Bastille, along the Grands Boulevards, up to Porte Saint-Denis, and, finally, back down to the Seine via Place des Victoires. The imposing fortification, 4,875 meters long, had a curtain wall 13 meters high, fronted by two moats. The bigger one, 30 meters wide and 8 meters deep, was right next to the wall, and filled with water. Before it was demolished in 1634, and its moats filled in, the wall protected a population of up to 275,000. Today, there is nothing left except a few areas of uneven ground.

The narrow Passage Sainte-Foy, starting at 236 Rue Saint-Denis (you have to imagine that this was inside the city walls at that time), is not much to look at. At the end of the passage, if you go up the steep steps bringing it level with Rue Sainte-Foy, you will have climbed up onto the rampart's covered way. In fact, Rue Sainte-Foy used to be called Rue du Rempart. Walk a few yards down Rue Sainte-Foy on the right-hand side as far as Rue Chénier, which will then take you straight to Rue d'Aboukir and Rue de Cléry, both parallel with one another. You are now outside the city wall. Rue d'Aboukir was built on the embankment of the big moat when the rampart was demolished, and Rue de Cléry follows the former path along the counterscarp, the covered way outside the enclosure. As you can see, a short stroll is all that is required in the 21st century to walk through a wall, cross a moat full of water, and jump out of the city into the "country"!

ROCOCO HOUSE NARROWLY ESCAPES HAUSSMANN'S PLANS

HÔTEL DE SAINT-CHAUMOND

226 RUE SAINT-DENIS, 131 BOULEVARD DE SÉBASTOPOL / 2nd

METRO: STRASBOURG-SAINT-DENIS

The porch at 226 Rue Saint-Denis opens into an unevenly paved courtyard, which reveals a fine, freestone façade at the far end.
This manor house (another story has been added) was built by Jacques Hardouin-Mansart in 1734 at the request of the Saint-Chaumond nuns at no. 224. They wished to put up some of their wealthier residents there, usually women involved in separation procedures.
The French Revolution proved fatal for the convent, and its chapel was closed. A certain Mr. Michelet set up his printer's shop there, and his son, Jules, later acclaimed as one of France's leading historians, was born there.
An escutcheon, flanked by two consoles supporting a splendid, wrought-iron balcony, crowns the main entrance to the manor house. A passage through the building leads to another courtyard where a second, more graceful façade, along with a work by Nicolas Pineau, portraying the delicate features of a woman's face, may be admired.
Another passage through a late 19th-century building leads from this courtyard to 131 Boulevard de Sébastopol.
As you can see, sometimes just an entrance is all that separates the winding streets of 18th-century Paris from the straight, austere boulevards designed by Haussmann (under Napoleon III he demolished older parts of Paris and replaced them with long, wide avenues).

The façade facing boulevard Sébastopol

A DANCER WITH CARRIAGE

CARYATIDS
39 RUE RÉAUMUR / 3rd
METRO: ARTS-ET-MÉTIERS

Loïe Fuller was more than a dancer, she was the essence of undulating movement floating through light. On stage, as her colorful entrechats reflected in a multitude of mirrors, her vast, gauzy veils swirled and fluttered reminiscent of petals, ocean waves, and elegant curves. She fascinated many; her admirers were numerous. Toulouse-Lautrec placed her in several stunning lithographs.
Born in Illinois in 1862 as Mary Louise Fuller, Loïe was seen by French symbolists as an incarnation of utopia. Auguste Rodin and Hector Guimard were among her friends. How could one not notice the influence of Art Nouveau in her swathes of floating chiffon and in the shimmering colors which she brought to life on stage?
Although no stunning beauty, the petite Fuller certainly had a lovely face, as evidenced in the busts supporting the balcony on the fifth floor of this building designed in 1900 by Salard. Despite obvious variations, these two pieces by Pierre Roche clearly represent the dance artist who died in Paris on January 1, 1928 and immediately slipped into oblivion.
Inside the entrance to the building is a beautiful ceramic freeze with a complex foliage pattern inspired perhaps by Fuller's creativity, a sort of final tribute to Art Nouveau and to its muse.

A WHISPERING GALLERY

CONSERVATORY OF ARTS AND CRAFTS
270-292 RUE SAINT-MARTIN / 3rd
METRO: ARTS-ET-MÉTIERS
Tel: 01 40 27 27 03
www.arts-et-metiers.net
Opening hours: Monday to Friday, 1 to 8 PM, Saturday, 9 AM to 7 PM

The Conservatory of Arts and Crafts is not renowned for being the home of one of the oldest monuments of Paris. Admittedly, the 19th-century style of the buildings in Rue Saint-Martin is deceiving; nevertheless, parts of one of the biggest and earliest abbeys of Paris can be seen here.
Around 700, a basilica was built along an ancient road, later to become Rue Saint-Martin. After the Normans pillaged one of the monasteries in the 9th century, the place appears to have been abandoned until the middle of the 11th century when another abbey was founded, and rapidly developed into a large Benedictine monastery. Still standing on the corner of Rues du Vertbois and Saint-Martin is an imposing tower, a relic of the 13th-century wall. In the 19th century, because of a threat to demolish it, Victor Hugo was prompted into saying: "Demolish the tower? No! Demolish the architect? Yes!" Two fragments of the abbey wall, parts of a crenellated curtain wall, and a turret can be seen in Rue du Vertbois. Another tower serves as a well for a staircase at 7 Rue Bailly.
Beyond the entrance, on the right, stands a library with a glazed tile roof; it used to be the monastery refectory, built around 1230. Its rib vaults, supported by tall slender columns, are a marvel of ethereal grace.
Finally, a curious note to end your visit on. In the large hall where Lavoisier's laboratory equipment is on view, you might find it fun to stand at one corner of the hall, facing the wall, and whisper very softly to your "partner in crime" at the opposite corner of the room, also facing the wall. Unlike someone standing in the middle of the room, he will hear you very clearly. Legend has it that this was how the monks heard the confessions of people suffering from contagious diseases.

THE LADY WITH THE BAG

CARYATID
57 RUE DE TURBIGO / 3rd
METRO: ARTS-ET-MÉTIERS

Rising four floors, the immense female silhouette overlooking 57 Rue de Turbigo is stunning to say the least. This sculpture in ancient garb has wings which seem to support the balcony overhead. The left hand holds a sprig of myrrh and the right hand holds a small handbag, typical of those in vogue in the Second Empire. At the entrance to this thoroughfare lined with businesses and shops, it offers a reassuring representation of Charity, ever ready to give to the needy.

And yet, this caryatid is one of the capital's most mysterious. It was nicknamed "the genius," "the angel of the bizarre," and even "the lady with the bag" in the interwar period. In 1984, Agnès Varda made it one of the stars in her short film about Paris' caryatids. Fifteen years later, it showed up in Cédric Klapisch's film *Peut-Être* (Perhaps), beneath the windows of the hero of the film, Arthur – a veritable landmark for the spectator who must navigate between two periods in very different sets.

As for its unusual proportions (the largest caryatid in Paris), it was designed by Auguste Émile Delange, who entered it in 1851 for the contest at the Beaux Arts (School of Fine Arts). It was intended to be a tribute to the physicist Fresnel, the inventor of the lighthouse lens. Standing on a base decorated with truncated pyramids, possibly an allusion to the legendary lighthouse of Alexandria, the lady of Rue de Turbigo quite recognizably figures as an element in his composition, leaning on a square tower holding a large storm lamp. When the building was erected in 1850, Delange integrated the giant with spread wings, a sort of oversized signature, that of an audacious man who, today, has been all but forgotten.

A UNION IN THE TEMPLE

14 RUE DE LA CORDERIE / 3rd
METRO: TEMPLE

A bend in Rue de la Corderie forms a picturesque square, lined with old buildings. It was formerly Cour de la Corderie, taken over by craftsmen in the 18th century, in the Temple enclosure. Writer Jules Vallès declaimed: "Do you know the damp square between the Temple and Château-d'Eau (Place de la République), not far from the City Hall, was boxed in by four rows of houses? Small shopkeepers occupy the ground floor, and their children play in the street. Carriages never come down here. The attics are full of poor people. This empty triangle is called Place de la Corderie. Take a good look at the house backing onto the faubourg barracks and overlooking the market. It looks quiet compared to the other houses. Go to the third floor and through a door, likely to fall off at the slightest knock of a shoulder, and enter a large, bare room, resembling a schoolroom. Greet the new Parliament! This is the revolution, sitting on the benches, leaning against the walls, resting its elbows on the rostrum, dressed in working men's clothes! This is where the International Working Men's Association holds its meetings, and the *Fédération des Corporations Ouvrières* (Federation of Working Men's Corporations) arranges to meet people."
Created in London in 1864, the International Working Men's Association was represented in Paris in 1865 at 44 Rue des Gravilliers. It had to move several times because of frequent police raids. It finally settled at 14 Rue de la Corderie in 1869. The signal to start the Paris Commune (a Republican uprising against the Versailles government) was given here on February 16th, 1871.
Cité Dupetit-Thouars, an attractive cul-de-sac, is where Italian film director Luigi Comencini shot some of his film *La Bohème*.

Cité Dupetit-Thouars

RUE
DE LA
CORDERIE
CYVOCT
- Plomberie - Chauffage
14
SORTIE
VOITURES
JOUR
NUIT
SORTIE
VOITURE
STATIONNER

CRIME ON STAGE

THÉÂTRE DÉJAZET
41 BOULEVARD DU TEMPLE / 3rd
METRO: RÉPUBLIQUE

Cinema enthusiasts will be surprised to learn that a theater, dating from the good old days of the "Boulevard of Crime", like the one portrayed in French film director Marcel Carné's film, *Les Enfants du Paradis* (Children of Paradise), has reopened its doors. Théâtre Déjazet is the only playhouse to have escaped Haussmann's city planning operations in 1862, when more than twenty were razed, wiping out one of the most fun-loving areas of Paris. Try to imagine, near the beginning of Boulevard du Temple, on the site of Place de la République, a road lined with theaters where tightrope walkers and mimes, first- and second-rate actors took part, nonstop, in light comedy and high tragedy. Crimes were "committed" on stage all along the boulevard to make the audiences cry. Originally, the building housed a royal tennis court, built by architect Belanger for Count d'Artois in 1786. The Louis XVI building overlooking the street is still there today, but without its pediment. It became, in turn, a bathhouse, a ballroom, and, finally, in 1842, a theater, *Les Folies Meyer*. Actress Virginie Déjazet, who excelled in male and female roles, bought the theater in 1859, and had it named after her. Then, French playwright Victorien Sardou looked after it for a time.

After World War II, it became a cinema, and in 1986, when it was about to be closed down, Hervé Trinquier took out a lease in his name, and added the initials TLP – *Théâtre Libertaire de Paris* (Libertarian Theater of Paris) – in memory of its former owner. Since then, one-man shows and musical comedies, in the grand tradition of Boulevard du Temple shows, are still put on. In an effort to revive the spirit of the past, the interior walls have been hung with funny frescoes – after Daumier, a renowned 19th-century painter and caricaturist – recalling the times when crime walked the streets of paradise.

THE GARDEN
BEHIND THE BOAR

SAINT-GILLES-GRAND-VENEUR GARDEN
RUE DU GRAND-VENEUR (ENTRANCE AT 9 RUE DES ARQUEBUSIERS) / 3rd
METRO: SAINT-SÉBASTIEN-FROISSART OR CHEMIN-VERT

This garden, located behind the Hôtel d'Ecquevilly, was built in 1637 for Mrs. de Martel, a widow. It is noted for its tranquility. Four squares of grass bordered by rose bushes are greatly appreciated by neighbors who enjoy relaxing here on sunny days.
In the late 17th century, a then larger garden was designed by Le Nôtre for the new owner, Louis Boucherat, France's powerful chancellor. Aside from the orangery in the courtyard of 11-13, rue des Arquebusiers, nothing else remains. By the early 18th century, Mme de Harlay, Boucherat's daughter, had started selling off parts of the estate, thus reducing the size of the garden. The façade behind the manor, albeit a bit overpainted, has nevertheless kept its original elegance. The front building offers us an impressive boar head indicating that as of 1733, the squire of the property was the king's captain of the royal boar hunt, one Augustin Vincent Hennequin d'Ecquevilly. Bearing the title "*le Grand Veneur*" (master of the royal hounds), the hunting captain left his name to these splendid buildings.
The wood paneling, which must have been sumptuous, was unfortunately dispersed in 1823 when the property was taken over by Franciscan nuns. The hunting horn that decorates the entrance to the modern apartment complex located on Rue des Arquebusiers is a reminder of the former owner's occupation.

ROOM FOR ENLIGHTENMENT

LIBRARY OF THE AMIS DE L'INSTRUCTION (HÔTEL DE GOURGUES)
54 RUE DE TURENNE / 3rd
METRO: CHEMIN-VERT OR SAINT-SÉBASTIEN-FROISSART
Tel: 01 42 71 03 43
Open Saturdays 3PM to 7 PM, 1st and 3rd Sundays
of each month from 10 AM to 1 PM, and by appointment

In the 19th century, Paris had numerous reading halls. For a fee, one could read books or dailies in a heated and well-lit environment, a veritable luxury. In 1861, in an effort to improve the education of the poorest, the lower and working classes of the Marais district, local workers and artisans – jewelers, bronze workers, opticians, and engravers – founded a library association, the *Bibliothèque des Amis de l'Instruction*. The lithographer Jean-Baptiste Girard, who initiated the idea, courageously set up his own bookshelves at the district town hall in the Temple, then at the École Centrale des Arts et Métiers.
By 1875, the city of Paris began subsidizing the initiative. In 1884, the library moved to its final home, the four small rooms in the venerable Hôtel de Gourgues, built circa 1640. Its holdings now total some 20,000 publications consulted by its avid readers. It is an intact and moving example of popular libraries launched by private associations, and which later became municipal.
The library's interior décor has been conserved. It still has its red floor tiles, the lending counter still has its counterweight lamp, the reading table is still covered, and there are still eight chairs. It is a warm and charming sanctuary in which the still very active association holds readings. They continue to provide fine moments of literary conviviality.

A RESTING PLACE FOR OLD STONES

SQUARE GEORGES-CAIN
AND MUSÉE CARNAVALET - HISTOIRE DE PARIS
CORNER OF RUE PAYENNE, RUE PARC-ROYAL AND RUE DE SÉVIGNÉ, 23 RUE DE SÉVIGNÉ / 3rd
METRO: SAINT-PAUL
Tel: 01 44 59 58 58
Open Tuesday to Sunday from 10 AM to 6 PM

Until 1913, Hôtel Le Peletier de Saint-Fargeau gardens were the site of a mail delivery station, which delivered mail throughout most of Paris. The dark building deserved to be demolished, but the two doors with their curvilinear pediments most certainly did not. They opened directly onto the street, and served as a side entrance to the gardens in the 18th century.
The Square, quiet and peaceful today, was named after a former curator of the nearby Carnavalet Museum, which uses the place as a retirement home for cumbersome old stones. You will find a clock pediment, fixed to the right-hand wall. It comes from the Tuileries Palace, burnt down in 1871. Just below the pediment is a carving of a group, dating back to the reign of Louis XIV (known as the Sun King), from the door of Château de Saint-Germain-en-Laye. You can also admire a ceiling rose taken from the former Paris City Hall, columns from the Tuileries, and, in the middle of garden, a finely sculpted bronze statue which once graced the Saint-Cloud gardens. On the left, the ground-floor building bordering the Square was originally the Hôtel Le Peletier de Saint-Fargeau orangery. Its central pediment is decorated with a representation of Truth, whose mirror, long gone, was angled towards the figure of an old man – a symbol of the destructive nature of Time – on the rear façade of the manor house at the far end of the Square.

For many years, stones were stored in the orangery. This building now houses the museum's archaeological collections. The items on display were unearthed during the 1990-1996 dig at the Parc de Bercy site. Furniture, several oak canoes, a hunter's bow, stole and flint tools, figurines, decorated ceramics, and miscellaneous tools, are among the items which illustrate life in the discovered riverbank village which dates back to the Neolithic period. Numerous sculptures, steles, figurines, bronze items, pottery, glass, and large frescoes, all from the 2nd and 3rd century AD, attest to the rich history of the Roman period of the city.

THE CRIME OF 1407

IMPASSE DES ARBALÉTRIERS
38 RUE DES FRANCS-BOURGEOIS / 3rd
METRO: SAINT-PAUL

Uneven paving stones, boundary stones, corbels – all, or almost all, characteristic of medieval streets – are to be found in the picturesque Impasse des Arbalétriers. It was once the side entrance to the Barbette residence where Queen Isabeau of Bavaria (wife of Charles VI, King of France) lived in the early 14th century, and which no longer exists today. The path, now a cul-de-sac, led to a field where the crossbowmen used to train.

Historians have it that Louis d'Orléans (brother of Charles VI and long-standing rival of Jean sans Peur) was assassinated by Jean's henchmen on this very spot on November 23rd, 1407, as he was returning from a visit to Queen Isabeau of Bavaria (see p. 18). This cul-de-sac is not a true dead-end street as it connects to a vast courtyard, which opens onto Rue Vieille-du-Temple.

ESTABLISHING SEA LEVEL

FONTAINE DU CHAUME

CORNER OF RUE DES ARCHIVES AND RUE DES FRANCS-BOURGEOIS / 3rd

METRO: RAMBUTEAU

A rather unassuming edifice stands at the corner of Rue des Francs-Bourgeois and Rue des Archives, ensconced in the Soubise Palace. It barely attracts the attention of passersby.
This convex wall with pediment and doorway was originally a water fountain providing housewives and water carriers with their daily supply of water.
Architect Jean Beausire, who designed several other similar structures, drew the plans for this small, elegant structure, built in 1710. This fountain replaced the one built in 1628, which had been condemned by city authorities for health reasons.
The prince de Soubise, who commissioned the neighboring palace, ceded to the City a portion of his estate for the widening of Rue de Paradis (now Rue des Francs-Bourgeois) and for the construction of the fountain.
A worn, nearly invisible inscription with gold letters on black marble serves as a memorial to his generosity. The text in Latin reads: "*Ut daret hunc populo fontem cerbatam uterque: Subisuis posuit moenia, praetor aquas*" (In the year 1706, by common accord, Soubise ordered this edifice to be built, and the city councilors provided the water to give this fountain to the people).
A rectangular plaque some fifteen centimeters wide is set into the ground. Notice the emblem of the city of Paris, a boat. Further down, you will notice another wider plaque, decorated with pilasters and a volute. Its inscription bears a line of numerals and the word *repère* (marker). This is the work of Baron Haussmann. On May 31st, 1856, this famous prefect of Paris ordered that sea level elevations be mapped out citywide. His order required that, "verified elevations be inscribed upon cast iron markers along with the crest of the City of Paris, and placed at intersections and street corners, at the base of monuments, upon the walls of city docks, and other places deemed necessary [...]". This plaque specifies the sea level measured in the port of Marseille, the difference with the zero level of the Pont de la Tournelle taken in 1719, and another differential with the virtual map, "exceeding 50 meters above the established level of the water in Paris' Bassin de la Villette [...]." From the time of this survey to today, the (virtual) topographical map of Paris bobs between the two water levels. From Marseille to Paris, there is but one step, or rather, the difference of a few meters.

HERE'S LOOKING AT YOU!

GROTESQUES
2 AND 4 RUE RAMBUTEAU / 3rd
METRO: RAMBUTEAU OR HÔTEL-DE-VILLE

In 1839, the first stone for Rue Rambuteau was laid by Flamand Devergie, as indicated by the engraving on the building at no. 21. That same year, several dozen yards away, the city of Paris expropriated a plot of land and building located on Rue du Chaume. It then sold it to Jacques Nicolas Piollet. It was this Parisian developer who erected the two buildings in 1842. Their freestone façades are unique in Paris.
Perhaps it was to show off his know-how or perhaps it was to surprise his buyers, in any case, Mr. Piollet decided that each window on the second, third and fourth floors should be graced by a pair of amusing carved heads. Executed in the then very fashionable Troubadour style, this series of grotesques was probably intended an allusion to the history of the neighborhood and the nearby Hôtel de Soubise chosen to house the kingdom's archives.
The sculptor did not fail to place over all these windows a small medallion with the owner's initials, nor did he fail to have a bit of fun by slipping in, among the 84 heads, a mustached figure wearing a workman's cap, a mason perhaps, or a stonecutter, unless it was the boss himself!

THE OLDEST HOUSE IN PARIS?

NICOLAS FLAMEL'S HOUSE
51 RUE DE MONTMORENCY / 3rd
METRO: RAMBUTEAU

For a long time, the very medieval-looking house at 3 Rue Volta was thought to be the oldest house in Paris. All the books on the history of the city contained a picture with the following caption: "The oldest house in Paris", and postcards with the same title were printed in their thousands. It took the perseverance of a historian, who researched the subject, to put an end to the legend in 1979.
The house in Rue Volta proved to be nothing but a pastiche, built by a citizen of Paris in 1644.
Alas, the oldest house in Paris "only" dates from 1407! Its somber, austere façade can be seen at 51 Rue de Montmorency, not very far from Rue Volta. The house was built by a certain Nicolas Flamel, a scribe at the University of Paris, who financed free lodgings for agricultural workers and fruit and vegetable growers from nearby areas with rent collected from the shops on the ground floor.
The words engraved on the string course along the front wall, while the benefactor was still alive, continue to bear witness to that undertaking: "We men and women, living under the roof of this house built in the year fourteen hundred and seven, are honorably bound to recite one Paternoster and one Hail Mary every day, and to ask God, in His grace, to forgive the sins of the poor departed. Amen."
Flamel's initials can be seen on the pillars whose bas-relief sculptures, although restored in 1929, are in a very bad state today. *Ora et labora* ("pray and work") was the motto of Nicolas Flamel's house, the oldest in the capital... for the moment.

A MOVING GATEWAY

DOORWAY TO THE LINEN MERCHANTS' GUILD
22 RUE QUINCAMPOIX / 3rd
METRO: CHÂTELET

Rue de la Reynie opens into a small square overlooked by a narrow, modern façade composed of five windows and an elegant, and obviously historic, doorway.
The doorway used to grace 6 Rue Courtalon, once the *Hôtel des Marchandes Lingères* (the lady linen merchants guild headquarters) which opened onto Place Sainte-Opportune. In the early 20th century, a street widening plan called for the destruction of this manor house. Astute historians lobbied for the preservation of the porch entrance and its black marble medallion carved with the words "*Bureau des M. Lingères, 1716*" (literally, the office of lady linen merchants). It was dismantled and taken to the corner of Square des Innocents where only drafts would cross its threshold... In 1977, it emigrated to Place Edmond-Michelet, and then was finally moved a few yards away to its present-day position.
The Parisian linen merchants' guild was made up of women dealing in linen canvases, fine linens, hemp, thread, lace, and generally any other article made in cloth. These merchants ran the fabric market known for its ever-adorned statue of Saint Veronica, the industry's patron saint. Interestingly, of the 124 other known job sectors in Paris, it was the only one to have been the exclusive domain of women.

The doorway of the lady linen merchants guild in 1902, Square des Innocents

A MULTIPURPOSE TOWER

SAINT-JACQUES TOWER
SQUARE DE LA TOUR SAINT-JACQUES, 39 RUE DE RIVOLI / 4th
METRO: CHÂTELET

Tour Saint-Jacques (Saint James) is a well-known landmark, easy to recognize. This was also the case for pilgrims of Saint James who set off from here for Santiago de Compostela in Spain (world-famous pilgrimage in the Middle Ages, shrine of Saint James).
It used to be the bell-tower of Saint-Jacques-la-Boucherie Church, which took 25 years to build (1508-22). A large statue of Saint James was placed at the top to guide the pilgrims.
The church suffered considerable damage during the French Revolution. The tower's wooden framework was burnt down in order to remove the bells, which, as they fell, smashed the vaults into pieces. The church was then sold to a man who demolished it, sparing only the tower.
A second-hand clothes market was set up on the site of the church, and the top of the tower was rented to a metal founder, who cleverly took advantage of its location by melting down the lead and pouring it from the top of the tower into a tub of water at the foot of building.
Repurchased in 1836 by the City of Paris, the tower was restored in 1852 by Ballu, who put the statues back on the top and the saints in their niches. A few years later, at the time of Haussmann's city-planning operations, the base of the tower was placed on a mound, underpinned, and had steps built around it. At that time, Pascal's statue, a reminder of the essays he wrote in 1648 on the weight of air, was installed under the archway. However, it was not under the Tour Saint-Jacques that the scientist and philosopher carried out his experiments, but in Saint-Jacques-du-Haut-Pas Church (5th arrondissement), but why quibble over a minor detail?
A meteorological station shares the top of the edifice with a few kestrels who have taken up residence there!

A 17TH-CENTURY METRO STATION

THE VAULTS OF CHÂTELET METRO STATION

METRO: LINE 7 TO LA COURNEUVE, EXIT RUE SAINT-MARTIN / 4th

Vaults slightly higher than the tunnel can be seen from the platform at Châtelet metro station. The fact that they date back to the 17th century makes them the oldest architectural element of the entire Paris Metro!

In 1642, on this very spot, Louis XIII parted with a piece of land between Pont Notre-Dame and Pont au Change. The only obligation incumbent upon the new owner, the Marquess of Gesvres, was to build a quay supported by a series of arches. Well situated, overlooking the Seine, the quay rapidly became a haunt for pickpockets and other disreputable individuals. In 1860, its openings were walled in, and its sunny, sheltered spots, afforded by the vaults built in front of the port, were forgotten. Only a few engravings and a painting by Hubert Robert (18th-century painter and engraver) serve as a reminder of the existence of those dark galleries.

Around 1921, engineers discovered the old vaults on the edge of the Seine while working on the site of the Ivry-Villette Metro line. The rubble, piping, and sewer outlets obstructing them were carefully cleared out, and, at the request of the experts on the City Committee for Old Paris, the vaults were preserved. They are still there today, and the best view of them is from the footbridge between the two platforms. Reproductions of 18th-century engravings of those sunny, sheltered spots are also on display.

THE GOLDEN EAGLE INN

CAFÉ DE LA GARE
41 RUE DU TEMPLE / 4th
METRO: RAMBUTEAU

Poet and precursor of surrealism, Guillaume Apollinaire was an unrepentant "stroller on both banks", and particularly liked the austere, evocative atmosphere of the Golden Eagle Inn in Rue du Temple. Today, the building houses the Café de la Gare theater and dance studios. In the 19th century, it was a coach inn. The courtyard had a wide timbered awning to shelter the coaches and carriages that stopped there.
Entering the courtyard, you will see a magnificent Louis XIII staircase on your right. The courtyard looks surprisingly majestic. In fact, in the 17th century, the old inn was a beautiful manor house, and what remains today are the main body of building and its left wing. For a long time, the dilapidated state of the place called to mind the postwar Marais district, where fine residences, occupied by a working population, used to house garages, workshops and various craft industries, a factor which helped save them from demolition, and, since the 1960s, often brought about their restoration. Despite the lack of upkeep, there are still a few interesting relics, in particular some splendid Louis XIII ceilings with painted beams, discovered in 1971 on the first floor of the main building, that can be viewed from the courtyard.

POLYCHROME AND RARE

JACQUES CŒUR'S HOUSE
38-42 RUE DES ARCHIVES / 4th
METRO: HÔTEL-DE-VILLE

Rue Sainte-Croix-de-la-Bretonnerie and Rue des Blancs-Manteaux were once connected by an alley so narrow that no cart could enter it, Rue de l'Homme-Armé (literally, the armed man street). Incorporated into Rue des Archives during the street-widening program in the 19th century, the only remnant of the street is this 15th-century house. Although commonly called Jacques Cœur's house, the building really ought to be attributed to his son Geoffroy, whose arms were probably incorporated in the design of the stained glass windows.
Marie Cœur, who was Geoffroy's daughter and Eustache Luillier's wife, was the 16th-century occupant. 17th-century historian Henri Sauval described the beauty of the façade, "pierced by mullioned windows and decorated with red bricks engaged with a diamond-pattern network of black bricks coated with a lead varnish." Although it underwent significant alterations over the centuries carried out by various owners, the work undertook in 1971 removed the plaster and exposed most of the red and lead bricks that captivated Sauval as well as vestiges of the mullioned windows. This elegant and joyous façade received a careful and respectful restoration. It is an extremely rare case of polychrome architecture in Paris.

HIDDEN TREASURE

RUE DU TRÉSOR
26 RUE VIEILLE-DU-TEMPLE / 4th
METRO: SAINT-PAUL

In 1882, while Hôtel d'Effiat was being demolished, a copper vase was unearthed from the rubble. It contained gold coins dating back to the reign of John II (King of France, 1350-64, known as John the Good) and to the reign of Charles V (King of France, 1364-80, known as Charles the Wise), the equivalent of 7,882 pounds sterling. When this treasure-trove was put up for sale, the Carnavalet Museum bought the vase and a few of the coins.
The road, being built at the time on the site of this manor house, was intended to create the junction between Rue Vieille-du-Temple and Rue des Écouffes; it was very aptly called "Rue du Trésor". Today, unremarkable buildings flank this cul-de-sac closed by a 19th-century fountain. Hôtel Effiat, which stood at the far end of this dead-end, was demolished in 1882. A doorway at one side of the street's back wall opens into a passageway to Rue des Écouffes. Around 1930, journalist Marius Richard described it as follows: "Let us continue our way through the passage whose doors may or may not be closed in the evening. The walls are all scraped and pitted by one wonders what... Neighborhood residents here must have very sharp elbows. Winter is the best time to enter this gullet, as a nasty wind blows in rain mingled with the grimy gas-lamp light, and creates a cutthroat ambush of a draught to slay the best of us."
Renovated in 2004, the tree-lined cul-de-sac is now a pleasant corner of the Marais.

THE BASTILLE
IN BITS AND PIECES

PLACE DE LA BASTILLE, SQUARE HENRI-GALLI, BASSIN DE L'ARSENAL / 4th
METRO: BASTILLE AND SULLY-MORLAND

What's left of the Bastille fortress today? Very little indeed! No time was lost in razing it to the ground, and most of its stone was sold in order to build blocks of flats and the Pont de la Concorde.

Only a few signs of the Bastille remain. Small, square paving stones at the start of Rue Saint-Antoine mark out its actual site, and at 3 Place de la Bastille, there is a map showing the exact position of the fortress and the formidable fortifications that surrounded it.

In 1898, an important discovery was made when the first Metro line was being built. The foundations of the tower of "liberty" were discovered between 211 and 236 Rue Saint-Antoine. They were dismantled, stone by stone, reassembled in Square Henri-Galli, and are still there today.

Another relic, part of the old moat wall now serving as a retaining wall for Boulevard Bourdon, can be seen at the junction of Canal Saint-Martin and Bassin de l'Arsenal, on the right-hand side looking towards the Seine. Inside the Bastille metro station, on the platform of line 5 going to Bobigny, some stones from the counterscarp wall of the Bastille moat are on view.

Finally, there are the "Bastille bells", installed in 1764. Later, they were saved from being melted down, and, for a short time, could be heard ringing in a café on the Place. Today, they belong to the State, and are on display in the Isle-Jourdain bell museum in the southwest department of Gers... a long way from the Bastille!

Square Henri-Galli

THE WALL OF PHILIP AUGUSTUS

RUE DES JARDINS-SAINT-PAUL / 4th
METRO: SAINT-PAUL

One side of Rue des Jardins-Saint-Paul is lined with the old buildings of the antique-dealer "Saint-Paul village" area. On the other side is an open field for sports activities, protected by a high wall complete with two towers. This is the largest remnant of the enclosure built by Philip Augustus in 1190, more than eight centuries ago.
The wall owes its strength to the mixture of sand and rubble holding the outside facing stones together. The reason why so many parts of the enclosure were preserved throughout Paris is that rapid urban growth led to the absorption rather than the destruction of the fortifications, often used as supporting walls. Thus, several parts of the wall can be seen – concealed and preserved – at the back of courtyards or workshops. The 70-meter wall along Rue des Jardins-Saint-Paul is an impressive sight. To get an exact idea of how it looked in the Middle Ages, you have to imagine a wall with crenellations, somewhat higher than it is today.
At one point, Paris city officials had plans to turn the grounds into a public garden with an underground car park. But the project drew the ire of locals, whose lobbying efforts resulted in the construction of outdoor sports facilities and a playground for children. Once again, warfare, albeit on a small scale, in the shadows of Philip Augustus' fortifications...

SOME CANNONBALL!

HÔTEL DE SENS (FORNEY LIBRARY)
1 RUE DU FIGUIER / 4th
METRO: PONT-MARIE OR SAINT-PAUL

The scarcity of fine architecture around Hôtel de Sens, with its appealing jagged silhouette, makes it seem quite out of place. Houses on the south side of Rue de l'Hôtel-de-Ville did not escape city planning of the 1950s. Some of them dated back to the 15th and 16th centuries, but were, nevertheless, demolished. Hôtel de Sens, built for the archbishops of Sens, and now the Forney library, is undoubtedly a survivor of the storm. Erected in the 14th century, the mansion was completely altered by Archbishop Tristan de Salazar in 1474.
In the late 17th century, it housed various artisans and commercial establishments. In the 18th century, stagecoaches left from here for the cities of Dijon, Auxerre, Bar-sur-Aube, Belfort, and so on. Then it became a laundry, a fruit and vegetable preserving factory, a rabbit-skin cutting workshop, an optician's, a jam factory, and, finally, a glass factory.
When the City of Paris acquired it in 1911, it was very dilapidated. Entire portions were completely rebuilt in medieval style. Recently, the building was so thoroughly cleaned that traces of a fresco (from a chapel which no longer exists) were washed off the walls overlooking the courtyard!
One hot day in the revolutionary times of 1830, a wayward cannonball embedded itself in the eastern façade of Hôtel de Sens. It is still there today, with the date of the event engraved underneath.

RENDEZVOUS UNDER THE ELM

SAINT-GERVAIS-SAINT-PROTAIS ELM TREE
PLACE SAINT-GERVAIS / 4th
METRO: HÔTEL-DE-VILLE

Have you ever noticed the elm tree in front of Saint-Gervais-Saint-Protais Church? Its history goes a long way back.

Try to imagine the district as it was before Baron Haussmann's city planning began – a maze of old streets. They had quaint names such as Rues de la Tisseranderie (weaving trade), de la Mortellerie (stone-breaking), du Pourtour (periphery), du Monceau – often referring to a craft, a physical characteristic, a locality – and were centered around Place Baudoyer, five times narrower than it is today. Rue Monceau opened out in front of the church to form a small square, in the middle of which the Saint-Gervais elm was planted, a little to the left of the present site.

In the Middle Ages, people settled legal disputes under this tree, or gathered there to chat after Mass. Debts were paid and duels were arranged beneath its foliage. It was a convenient place to meet, and the expression: "Rendezvous under the elm" was a familiar phrase to Parisians for a long time. The Saint-Gervais factory used to finance the annual upkeep of the tree.

History does not tell us what happened to the old elm tree, and it was not until March 10, 1914 that another one was planted.

The elm was often the subject of paintings and engravings, the most original of which can still be seen on the second-floor balconies of buildings adjoining the church (2-14 Rue François-Miron / 17 Rue des Barres). Inside these homes, many fireplaces' back hearthstones are still ornamented with elms, which can also be found carved on four of the wooden choir stalls in Saint-Gervais Church.

An edge-tool maker's sign in Rue du Monceau was an elm, and, in the Carnavalet Museum, it continues to honor the memory of one of the most fragile monuments of Paris.

FOREVER UNITED

SITE OF THE HOUSE OF HÉLOÏSE AND ABELARD
9 QUAI AUX FLEURS / 4th
METRO: HÔTEL-DE-VILLE

Who has not heard Héloïse and Abelard's distressing story of thwarted love? It has been told on stage so many times that the actors themselves have also become mythic figures. And yet this Parisian version of Romeo and Juliet really took place. Héloïse and Abelard met on Île de la Cité. A plaque on the (approximate) site of the lovers' residence on Quai aux Fleurs announces: "Former home of Héloïse and Abelard [in] 1118, rebuilt in 1849". A little further on, you will see two 19th-century medallions bearing portraits of the immortal lovers.

Abelard, born in Nantes, arrived in Paris in 1100 to receive tuition from Guillaume de Champeaux. He became an eminent teacher, and readily accepted a request from Fulbert, canon at Notre-Dame, to give lessons to his niece, Héloïse. The young lady was 18 years old whereas Abelard was 39, but this did not stop pupil and tutor from falling passionately in love.

Fearing the canon's anger, the lovers fled to Brittany where they had a son before returning to Paris. Meanwhile, Fulbert had been preparing his revenge: he hired men to catch and castrate Abelard. From that time on, Abelard devoted himself entirely to spiritual matters; he became a monk and founded the Paraclete oratory. Héloïse became a nun at Argenteuil Convent.

On Abelard's death in the Saint-Marcel monastery of Châlon-sur-Saône in April 1142, Héloïse had his remains secretly transferred to the Paraclete. Twenty-two years later, Héloïse died and was buried beside Abelard in his coffin. The scandal was not discovered until centuries later when, in 1630, an abbess took it into her head to carefully sort and separate the lovers' bones.

Today, they are together again in Père Lachaise cemetery. Roses are regularly laid between the recumbent statues of Héloïse and Abelard, a sign of admiration for two lovers who were forced to part, but now reunited forever.

A MOCK MEDIEVAL HOUSE

1 RUE DES CHANTRES, 1-3 RUE DES URSINS / 4th
METRO: HÔTEL-DE-VILLE OR CITÉ

A house on the corner of Rue des Chantres and Rue des Ursins attracts attention because it looks very old. It is one of the rare houses to escape Baron Haussmann's city-planning operations which destroyed much of Île de la Cité, except for Place Dauphine and a few streets near Notre-Dame.
This house down by the quay was still a funny, oddly-shaped little place when architect Fernand Pouillon began to restore it in 1958. In fact, the architect transformed it into a curious copy of a medieval house, as he recounts in his memoirs: "After a year's work, the ruin, demolished bit by bit, was replaced by a clever pastiche of deliberately ill-assorted architectural items, which have been both envied and admired ever since by people dreaming of a view over the Seine."
The originality of the house lies in the splendid antique pieces, of various origins, which Fernand Pouillon incorporated into his building. Some of them can be seen from the street (stained-glass windows, wrought-iron bars). Also to be noted are the tower-cum-stairwell, the two mullioned windows to the right of the steps, and the door at the top of the steps in Rue des Ursins, all very medieval-looking.
The architect lived for only a year in this amazing house, which was then occupied by the Aga Khan. Today, the small house in Rue des Chantres blends in with the scenery; although not an ancient dwelling, it is a real masterpiece by a talented architect.

TOMBSTONES TO KEEP YOUR FEET DRY

26 RUE CHANOINESSE / 4th
METRO: CITÉ

At the heart of one of the rare spots spared by Baron Haussmann, Rue Chanoinesse is reminiscent of the cloister of Notre-Dame, where Chanoine monks or canons, safe inside a closed guarded domain until the 18th century, were able to dedicate their lives to work and meditation. Canons used to live at nos. 22 and 24, buildings which open into the street via two wide doorways leading to courtyards. The latter building now bears the façade of an authentic, 18th-century, wine merchant's shop, and you can still taste the juice of the vine here, as a restaurant, *Le Vieux Paris*, keeps up the tradition.

At no. 26, there is a small, narrow courtyard common to several buildings. In the past, this may have been a passageway into Rue des Ursins, and has become a cul-de-sac today. It is lined with reused columns. However, the main interest of the place lies in the long flagstones on the ground, on which traces of Gothic script can be detected. These flagstones are, in fact, tombstones from some religious establishment on Île de la Cité. They were used for drainage, and as a result, generations of Parisians, without much regard for the deceased, were able to keep their feet dry!

ALL ROADS LEAD TO NOTRE-DAME

THE ZERO KILOMETER MARKER FOR FRENCH HIGHWAYS

PLACE DU PARVIS-NOTRE-DAME - PLACE JEAN-PAUL II / 4th

METRO: CITÉ

Not far from the cathedral Notre-Dame-de-Paris, embedded in the concrete, is an odd little circular plaque, in the middle of which is a copper octagon engraved with a compass rose. While it is easily recognizable as the national zero marker for all roads in France, its age is less well known.

Back in the days when the cathedral's esplanade teemed with innumerable stalls and workshops, at this very spot there was a statue leaning against a wall, a larger-than-life male figure "holding a vessel in one hand and, beside him, a serpent." This description written in 1717 by Germain Brice leads some to think that it may have been Aesculapius. In any case, the religious connotation reference is quite certain.

Long ago, good Christians, when arriving in the city after a long trip, were expected to pay homage to Saint Christopher, the patron saint of travelers. A colossal statue of the saint stood in the cathedral. When voyagers asked for their way in Paris, there was always someone to reply that the illustrious Monsieur Gray could show them the way. This was how Parisians playfully referred to the statue with its gray patina.

But by 1748, "Monsieur Gray" had been whisked away and replaced by a triangular post bearing the arms of the Chapter of Notre-Dame. This post was the starting point for a network of milestones set up roughly every two kilometers. The plaque that replaced the post was unveiled on October 10, 1924. Today, thousands of tourists come to stand on it and make their wish. Legend has it that making a wish from this spot ensures a return at least once more to the city of lights.

THE LIVING AND THE DEAD

SAINT-SÉVERIN CHARNEL HOUSE
RUE DES PRÊTRES-SAINT-SÉVERIN/ 5th
METRO: CLUNY-LA SORBONNE, RER: SAINT-MICHEL

The rare visitors to a little square next to Saint-Séverin Church may notice some singular-looking Gothic buildings at the far end on the right. This curved corridor with its pointed roofs is not a cloister but a charnel house used in former times to deposit remains from the communal grave that once occupied this site. It is the only one left in the entire city. The charnel house was built in the late 15th century around the Saint-Séverin cemetery. It was customary for the dignitaries of the parish to be interred beneath the arcades, while the draughty space under the roofs was reserved for "less high-ranking" corpses taken from the communal grave.

However, at Saint-Séverin, the living very soon took over from the dead. In the 17th century, some of the arcades were filled in with stained glass so that the churchwardens could hold their meetings there, and lodgings were installed for the priests above one of the arcades. By the 18th century, the disused cemetery was surrounded by nothing but blind arcades, blocked up by stone walls. In 1840, some of them were demolished to make way for a presbytery. It was not until 1920 that the remaining vaults were restored by architect Bévière.

IN THE MASTER'S SHADOW

SALVADOR DALI'S SUNDIAL
27 RUE SAINT-JACQUES / 5th
METRO: CLUNY-LA SORBONNE

Noon, Tuesday, November 15, 1966, Rue Saint-Jacques, marked the "first event of the 21st century."
Perched high in the air in a cherry picker, Salvador Dali, "the master," unveiled this sundial, a new, timeless and immanently spiritual piece. As there was little sunshine that day, a spotlight was brought in to shine on the needle and, thus, create the requisite shadow while a brass band from the Beaux-Arts played.
The artist chose to cast his gift to the city of Paris in concrete. The composition features a scallop-shaped face, a reminder of the many pilgrims that took the Rue Saint-Jacques on their way to Santiago de Compostela. The flame-shaped eyebrows recall the hot rays of the sun, while the hair, pulled back onto the neck, flows down to the shoulders.
One can reproach this "eighth wonder of the modern world" for lacking accuracy, after all, isn't that what makes it so charming?

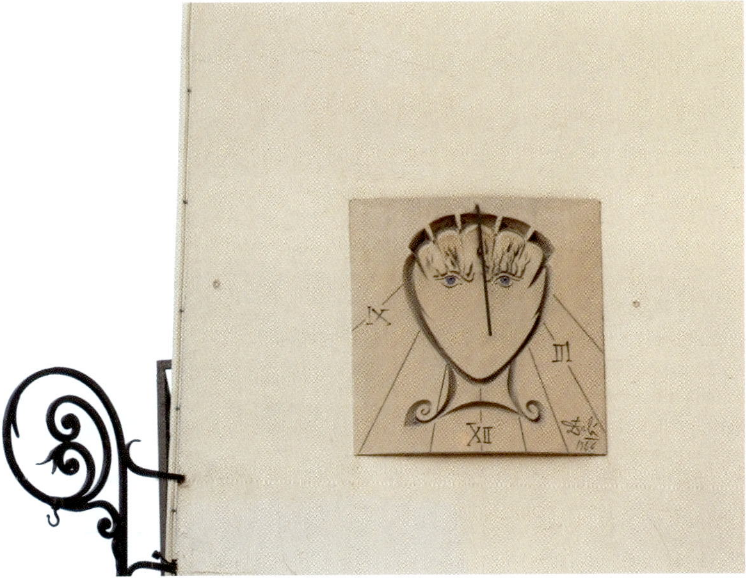

UNDER SAINT JULIAN'S PROTECTION

SIGN
42 RUE GALANDE / 5th
METRO: MAUBERT-MUTUALITÉ

Most of the city's old signs either vanished or wound up in the collections of the Carnavalet Museum. It is, therefore, astonishing to see this bas-relief over the entrance to the cinema. Standing up in a boat, is a haloed male figure flanked by two rowers and, on the bank, is a small house overshadowed by a tree beside a dangerous river, a description of the place where Saint Julian the Hospitaller and his wife did their penance. To expiate his sin of murdering his own parents, he ferried the poor across the river and gave them shelter. One day, a leper came to ask Julian to ferry him to the other side. The leper was, in fact, Jesus who promised the couple that they would go to heaven.

Saint Julian was known as the patron saint of travelers. In Medieval times, many innkeepers thought it wise to place their establishments under his protection. It was long thought that this sculpture had originally belonged to nearby Saint-Julien-le-Pauvre church as its doorway was demolished in 1675. But according to historical documents which refer to it as "the house beneath the sign of Saint Julian" (1380) and elsewhere as the "house where presently a stone is carved in the image of Saint Julian" (1441), the sign must predate that supposition, thus making it the oldest sign in the city of Paris.

THE POPE'S ABODE

THE OLD COLLÈGE DES BERNARDINS
20 RUE DE POISSY / 5th
METRO MAUBERT-MUTUALITÉ
Tel: 01 53 10 74 44
Free general admission to the nave. Guided tours of the buildings on Mondays, Wednesdays, and Fridays at 11 AM and 4:30 PM

Opened to the public in 2008, the old Collège des Bernardins, an exquisite example of Cistercian Gothic architecture, is one of the largest medieval edifices in Paris. This institution of learning was founded in 1244 by Englishman Stephen Harding, abbot of Clairvaux.
The school was completed in 1253.
It comprised several buildings with four levels. They housed classrooms, refectories, and dormitories. In 1320, the Cistercian Order took over the property. In 1338, it began building a church which was never finished. Declared national property in 1790, it was used as a salt storage house, then turned into a school, and, still later, into a fire station.
The *logis du pape* (literally: the pope's abode), was the only structure untouched by the demolitions in the street-widening programs that created Rue de Poissy and Rue de Pontoise in 1806 and then Boulevard Saint-Germain in 1855.
Since 2001, it has been Paris diocese property. The crumbling building's harmonious proportions were restored thanks to the joint talents of architect Hervé Baptiste from the national Monuments Historiques, and architect Jean-Michel Wilmotte. The original flooring was restored, the second gable with its rose window was rebuilt, and the roof with its 110,000 tiles of six different colors was restored to its original height. In its rafters, today, are two auditoriums.
One must go into the main nave on the ground floor (70 meters long, 14 meters wide) to appreciate the balance: thirty-two columns – two of which remain unfinished – support the barrel vaults. Polychrome traces give an idea how the place must have looked in medieval times. A little further off, one can get a glimpse of the old sacristy built in 1360 to connect the church to the monastery. It houses a copy of the tombstone of a German monk named Günter who died in 1306, as well as a stone carving depicting the touching profile of a medieval man. Two other 14th-century pieces were found in the building's foundations. One was a headless female statue placed in the niche of the 18th-century staircase, and the other was a polychrome Christ which can be admired in the nave.
The cellar, which had been filled in to prevent the building from sinking, was completely cleared of rubble and consolidated by incorporating 350 micropiles. It is now divided into several classrooms.
The college aims to foster exchanges and conviviality. It sponsors exhibitions, classes, and conferences, thus returning to its original function.

ARCH OVER
A LOST CANAL

BIÈVRE RIVER CROSSING VESTIGES, POST OFFICE
30 BIS RUE DU CARDINAL-LEMOINE / 5th
METRO: CARDINAL-LEMOINE

Paris has many well-known remnants of the 12th-century city walls built by King Philippe Auguste. Portions of towers and walls were often integrated into later constructions. Sometimes, however, archeologists make new discoveries.
Take for example the arch and the canal unearthed in 1991 at the construction site of the Saint-Firmin seminary, razed prior to WWII. Archeologists were called in and they identified vestiges of a crossing on the Bièvre River diversion canal.
This river, which has its source near Guyancourt, a stone's throw from Versailles, enters southern Paris near the Poterne des Peupliers and meanders its way northwards through the 13th arrondissement. In the 12th century, it cut past the Saint-Médard church and through the Saint-Marcel faubourg, then through the Sainte-Geneviève abbey and the Saint-Victor abbey. It flowed into the Seine River near today's Pont d'Austerlitz.
Around 1150, clerics from Saint-Victor received authorization to deviate the course of the Bièvre River to power the monastery's mill and water its gardens. When Philippe Auguste's ramparts were erected, an arch was built over the monks' canal.
That archway can now be seen in the basement of a local post office. During the reign of Charles V, trenches were dug to improve the city's defenses and the canal was diverted straight to the Seine. The canal later became an open-air sewer, but by 1674, was filled in and covered.

CIRCUS GAMES

LUTETIA ARENAS
49 RUE MONGE/RUE DES ARÈNES / 5th
METRO: CARDINAL-LEMOINE

The last remains of the great Lutetia arenas, long since buried underground, are hidden away in the middle of a square. And yet, those arenas, nearly nineteen centuries old, have never really been forgotten. Even people living in Middle Ages used to talk about the "enclosure of the arenas." Memories of them only began to fade when the ground on the site was leveled off, making their exact location increasingly uncertain. In 1869, the underlying remains of the arenas were discovered. However, despite the efforts of a very active Society for the Arenas, the site was filled in, and a depot installed for the Omnibus Company. Buildings erected along Rue Monge accounted for the disappearance of a good third of the arenas. It was not until 1883, after a vigorous campaign led by Victor Hugo and Victor Duruy, that the last remains of the arenas were discovered. They were finally restored in 1917-18.

The amphitheater and its stage were built on the slope of Montagne Sainte-Geneviève at the beginning of the 2nd century. This meant that many of the tiers could be built into the hillside itself. The steps surrounding an oval arena faced a big podium equipped with a wall with recesses where a succession of different kinds of entertainment could be presented: circus games, mime, drama, and so on. In its time, this amphitheater was the second biggest circus in Gaul before its decline towards the 4th century, when it served as a quarry for the inhabitants of the area.

AWAY FROM PARIS

THE MOSQUE OF PARIS
2 PLACE DU PUITS-DE-L'ERMITE / 5th
METRO: MONGE
Open to the public every day except Fridays
from 10 AM to 12 PM and from 2 PM to 6 PM (7 PM in summer)

Visit the Mosque of Paris on a hot summer day to get the feeling you are truly elsewhere. Located near the Latin Quarter, this lively place is open to the public for a small admission fee. Visitors cross several corridors then the patio surrounded by its cloister. Look up and admire the Malekite-style minaret, towering 33 meters over a Paris which now seems miles away!

The Paris mosque was the brainchild of Sultan Abdülhamid II, Caliph of Constantinople, who wished to honor the great number of Muslims who perished in World War I. France granted substantial funding for the project, and the City of Paris donated a one hectare plot of land (about 2 1/2 acres) beside the Jardin des Plantes. Construction spanned four years, from 1922 to 1926, under the direction of three French architects Charles Heubès, Robert Fournez and Maurice Mantout, after the plans laid out by Maurice Tranchant de Lunel. Most of the building materials were imported. Some 450 North African craftsmen worked to assemble them. Respecting traditional mosque architecture, the Paris mosque contains designated areas for worship, study, and social activities. The prayer hall was designed to hold up to 600 worshipers. It contains Persian carpets, a copper and wrought-iron chandelier from Fez, and the famous mihrab pointing in the direction of Mecca. The wooden minbar (pulpit) was donated by King Fouad I, in 1931.

The walls of the galleries off the patio are decorated with blue mosaics. The cedar door is a copy of the doorway at the Bou Inania mosque in Fez. A fountain gurgles in the middle of the patio.

Further off, a courtyard with green hexagonal floor tiles – for green is the color of Islam – and a delightful garden with fountains, basins, and terraces, invites you to continue your journey. Shooting off from this hub are halls occupied by the Institute of Muslim Studies. Its library is a veritable treasure house.

The tour does not stop here for those who might enjoy the sweet pleasures of the mosque's Turkish baths or the tea room's delicious pastries served with piping-hot mint tea.

DOWN BELOW, ON THE MOUNTAIN...

ROCK GARDEN IN LE JARDIN DES PLANTES
RUE JUSSIEU/RUE GEOFFROY-SAINT-HILAIRE / 5th
METRO: JUSSIEU
The rock garden is open from 8:00 AM to 5:30 PM, April to October 30th

The little rock garden does not immediately spring into view as you first glance over the vast Jardin des Plantes. The reason for such unobtrusiveness is because this delightful place is a sunken garden, located three meters below the terraced gardens in order to create hilly ground, a feature which is altogether atypical of the neat flower-beds of Jardin des Plantes.
At the beginning of the thirties, the Museum botanists came up with the idea of presenting mountain plants in the heart of the capital, in surroundings as similar as possible to those of their natural environment. The undertaking had its complications as the plants grown in the garden did not all originate from the same part of the world. The ambition was to cultivate both mountain flora as well as plants from Mediterranean areas.
Light, warmth, humidity, soil types – each plant requiring specific conditions which could not be left to chance.
The garden is protected from sudden changes in weather conditions and from harsh winds, thanks to its hollowed out terraces and the big trees along Allée Cuvier and in the nearby zoo. The gardeners make the most of the northern or southern

exposures and the permanently shady areas of this little, sheltered valley. Within just a few meters, temperatures can range from 15 to 20°C, what one would call a micro-climate! More than 2,000 plants from the Alps, the Pyrenees, Corsica, as well as the Himalayas, Japan and China, all cultivated on a few acres of rock garden with little streams running through it, appear to appreciate this sanctuary in the heart of Paris.

If you go through the underground passage which starts in the Botany School gardens and crosses Allée Cuvier, you will come up into the heart of the rock garden, between the Cévennes massif and that of the Pre-Alps. Columbines, cornflowers, foxgloves, alpine sea holly and asters bring touches of bright color to these massifs, whose most precious flower remains the edelweiss, the "star of the snows", an uncommon sight in Parisian parks and squares. Opposite, along the zoo wall, there are rocks from the Balkans and the Mediterranean, scattered with lavender and rosemary. On the same side, towards the far end of the garden, you will see the massifs of the Caucasus and Corsica as well as rocks from Japan and China, and as you return to the entrance you will go past rocks from the Himalayas, North America and the Pyrenees. Opposite the Pyrenees massif, in the middle of the garden, stand the rocks sheltering cacti and succulents.

Towards Rue Geoffroy-Saint-Hilaire, behind the greenhouses, you can still see the Coypeau hillock, originally a dumping ground in medieval times.

The iron and bronze gazebo at the top was built in 1786 by the garden iron smith, according to Verniquet's plans. This is one of the first iron structures in the world, all the more exceptional since this was more than half a century before the achievements of Victor Baltard, also a forerunner in that area (he built the main buildings for Les Halles market). Beneath the cornice, there is an inscription in Latin: "*horas non numero nisi serenas*" (I only count the hours of happiness).

It refers to an ingenious device, no longer here today, that used to tell the time according to the sun. It consisted of a small Chinese drum placed in the hollow of a globe at the top of the belvedere. A horsehair thread, burnt under a magnifying glass set according to the meridian, triggered off a clock mechanism which struck the drum at midday. Naturally, the horsehair thread had to be changed every day!

THEY SELL HORSES, DON'T THEY?

FORMER HORSE MARKET
5 AND 11-13 RUE GEOFFROY-SAINT-HILAIRE / 5th
METRO: SAINT-MARCEL

A century ago, there were about 80,000 horses in the capital, putting Paris ahead of the Meuse, the most "horsy" department in the country. Boulogne draught-horses pulled heavy loads along the quays. Percherons trotted by with omnibuses in tow, and the Anglo-Normans proudly clopped up the streets of the uptown districts.

The big Paris horse market, decided upon by Louis XIII in 1641, used to stand on the present site of Boulevard Saint-Marcel and Boulevard de l'Hôpital, where it remained until 1908, when it was transferred to the Vaugirard slaughterhouses.

The market was supervised from a building at 5 Rue Geoffroy-Saint-Hilaire, which can be seen from Boulevard Saint-Marcel. This lovely Louis XV house was built between 1760 and 1762, under the orders of Police Lieutenant General Sartine.

On either side of the center window, a crane and a cock, symbols of patience and vigilance, stand face to face.

At nos. 11 to 13, the inscription on the façade beneath the head of a horse declares the following: "Dealers in thoroughbreds, ponies of all kinds and shire horses." This building, along with the house at no. 5, is all that remains of the market.

THE HOSPITAL BAKERY

HÔTEL SCIPION
13 RUE SCIPION / 5th
METRO: LES GOBELINS

Square Scipion with its low-roofed houses has been miraculously preserved. It was widened and restructured in 1985, and is ornamented with a large, terra-cotta bas-relief by Alexandre Charpentier, a reminder of the bakery trade. Opposite stands the solidly-built façade of a 17th-century building with tall windows and wrought-iron work. The center door has a round opening with a grille over it, bearing the following inscription "*S(ainte) Marthe, maison de Scipion*" (Saint Marthe, House of Scipion). If you push open the door, you will find yourself in a big courtyard, similar to that of a coach house because of its width. The right wing, more low-roofed and older than the rest, is an outstanding, very well restored Renaissance edifice. It has stone arches on the ground floor, and, on the floor above, terra-cotta medallions, casts of the original medallions kept in the Public Health and Welfare Museum, which, until a few years ago, was housed here. The Central Bakery for Paris hospitals used to occupy these buildings (from the 17th century onwards), which explains why there is so much space and why the entrance is so exceptionally high.

The manor house was built in the 16th century for a certain Maurice de Bullioud, and then bought by Scipion Sardini, hence the name. The Genoese gentleman's sympathies were with Catherine de Médicis and Henry II, and he was probably responsible for having the terra-cotta medallions installed on the façade of the right wing. No serious claims as to the making of these medallions have been recorded. Some mention the Juste atelier (family of 16th-century sculptors renowned for their ornamental, Renaissance style), but do not provide much in the way of proof to support their theories.

In 1613, the manor house was rented to a mental hospital for the indigent. It next served as a nursery for the children of needy families, before becoming an apprentices' workshop and tapestry factory.

THE THIRTY-THREE AT NO. 34!

OLD SEMINARY OF THE THIRTY-THREE
RUE DE LA MONTAGNE-SAINTE-GENEVIÈVE / 5th
METRO: CARDINAL-LEMOINE

A heavy, 18th-century door opens into a passage leading to a courtyard resembling a small street. Unevenly paved alleys lead up to buildings of different heights.

This is the Seminary of the Thirty-Three, established in 1657 in the former Hôtel d'Albiac. This little-known college of the Latin Quarter gets its name from its thirty-three grant recipients, the number referring to the age of Christ when he died.

The part overlooking the street was built by Germain-Éloi Legrand in 1737. At the far end of the courtyard, architect Charon erected an elegant building with big arcades. The upper stories are reached by a staircase, with a wrought-iron balustrade, down which we can imagine the seminary students racing out of classes. A curious feature is the tiny door, between the ground and the floor above. It opens onto the other side of the college for access to Impasse des Bœufs.

The smaller buildings, although added during the 19th century, blend in well with those around them.

As the evening darkness begins to fall, the courtyard of the Thirty-Three, under the pale lamplight, gives you an idea of Paris as it looked in the 18th century with its twisting, mysterious alleys.

THE LAST ROOD SCREEN

SAINT-ÉTIENNE-DU-MONT CHURCH
1 PLACE SAINTE-GENEVIÈVE / 5th
RER: LUXEMBOURG

A rood screen, the only one of its kind in Paris, lies hidden within the walls of Saint-Étienne-du-Mont Church. It was used for reading from the Gospels, before the pulpit was created. When pulpits had completely supplanted rood-screens, the latter were usually destroyed.
In the middle of the 18th century, some parishioners from Montagne Sainte-Geneviève demanded that the Saint-Étienne-du-Mont rood screen be demolished.
One of them even offered three thousand silver pounds to pay for the job! Despite the lightness of the structure concealing the chancel, members of the congregation most enamored of modernism felt the structure was inappropriate. Fortunately, Providence intervened; ardent reformers were discouraged from destroying the rood screen which is still in almost perfect condition.
Antoine Beaucorps built this marvel in 1541. Essentially Renaissance, the rood screen comprises one 9-meter, depressed, basket-handle arch on the transept side, and three archways joined by two slender pillars on the chancel side, and is designed so as to leave the nave in full view. You will appreciate the sculpture on the two flights of steps on either side of the platform with its ornamental openwork balustrade.
In the corner-pieces of the arch facing the transept, the two winged female figures used to carry the nails of the Passion and the Crown of Thorns, symbols which were replaced by a crown of olive and oak leaves in 1794. Notice also the beautiful pulpit, as well as the organ case, dating back to 1630.

RUE DES MARIONNETTES

277 AND 284 RUE SAINT-JACQUES / 5th
RER: PORT-ROYAL

At no. 284 Rue Saint-Jacques, opposite the magnificent Val-de-Grâce Chapel, an unusual relic of old Paris is hidden away in a modern building behind a pane of glass: a stone portal which, until the French Revolution, served as an entrance to the convent of the Incarnation Carmelites. When the apartment block was built in 1978, the portal as well as a small manor house, which can be seen from 6 Rue du Val-de-Grâce, were in danger of disappearing. As a result of various protests, the *tabula rasa* enthusiasts were urged to exercise restraint. The portal was dismantled, stone by stone, and reassembled in the place where you see it today. The manor house, built for sculptor François Scelles in 1796, was also saved. It has an attractive façade, crowned with balusters. During excavation works, vaulted, underground channels were discovered near the cellars of the manor house. They were part of the system which carried water from Arcueil to a fountain in Rue Saint-Jacques, known as the "Carmelites' Fountain".

At no. 277, through one of the two houses flanking Val-de-Grâce Chapel, there is a paved alley, lined with guardstones and ending in a cul-de-sac. This used to be Rue des Marionnettes, formerly linking Rue de l'Arbalète with Rue Saint-Jacques. The passage of time does not appear to have affected this old street, a veritable fossil of a road.

OLD STONES

SCHOOL OF MINES AND MINERALOGICAL MUSEUM

60 BOULEVARD SAINT-MICHEL / 6th

RER: LUXEMBOURG

Tel: 01 40 51 91 39

Open Tuesday to Friday from 1:30 to 6:00 PM,
Saturdays from 10:00 AM to 12:30 PM and 2:00 to 5:00 PM

Many diamonds are cut to reveal their brilliance; others are irreparably damaged by careless hands. The dazzling sort can be admired at the school of mine's mineralogy museum. Upstairs, an 80-meter gallery holds most of the 85,000 pieces. The Musée de Minéralogie de l'École des Mines has one of the richest collections in the world. The formerly beautiful Hôtel de Vendôme belongs to the second category. Commissioned by the Chartreux monks, whom Saint Louis moved here in 1257, the mansion was built in 1707 by architect Le Blond, on a street then named *Rue d'Enfer* (Hell Street). In 1714, the tenant was Marie-Anne de Bourbon-Condé, the Duchess of Vendôme. The mansion still bears her name. In 1816, the École des Mines became the next tenant, then, after the administration purchased the property, architect Duquesney enlarged the structure from 1840 to 1852. In addition to the portion overlooking Boulevard Saint-Michel, the mansion had two wings that had to be shortened in 1860 to accommodate the construction of a new boulevard. Today, nothing remains except the lovely 18th-century façade next to the Luxembourg Gardens.

A SNOW-WHITE ELEPHANT

CAROUSEL
LUXEMBOURG GARDENS / 6th
RER: LUXEMBOURG

Not far from the children's playground in Luxembourg Gardens is a charming, old-fashioned carousel. It's Charles Garnier's *jeu de bagues*, (the ring game). The architect of the grandiose opera house sketched all the animals for this veritable museum piece which went into service in 1879. Beneath the green canvas tent top and the yellow sphere, generations of young Parisians have giggled and had great fun riding the twenty-two white, brown, and black ponies, the three pairs of stags, elephants, and giraffes, and the two carriages.

Under its roof that casts a cooling shadow,
the carousel keeps circling for a while
with brightly painted horses, [...]
Though some of them are pulling carriages,
still all show pride and boldness in their mien;
a vicious-looking lion, all in red, goes with them,
and now and then appears a snow-white elephant.

When Rainer Maria Rilke wrote those verses back in 1905, a player piano pounded out melancholy tunes for the spinning carousel. But in 1917, park officials found the noise offensive and banned the music. The crank handle was replaced with a humming electric motor that gave a different ambiance for children's attempts to grab rings hanging from a wooden shank held by an employee. Yesteryear's candy prize for the most nimble is now but a lovely memory.

COURTYARD-CUM-GARDEN

ZADKINE MUSEUM
100 BIS RUE D'ASSAS / 6th
RER: PORT-ROYAL
www.zadkine.paris.fr
Open every day except Mondays from 10 AM to 8 PM

A narrow passageway between some tall buildings leads to the entrance of the secluded Zadkine museum at the far end of a courtyard-cum-garden. Ossip Zadkine lived here from 1928 until his death in 1967. Born in Russia in 1890, he arrived in Paris at the age of nineteen. To begin with, he lived in La Ruche (see p. 186), then in Rue de Vaugirard and Rue Rousselet, and, in 1920, he exhibited his work for the first time. This success was followed by others; Zadkine exhibited forty-seven sculptures at the 1937 International Exhibition, and went to New York in the same year to show his work at the Brummer gallery.
Zadkine returned to New York to escape from the Nazis during the World War II, and devoted a lot of his time to teaching. His work, very much in the public eye, was the subject of a retrospective held in the National Modern Art Museum in 1949. Apart from Zadkine's work, a walk in this garden in Rue d'Assas brings to mind the countless other little backyards where Montparnasse artists, the famous "Montparnos", lived and worked before World War II.
The sculptor's secluded, 19th-century home was converted into several small exhibition rooms. Contemplating Zadkine's sculptures – skillful entanglements of shapes in wood, stone or bronze – is a moving experience. The original, poignant plaster cast of the monument dedicated to Vincent van Gogh is a masterpiece of sensitivity.
There is a welcoming bench in the garden where statues of all sizes have been installed, often by Zadkine himself. Mingling with the trees and the ivy, his work – sober, sensual, and out of the ordinary – is a tribute to nature.

THE HOUSE OF RETORTS

FORMER HÔTEL DE PHILIPPE DE VENDÔME
25 BOULEVARD DU MONTPARNASSE / 6th
METRO: MONTPARNASSE-BIENVENÜE

In the 18th century, Rue de Vaugirard wound its way past huge properties, with beautiful French-style gardens, and more modest, country cottages. Montparnasse was still a hillock with muddy paths zigzagging up and down.
The residence at 25 Boulevard du Montparnasse is a fine example of that period. Now in disrepair and heightened by several stories, it used to be surrounded, in the days of its glory, by a small park opening onto Rue de Vaugirard through a heavy portal.
On the south side, go through a double wrought-iron gate into a tiny courtyard where you can admire, unfortunately too close-up, the classic layout of the façade ornamented with delicately-carved *mascarons* (faces). You can get a good view of the entire north side of the manor house from the courtyard at no. 23.
The house was built in 1712, and a certain Catherine Bonot became its owner the following year. After that, there was a succession of occupants: Count de Béthune followed by Prince de Condé in 1716, and then Philippe de Vendôme in 1722. Philippe de Vendôme, a renowned libertine and brother of the Duke de Vendôme, was France's Grand Prior of the Knights of Malta. A high-ranking dignitary ruling supreme over the Temple and its members, later to be scorned by Louis XIV, Philippe ended his life in his manor house in Rue de Varenne, betrayed and ruined by his servants, and deserted by all those who had loved him during his hours of glory.
What was he doing in Rue de Vaugirard, when his real home was in Rue de Varenne? Like many of his contemporaries, he was perhaps trying to discover the key to the philosopher's stone.
On Philippe de Vendôme's death in 1727, the notaries, while making an inventory of the deceased's belongings, discovered a room full of retorts, flasks and filters, the tools of someone dabbling in the exalting, if not exact, sciences.

SAINT VINCENT DE PAUL'S SHRINE

CHAPEL OF THE PRIESTS OF THE LAZARIST MISSION
95 RUE DE SÈVRES / 6th
METRO: VANEAU
Open every day from 7 AM to 6:30 PM

The Lazarists' chapel, with its rather plain, pedimented façade, is a fine, recently-restored, 19th-century building. As a replacement for the Saint-Lazare priory (Rue du Faubourg-Saint-Denis) after the French Revolution, the priests of the Mission were given the former Hôtel de Lorges. The chapel you see today was built on part of that site (1826-27).
The stained-glass windows give a picture-book account of the life of Saint Vincent de Paul. Born on April 24th, 1581 in Pouy, near Dax, he was ordained priest in 1600, and devoted his life to both study and adventure. Captured during one of his journeys, he was sold as a slave in Tunis. He converted his master, escaped, and returned to Paris. He became chaplain to Queen Marguerite de Valois (whose marriage to the future Henry IV was one of the causes of the massacre of Saint Bartholomew's Day), then parish priest in Clichy-la-Garenne, before becoming private tutor to the illustrious Gondi family. In 1617, moved by the poverty he saw around him, he founded the "Brotherhood of Charity" in Châtillon-les-Dombes; people throughout the world benefited from it. "Mr. Vincent" died on September 27th, 1660 and was canonized by Pope Clement XII on June 16th, 1737.
The interesting items in this chapel include a Cavaillé-Coll organ, a series of paintings by "Brother François", pupil of Ingres, and, above all, a silver shrine, visible as soon as you enter, in which the relics of Saint Vincent de Paul are preserved.
A staircase concealed in the masonry affords a good view of this exceptional piece of silver work, created by silversmith Odiot in 1830. The 2.25m by 0.65m shrine contains a wax statue, dressed in priestly garments and holding a cross which Vincent may have used to comfort Louis XIII during the last hours of his life.

BLOODSHED AT THE CARMELITE CONVENT

SAINT-JOSEPH-DES-CARMES
74 RUE DE VAUGIRARD / 6th
METRO: SAINT-PLACIDE

The beautiful, domed façade of Saint-Joseph Church can be seen at the far end of a courtyard through a metal gate. On the right, a passageway gives easy access to the door into the building, hidden from view.

The Carmelites, originally from Spain, settled in Paris in the early 17th century. During the 18th century, the Rue de Vaugirard monastery was extended between Rue du Regard, Rue du Cherche-Midi and Rue Cassette. The monks cultivated the herbs for the famous lemon balm water (marketed under the name of "*Eau des Carmes Boyer*") in their enormous garden. However, this peaceful, rural life was to be disrupted by bloodshed.

As a result of the law of August 17th, 1792, whereby all the monasteries had to be vacated, the Carmelite monastery was converted into a prison. More than 150 priests refusing to take an oath to uphold the Constitution were imprisoned there.

As the Prussian army advanced, so revolutionary fervor mounted in Paris; the prisoners were accused of spying for the enemy, and their heads were demanded by the revolutionary Saint-Sulpice branch. On September 2nd, 1792, armed men led by citizen Maillard entered the prison screaming for the death of the prisoners. The massacre lasted three days. After a sham trial, pikes, swords and makeshift weapons were used to kill 118 monks in the gardens near the steps, still there today. In the crypt, there is a very dramatic presentation of the remains of these men, disinterred from a grave that had been dug in the garden. A macabre detail: not a single skull is in one piece. On the upper floor in one of the former cells, a relic – traces of blood from the executioners' pikes – is protected by a wooden frame.

THE TIME ACCORDING TO SAINT-SULPICE

THE CHURCH GNOMON
PLACE SAINT-SULPICE / 6th
METRO: SAINT-SULPICE

Outstanding in many ways, Saint-Sulpice Church has a gnomon – a somewhat worldly item for a church – in the left wing of its transept. The white marble, astronomical measuring instrument, is an obelisk with a line of copper leading away from it, embedded in the floor. When the sun shines, the ingenious device indicates the "true" midday hour and the approximate date. Completed in 1727, the meridian line was improved upon by Pierre Lemonnier in 1744. In order to use it in winter as well, he built an obelisk ten meters high, linking it with the gnomon's eye located 25 meters above the ground in a transept window facing south. The copper line embedded in the floor is meant to represent the Paris meridian, the accuracy of which people with a rational turn of mind are quick to contest. What does it matter, as long as the time spent wandering round the square is a happy time!

LAYERED CHURCHES

SAINT-SULPICE CHURCH CRYPT
PLACE SAINT-SULPICE / 6th
METRO: SAINT-SULPICE

The walls of this crypt, in which concerts are often held, reveals the outline of a much older parish church that stood between the 14th and 16th centuries. By the 17th century, plans had been drawn up to replace the older structure by an edifice more in proportion to "the number and the piety" of the parishioners. The plans were for outward and upward expansion.
In terms of size alone, the new Saint-Sulpice church (the one still standing today) not only dominated the neighboring buildings, it required worshipers to climb a set of stairs to enter the church. The old church building was not entirely demolished; portions of the new church were built over the old pillars, up to four meters in height, to form the foundation of today's church.
It is down in this lovely 5,000-square meter underground crypt (approximately 54,000 sq. feet) that one may admire the old church's bell tower staircase, and an old well. Montesquieu, Mme de La Fayette, and other celebrities were buried in this crypt.

LARGER NUMBERS

FORMER BROTHELS
15 AND 36 RUE SAINT-SULPICE / 6th
METRO: ODÉON OR SAINT-SULPICE

A law promulgated April 13, 1946 forced the closure of all "houses of pleasure" in France. The capital,with no shortage of brothels, was suddenly deprived of its Sphinx, Chabanais, One Two Two, and countless other houses of ill-repute.
After the Liberation, the city had no fewer than 195 bawdyhouses employing some 1,150 "working girls." Some of these establishments offered their customers particularly refined decors and furnishings. The Sphinx had its Egyptian room. The house at 32 Rue Blondel still has sumptuous mosaics. Some offered inventive themes, for example a train compartment complete with sound effects, rolling country sides views, a ticket collector, and a "madonna of the sleeping cars."
Discretion was the hallmark of other establishments distinguishable only by their street numbers painted larger than other addresses'. Such was the case of two homes on Rue Saint-Sulpice. Located very close to the church and religious articles shops, they were frequented by certain clerics, described by Alphonse Boudard in his novel *La Fermeture*. "The doorbell rings and the assistant madame looks out the peephole, opens the door, then leads the way to the available girls. A maze of corridors prevents awkward encounters." The area surrounding the church was also frequented by regulars at 27 Rue de l'Échaudé, and salesclerks frequented those on Rue Mazarine, Rue Grégoire-de-Tour, Rue Monsieur-le-Prince, and Rue Dauphine.

THE REVOLUTIONARY METER

36 RUE DE VAUGIRARD (TO THE RIGHT OF THE PORCH UNDER THE ARCHES) / 6th
RER: LUXEMBOURG

Defined as the ten-millionth part of the meridian circle between the North Pole and the Equator, the meter was brought in by the Convention (responsible for the Proclamation of the Republic in 1792) in 1795 to replace the toise and the foot. The creation of a common unit was really revolutionary when you think that, under the Ancien Régime, the foot was divided into a variable number of inches, and had varying lengths depending on where you lived.
Adopting the meter meant mastering the decimal system, not an easy task in view of the degree of illiteracy in France at the time. People could divide by 2, 4 or 8, by folding a piece of string once, twice or three times, but dividing by 10 was quite a different matter!
In order to acquaint the public with the new unit of measure, 16 marble standard meters were installed in the busiest parts of Paris between February 1796 and December 1797. There are only two left in Paris today, and only one is in its original position in Rue de Vaugirard. It is fixed to the wall of a private manor house taken over by the Department of Weights and Measures at the end of the 18th century.

TIME STANDS STILL

THE HOME OF AUGUSTE COMTE
10 RUE MONSIEUR-LE-PRINCE / 6th
METRO: ODÉON
Tel: 01 43 26 08 56
www.Augustecomte.org
Open Wednesday from 2 PM to 5 PM

Despite a sign indicating that philosopher Auguste Comte drew his final breath here, Rue Monsieur-le-Prince, few Parisians cross the threshold of this building which was home to the pope of Positivism. Past the carriage door, then to the right, is a door to a staircase. Upstairs, the former home of the master is open to the public and provides visitors an exceptional opportunity to view a bourgeois, 19th-century residence, for which time has stood still.

In the entrance hall, the oil portrait of Isidore Auguste Marie François Xavier Comte greets guests. His stern face contrasts with the more pleasant features of a young lady, Clotilde de Vaux, the great man's muse. Glass cabinets hold the personal belongings of Clotilde and her beloved, as well as published works, and photographs providing insight into the tumultuous life of Auguste Comte. Born in 1798 in Montpellier, he taught mathematics, then went to Paris where he encountered Saint-Simon (social philosopher famous for his system of utopia), whom he hired as his secretary. Comte taught his positivist philosophy from 1830 to 1842. He set forth the basis of Positivism, which can be summed up as a system tacitly refusing metaphysics and favors the notion that experience is the sole foundation for knowledge.

Comte's home became a pilgrimage for adherents to Positivism. As his apartment still contains his furniture and personal belongings, it feels as if he still inhabits the place. Some of the rooms were very accurately recomposed by Paulo Carneiro, about 1960. The living room is the most important of the rooms. It was here that took place, on numerous occasions, ceremonies of the humanist religion he had developed after the demise of Clotilde de Vaux. These included weddings, baptisms, and initiations. The study has the very desk upon which Comte composed his treatise on sociology, outlining the humanist religion. The bedroom, utterly simple, is lit by one courtyard window. It is perhaps the most moving room. The only decorative item is a basket of artificial flowers, a present from Clotilde de Vaux. The bed is still in its original place, an alcove. Surrounded by a few loved one, Comte drew his final breath on this bed on September 5th, 1857. Visitors are often surprised to find themselves whispering in this residence frozen in time. It almost seems that one tiny spark from a log burning in the hearth would be enough to bring him back to life.

REVOLUTION AT THE CONVENT

REFECTORY OF THE FORMER CORDELIER CONVENT
15 RUE DE L'ÉCOLE-DE-MÉDECINE / 6th
METRO: ODÉON
Open daily from 11 AM to 7 PM

The refectory, all that is left of the Cordelier Convent, is a fine example of flamboyant Gothic architecture, a rare sight in Paris. Founded by Franciscan monks in the 13th century, the convent was organized around a church, built in 1262 and the biggest in Paris since it covered the area occupied by today's School of Medicine. Construction of the refectory itself began in the second half of the 15th century, and was completed in 1506. However, the Cordelier Convent (the monks got their name from the knotted cord girdles they wore) is known more for its extra-theological activities. In the spring of 1790, the famous Cordeliers' Club, one of the most important political clubs of the French Revolution, began holding their public meetings here. More left-wing than the Jacobins (radical political group led by Robespierre during the French Revolution), the Cordeliers were led by Danton and Marat who lived nearby. Marat, who lived at no. 20, was buried in the monastery garden after his fatal meeting with Charlotte Corday. Behind a small metal door to the left of the main entrance, there are some 17th- and 18th-century graffiti on the walls between the 8th and 10th buttresses. They are highlighted by a very symbolic palm leaf, and immortalize the names of the monks connected with the school of convent theology.

The former refectory

GRIM REMINDERS

FORMER SCHOOL OF MEDICINE
15-21 RUE DE L'ÉCOLE-DE-MÉDECINE / 6th
METRO: ODÉON

Opposite the Cordeliers refectory, a nice surprise awaits adventurous explorers of Paris. A discreet entrance through the austere façade of the former School of Medicine leads to a peaceful and attractive courtyard. This building, constructed between 1877 and 1900 by Léon Ginain and Charles Duprez, is a propitious place for meditation and rest. The school stands on the site of the Cordeliers convent, as the cloister here so eloquently recalls. Was this intentional in the design? Alas, we do not know.

Visitors will be intrigued by the inscription over the door pointing to the Dupuytren museum. This museum, only visited upon appointment, contains a prestigious anatomical collection. It was named after the surgeon Guillaume Dupuytren. It opened to the public in 1835. Viewing the rows of skeletons or the jars containing monstrous fetuses may stun you. Pathologies (many of which disappeared thanks to medical progress), captured forever in time, in wood or wax, or in the form of "preparations", are absolute masterpieces.

This museum houses antique woodwork from the Académie royale de chirurgie (Royal Academy of Surgery). The oldest skeleton, presented to the Academy in 1752, is that of a woman afflicted with pregnancy-associated degenerative bone disease (osteomalacia). Her curled up remains bear witness to the immense pain she suffered. The brain of Leborgne, alias "Tan", rests in eternal peace in a glass jar. The famed Dr. Broca located the human brain's center of language by studying it. The mummified head of a bearded woman in a glass case continues to fascinate the museum's rare visitors. This is no place for the squeamish!

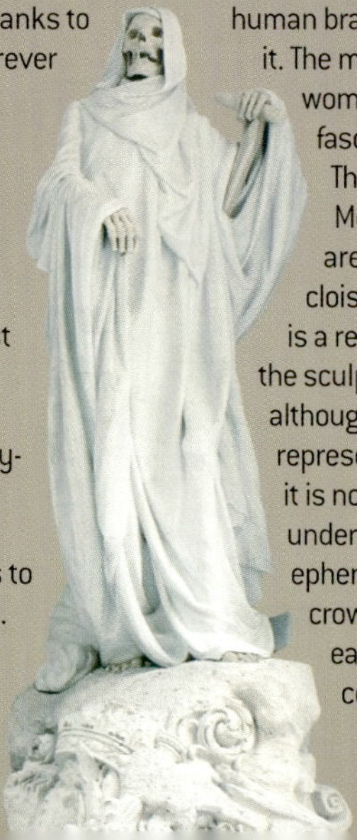

More serene sights carved in marble are placed in the middle of the cloisters. Standing out among them, is a remarkable statue chiseled by the sculptor Allouard in 1910. Frightful, yes, although a quite conventional representation of the Grim Reaper, it is none the less magnificent. Crushed under its feet are the symbols of man's ephemeral fancies and vanity (a princely crown, a bishop's crozier, money, etc.), each one is there to remind us of our common, inevitable fate.

NOTHING BUT A SHARP CHILL...

COUR DE ROHAN
RUE DU JARDINET, COUR DU COMMERCE-SAINT-ANDRÉ / 6th
METRO: ODÉON

The narrow Rue du Jardinet snakes between buildings up to the gates of Cour de Rohan, a peaceful, green space in an area devoted to tourism. The former, well-restored manor house, wrongly attributed to the archbishops of Rouen, has three small courtyards. The first one, Louis XIII in character, built in brick and stone, has a well in a recess on the left, complete with well-curb, gargoyle and pulley. A passage leads to the second courtyard where there is a wrought-iron mounting-block, the last one in Paris; ladies, abbots and old men used it to mount their horses.
In the third courtyard, a fragment of Philip Augustus' wall forms a terrace, which used to be the end of Rue du Jardinet, a cul-de-sac until 1791. Since the end of the 18th century, a wide door gives access to Cour du Commerce-Saint-André, just opposite the rear entrance of the famous *Procope* café. This passage was partly destroyed when Boulevard Saint-Germain was built; it used to join an old street, Rue des Cordeliers, near Danton's statue. Danton and his wife lived in the house at the top of the passage which Danton used to take to go to the *Procope*, long renowned for its passionate debating sessions.
Marat set up the l'Ami du Peuple printing works at no. 8, now a recently renovated shop, where, on the left at the back, you can see the base of one of the towers of Philip Augustus' wall (see p. 45).
At no. 9, sheep were used to test the guillotine, a revolutionary tool which, according to its inventor, Dr. Guillotin, would "standardize" methods used for putting the condemned to death. The doctor, a humanist when the fancy took him, asserted that the heavy blade sliding rapidly down between the two wooden uprights would painlessly cut off the heads of the prisoners, "who would feel nothing but a sharp chill on the nape of the neck".

A CHAPEL IN BITS AND PIECES

SQUARE LAURENT-PRACHE
RUE DE L'ABBAYE / 6th
METRO: SAINT-GERMAIN-DES-PRÉS

Saint-Germain-de-Prés Church is the remnant of an abbey of the same name, one of the most imposing abbeys in France. After two of its bell-towers had been knocked down during the French Revolution, and it had been converted into a saltpeter factory in the late 19th century, the church was in such a bad state that work to restore – and change the nature of – the edifice was undertaken several times during the 19th century. However, our main interest here concerns the remnants outside in Square Laurent-Prache. Exposed to the wind and the rain, the remains of a magnificent chapel, dedicated to the Virgin Mary, have been on view here since the beginning of the century. Perpendicular to the site of Rue de l'Abbaye, this jewel of a chapel was built in 1255 by the famous architect, Pierre de Montreuil, who was buried here some years later alongside his wife. The French Revolution left the chapel practically unscathed, whereas it was dealt a fatal blow during the 19th century. After serving as a granary, the chapel was restored to the church for the purpose of worship from 1795 to 1802, the year when Dr. Salbrune bought and razed it to the ground. He saved a few architectural items which he installed on the façade of his house, a strange way of paying tribute to a building he had just destroyed. After his house was demolished at the beginning of this century, some of the chapel's relics were recovered and placed in the square bordering Saint-Germain-des-Prés Church, making it a veritable museum of stones. Since then, there has been a general lack of concern regarding this beautiful chapel's remains, which continue to deteriorate.
The door of the edifice can be seen in Cluny Museum gardens, and, fortunately, a stained-glass window has been preserved, its kaleidoscope of colors glowing in one of the apses of Saint-Germain-des-Prés Church.

A MUSEUM OF STONES

ÉCOLE DES BEAUX-ARTS
14 RUE BONAPARTE / 6th
METRO: SAINT-GERMAIN-DES-PRÉS
Tel: 01 47 03 50 00

The School of Fine Arts opens into Rue Bonaparte through a wide courtyard surrounded by austere, 19th-century buildings. The school's various, easily accessed courtyards are havens of peace in the heart of Paris.
It was here, in the gardens, among the remnants of the Grands-Augustins Convent, that archeo-logist Alexandre Lenoir stored works of art which he managed to rescue from the hands of the revolutionaries, thus creating the first Museum of French Monuments. Various pieces of architecture, statues, medieval tombs were on view to the public in the "Élysée Garden", the latter making a considerable impression on generations of young romantics, many of whom became artists or writers.
The museum was closed in 1816, and became the School of Fine Arts.

Conversion work on the former convent was started by architect François Debret, and continued by Félix Duban until 1872. He installed pieces of architecture from the former museum all over the school, and some of them can still be seen in the main courtyard.
The architect placed the central projecting part of Anet Castle, built by Philibert Delorme for Diane de Poitiers, on the right-hand side of the church façade. The gates in front also came from the castle. Opposite, under the arches, are some of the remains of the magnificent Hôtel Legendre, built during the 15th and 16th centuries and demolished in 1844. Remains of the Tuileries are also scattered about.
The Petits-Augustins Church, built in 1617, is one of the rare remnants of the convent, and may be visited during exhibitions.
A corridor on the left gives access to the former cloister, converted by Duban into an antique-style atrium in 1836. The Mûrier courtyard echoes with the soothing sound of water from the central fountain.
The moldings on the walls are copies of the Parthenon sculptures. To the right of the Palais des Études, in another courtyard, you can admire some arches, unfortunately rather blackened, from Hôtel de Jacques Du Faur, or de Torpane, dating back to 1567. People strolling past are generally unaware that the School of Fine Arts has a garden, and, despite the passage of time, its attraction still lies in its air of romance.

CHOCOLATE: GOOD MEDICINE, GOOD BUSINESS

CHOCOLATERIE DEBAUVE ET GALLAIS
30 RUE DES SAINTS-PÈRES / 7th
METRO: SAINT-GERMAIN-DES-PRÉS

The first chocolate shop in Paris belonged to Sulpice Debauve, who had once served as the pharmacist to Louis XVI. It was in the heart of the Saint-Germain-des-Près faubourg, "near Rue Saint-Guillaume, in front of number 4 Rue Saint-Dominique." The sign over the shop read: *À la renommée des chocolats de France* (the best of France's chocolates). The smart businessman tempted his customers with such sophisticated and novel ingredients as Persian Salep "light and nutritious suitable for weak constitutions and susceptible chests, for persons afflicted by chronic ailments and nervous stomachs." It was the start of a huge success.
Purveyor to the king and known throughout Europe for his specialties, he opened sixty-five outlets for the sale of his products throughout France, with several in Paris.
By 1818, he had moved to Rue des Saints-Pères. Combining his previous profession with his current, he began producing "healthy" chocolates flavored with almond milk, vanilla, or orange blossom. Next, he created the "*Théréobrome*," a cold, instant chocolate, recommended for those with low stamina. In 1832, doctors recommended his analeptic chocolate to ward off cholera.
Ingenious Sulpice Debauve also invented dehydrated milk, however, was not able to to take advantage of his invention. After his death in 1836, the chocolate company was taken over by professionals who never betrayed the founder's wishes: make high-quality chocolate with beneficial and salutary qualities.
Awarded several prizes at universal expositions, the Chocolaterie Debauve & Gallais continues to welcome chocolate afficiados in its magnificent first Empire décor, designed by Percier and Fontaine, architects to Napoleon I.

FINAL RESTING PLACE

FORMER PROTESTANT CEMETERY
30 RUE DES SAINTS-PÈRES / 7th
METRO: SAINT-GERMAIN-DES-PRÉS

The apparently ordinary courtyard behind the iron gate by the chocolate shop is in fact a sanctuary, where for many centuries, Protestants were laid to rest. No holy graveyard could accept any members of the "so-called reformed religion." For a long time, Protestants had to bury their dead in their own cemeteries. They chose various places along Rue des Saints-Pères, in the Saint-Germain-des-Prés quarter. First, at today's number 51, then at number 49 near the Saint-Pierre-de-la-Maladrerie chapel (now the Ukrainian church, Saint-Vladimir-le-Grand), on the site of the small square beside today's Boulevard Saint-Germain. However, as the abbey wanted to acquire this plot of land for lepers, the Conseil d'État ruled that the cemetery had to be moved across the street. Thus, Protestants obtained their first official cemetery, funded entirely by the royal treasury. And on May 21, 1604, the first to be buried there was one Jean Ruffin, an 81-year-old printer, soon followed by many other Protestants, including some famous names such as the engineer and architect of royal buildings Jacques Salomon de Brosse, Jean Androuet du Cerceau,

the wife of Théophraste Renaudot, cloth dyers Gobelins, and Académie Française's founding secretary Valentin Conrart.
The Revocation of the Edict of Nantes in 1685 forced Protestants to bury their dead in secret places, in gardens on private property, and vacant lots. This practice lingered on even after the French Revolution had paved the way for freedom of religion.
This address, anonymous, discreet, and moving, is a rare example of the small private cemeteries that have since disappeared.

AND THEN THERE WAS LIGHT...

THE GLASS HOUSE
31 RUE SAINT-GUILLAUME / 7th
METRO: RUE-DU-BAC
For visits, write to the Association des Amis de la Maison de Verre (address above).

The glass house in Rue Saint-Guillaume is tucked away, well out of sight, in the courtyard of an 18th-century house. Avant-garde architect Pierre Chareau, admirer of the Cubists, together with Bernard Bijvoët, built this amazing, transparent house for Dr. Jean Dalsace in 1930. In fact, the glass structure came about on account of an unexpected complication.
The parcel of land where Dr. Dalsace planned to build his office and private apartment did not become available as planned. The top floor of the building on the site was occupied by an old lady who had no intention of moving! As it was impossible to demolish the building, Chareau built three, light-reflecting stories in the space of the former ground and first floors, and left the top floor intact. The surgery is on the ground floor, while an impressive-looking, two-level reception room, a dining room, a small sitting room, and a study are the next flight up, with the bedrooms and bathrooms above them.
The metal-latticed glass façade allows the light to flood into the house. Such transparency went against tradition because of its dismissal of the notion of inside and outside. However, this admirable house did not really set a trend, even though famous architect and city planner Le Corbusier was very impressed by it, and frequently visited the building site to make sketches of it.

The interior of the glass house is modular with sliding and pivoting panels and partitions. Chareau had an almost fanatical eye for detail, leaving nothing to chance. Even the soapdishes in the bathrooms bear the hallmark of their creator!

BEAUTIFUL JULIE...

SQUARE ROGER-STÉPHANE (FORMERLY SQUARE RÉCAMIER)
AT THE END OF RUE RÉCAMIER / 7th
METRO: SÈVRES-BABYLONE

The memory of Julie Récamier, a woman of wit and learning, and muse to Chateaubriand, lingers over Rue Récamier where, for a long time, under the Restoration of the Bourbons, she lived and held brilliant receptions in a small apartment on the third floor, overlooking a cloistered courtyard.
Men of letters such as Balzac, Musset, Hugo, Lamartine, all came to converse with this lady, whose intelligence equaled her beauty. René de Chateaubriand never failed to pay her a visit every day.
Rue Récamier was built on the site of the Abbaye-aux-Bois, demolished in 1906-7, and is now just a cul-de-sac leading to the unexpected sight of a pretty garden. The Square, laid out on the site of Hôtel de Vaudreuil gardens (7 Rue de la Chaise) which communicated with those of Abbaye-aux-Bois, is a delightful, peaceful place with raised flower beds, full of all kinds of fragrant flowers – rhododendron, heather, periwinkles – to scent the summer air.

MIRACLE MEDALS FROM RUE DU BAC

CHAPELLE DE LA MÉDAILLE-MIRACULEUSE
140 RUE DU BAC / 7th
METRO: SÈVRES-BABYLONE

It takes a dose of optimism and confidence in divine providence not to be weighed down by all the woes of this world. Indeed, they seem to have rained down upon 140 Rue du Bac. A tiny medal might work wonders. The chapel is never empty, and prayers are recited more fervently here than elsewhere.
On November 27th, 1827, Catherine Labouré – a young country girl who had come from her native Bourgogne to join the Saint-Vincent-de-Paul Sisters of Charity – is said to have seen a vision of the Virgin Mary in the Hôtel de la Vallière chapel.
"It was half past five in the evening.
In the silence following meditation, I thought I heard a noise coming from the gallery. When I looked, I caught sight of the Virgin Mary standing there, dressed for the evening, in glimmering white." Catherine was canonized in 1947.

A constant stream of pilgrims from all over the world comes to kneel for a few moments before the shrine containing Saint Catherine's remains. Other relics, such the chair the Virgin Mary is said to have occupied, are on view in the chapel.
Since 1832, millions of tiny miracle medals have been struck and sold. Until recently, they were obtainable from a vending machine. A notice states that the medal should "be worn and distributed, not as a lucky charm, but with faith and love". Was it really necessary to explain?

AN INDUSTRIAL SITE

23 RUE OUDINOT / 7th
METRO: VANEAU OR DUROC

Despite the fact that it is named after a general of the First Empire, Rue Oudinot always looks very peaceful. There is a surprise in store for you behind the door of an ordinary-looking, 19th-century building at no. 23. Push open the door and go down the long cul-de-sac, perpendicular to Rue Oudinot. This used to be an industrial site consisting of workshops built out of wood and brick, which have now been converted into flats. There is a fairly ordinary-looking house at the far end, past some clumps of bamboo. You will also find a few inviting benches where you can take a quiet rest in the courtyard.

TWIN MANSIONS

HÔTEL DESMARES, AGRICULTURE MINISTRY
78 RUE DE VARENNE / 7th
METRO: SOLFÉRINO

17 RUE DE LA GARE, CHÂTILLON / HAUTS-DE-SEINE
METRO: CHÂTILLON-MONTROUGE OR RER: FONTENAY-AUX-ROSES

Former country home in Châtillon.

The immensely popular actress Charlotte Desmares was the darling of the Comédie Française as well as of the Grand Dauphin, son of Louis XIV. Later, she became the mistress of Philippe d'Orléans, future Regent de France, who fathered her daughter. She then inflamed the passions of Antoine Hogguer, the Baron de Presles. The baron, member of the Swedish Royal Council of Commerce belonged to a family of wealthy Swiss bankers. As Antoine and Charlotte's fiery love affair could not decently be sealed in matrimony, the banker used common sense. While social conventions prevented the lovers from sharing the same roof, they didn't prevent them from being next-door neighbors. Hogguer purchased a parcel of land beside his mansion located at today's number 101 Rue de Grenelle, and commissioned architect François Debias Aubry to build a delightful mansion for the actress. A small door provided discreet access from one garden to the other. Today, the Hôtel Desmares is the main building at the Ministry of Agriculture.

Not one to do things half way, the baron ordered the same architect to erect a nearly identical mansion in the country, in what is now Châtillon. It was his gift to his beloved Charlotte. The home can be admired from the city park that it overlooks.

Hôtel Desmares.

THE WOLF AND THE EAGLE

HÔTEL DES INVALIDES / 7th
METRO: LA TOUR-MAUBOURG OR VARENNE

The stark military style of the Hôtel des Invalides always impresses visitors. It is hardly surprising, then, that words should have so little place in one of the temples of silence. Shall we give two examples?
In the main courtyard, on the east side, the sixth dormer window from the far end is crowned by carved stone. A wolf peeks out from forest vegetation. It would seem that Louvois, a minister under Louis XIV, who carried out the construction of the Les Invalides, was asked to remove his coat of arms that he had too generously placed throughout the royal military hospital. Being equally obstinate and vain, the minister managed nevertheless to make his mark here in the form of a stone rebus. The pun in French turns the syllables in his family name into subject and verb, thus: *le loup voit* (the wolf sees). In this case, the pun is heightened by the fact that the carved wolf is indeed watching the court(yard).
Nearby, the Nîmes corridor provides a direct view of the tombstone placed on Napoleon's grave on the isle of Saint Hélène. Brought to France in 1840 with the remains of the emperor on the frigate *La Belle Poule*, this tombstone in three sections was forgotten at the Cherbourg arsenal. In 1909, the relic was transferred to Les Invalides and placed in a side chapel among other funerary objects belonging to the emperor. The tombstone sections have been in their present place since 1977, surrounded by an iron gate, much as they were on the island of Saint Hélène beneath the willows. No words were ever carved upon them because Hudson Lowe, the emperor's jailor on the island, refused to allow the imperial name "Napoleon" to be engraved.

Time has not yet burnished
the narrow stone,
Beneath the green weave
of the ivy and bramble
One can make out... a broken scepter
Here lies... There is no name!
Ask the soil!
(Lamartine)

A BUILDING AS A BILLBOARD

LAVIROTTE ARCHITECTURE
29 AVENUE RAPP AND 3 SQUARE RAPP / 7th
METRO: ÉCOLE-MILITAIRE

Architect Jules Lavirotte's Art Nouveau façades are the finest in Paris, particularly those along Avenue Rapp. Born in Lyons in 1864, he was very gifted in his use of cement, and used to call upon the services of a leading ceramics expert, Alexandre Bigot, to overlay his buildings. It was for Bigot that Lavirotte erected the building at no. 29 in 1900. In order to please his associate, he gave full rein to his imagination. Straight lines were abandoned in favor of entangled, extravagant curves, which, even today, never cease to amaze passersby. This was the first time that ceramics had been used so extensively on a façade in Paris, and also an ideal opportunity to make a billboard of this six-story building, thus advertising Bigot's work at little extra cost!
The decoration round the front door is particularly audacious. It has foliage curved round it, and is topped by two small figures which flank the face of a woman with her hair in a graceful chignon. It might even be Mrs. Lavirotte's pretty face.
The entire façade is a mosaic of all sorts of surprising embellishments and motifs in brick, stone and ceramics.
Just nearby, at the far end of Square Rapp, Lavirotte put up another building, this time for himself, with a façade just as elaborately decorated.

29 Avenue Rapp

GLASS JEWELS

RENÉ LALIQUE'S HOME
40 COURS ALBERT 1er / 8th
METRO: ALMA-MARCEAU

In 1902, the architectural firm L. & A. Feine completed a rather disconcerting building for master glassmaker René Lalique. The relatively stiff neo-Renaissance style given to the façade contrasted sharply with the style of this artist who excelled in Art Nouveau. Although it includes organic elements in a few remarkable cast iron and carved stone pieces, it looks as if it were slapped onto the building to make up for the ensemble's stark verticality.
The interior, however, is more in line with his trademark style. Lalique set up his showroom here. He himself designed the furnishings and decorative pieces, which have long since been auctioned off. His art is only reflected now by the doorway with its elegant curves and its steel-encased glass complementing the arborescence of the stonework. Curious visitors who dare push through the doorway will admire the masterpiece of transparency in the main hall: the staircase and the elevator wrapped in brambles.

VICTIMS OF CHARITY

CHAPELLE NOTRE-DAME-
DE-LA-CONSOLATION
23 RUE JEAN-GOUJON / 8th
METRO: ALMA-MARCEAU
Open from 9 AM to 7 PM

In 1897, some patronesses had a long wooden shed built. It housed twenty-two medieval-style booths, decorated with painted fabric and oriflammes, and topped with a canopy. Huge crowds used to pack into the shed, and they were served by 70 ladies who were the cream of Parisian high society.

A tiny, 9m by 4m booth contained an exciting attraction: the cinematograph (a movie projector). As a result of a mistake by the operator, the tarred shed caught fire. The flames spread rapidly, and the burning fabric suffocated many of those vainly trying to escape. There was total panic; the poor people pushed, screamed, fought, and were trampled in a frantic attempt to escape the blaze. When it was over, one hundred and twenty-five victims – including one hundred and twenty women – were recovered from the debris. Generous donations from Parisians allowed the bereaved families to buy a plot of land where a magnificent chapel was built by architect Albert Désiré Guilbert in 1900. Squeezed between two tall buildings, the façade with its double stairway, is unusual. An inscription above the entrance (*"Ne vous attristez pas comme ceux qui n'ont pas d'espérance"*) gives the following advice: "Don't be saddened like people without hope."

The baroque interior is Louis XIV, and rather interesting. A beautiful marble mosaic covers the floor. The dome, supported by four massive, gray marble columns, is ornamented with a painting by Albert Maignan. Behind the high altar, in an atrium representing the Way of the Cross, the remains of the fire victims, who died out of love for charity, are buried beneath the cenotaphs.

Little known and hardly ever visited, Notre-Dame-de-la-Consolation Chapel, a memorial to a national catastrophe, houses the Italian Catholic Mission. The building was listed as a historic monument in 1980.

ART NOUVEAU ON EVERY FLOOR

ÉLYSÉES CERAMIC HOTEL
34 AVENUE DE WAGRAM / 8th
METRO:TERNES

Passersby are often surprised by this strange façade. In his *Envahissant Cadavre de la Plaine Monceau*, novelist Léo Malet compared it to a bathroom. The fired-sandstone and varnished-brick cladding spanning the seven floors of the building was the work of Jules Lavirotte, with the assistance of ceramist Alexandre Bigot and sculptor Camille Alaphilippe.

The architect's display of talent earned him an award in the city's 1905 façade contest. Erected in 1904 and originally planned for furnished room rentals for Logiluxe, a Parisian company, this building was first known as Ceramic Hôtel, then later became Élysées Ceramic. At the time when the Étoile area teemed with houses of ill repute, the hotel was a landmark in the sex industry. Wisteria, quince trees, and other climbing plants creep across the façade, whereas cockchafers placed here and there give an animal effect. The interior decoration, unfortunately disfigured long ago, is nonetheless tasteful done in a style incorporating the lines and curves of Art Nouveau (see also page 92).

AN AIR OF CHINA

LOO'S HOUSE
48 RUE DE COURCELLES / 8th
METRO: COURCELLES

A red pagoda right in the heart of Paris – a rather unexpected sight – stands on the corner of Rue de Courcelles and Rue Rembrandt. Contrary to popular belief, it was neither the former Chinese Embassy nor the traditional-style residence of a retired mandarin.
Young, well-born Mr. Loo came to study in Paris at the end of the 19th century. At the age of twenty-two, he set up an oriental antiques business, Place de la Madeleine. He quickly became the leading expert in Paris, and opened up new horizons for informed collectors as well as museum curators.

In 1922, Mr. Loo bought a private manor house on Rue de Courcelles, but it soon proved to be too small for his vast collections. The antique dealer then called in a French architect to build him the house of his dreams: a Chinese house in the heart of Paris. François Bloch oversaw the building work, and the house was finished in 1928.

TASTES
OF CHOCOLATE

HÔTEL MENIER
5 AVENUE VAN-DYCK / 8th
METRO: COURCELLES

This fanciful mansion with weeds and wild grass growing in its yard has long conjured up images of Sleeping Beauty's castle... and it very nearly was relegated to the stuff of fairytales. Slated for demolition, the old home, built for chocolate king Émile Menier by architect Henri Parent between 1872 and 1874, was saved in the nick of time by being listed on the historical register. It was then bought and carefully restored by the Compagnie Française de Crédit et de Rénovation.

Overlooking the Parc Monceau, the building is shaped like a backwards L. The main entrance in Louis XV style has imposing balustrades, grooved masonry and consoles, curves and reversed curves, all providing a very baroque effect with a few prominent elements. First, there is the carved face of Mercury in the keystone over the doorway, framed by lions' heads in the console above, but there are also the pediment's curious hippocampi, fauns, and female heads gracing window awnings, all attributed to Jules Dalou.
Inside the mansion, once past the vestibule and the grand staircase decorated with atlantes, we come upon three astonishing rooms: the dining room which has preserved its fireplace framed by a pediment and capitals, the Neo-Gothic billiards room upholstered in fine leather from Cordoba embossed with characters in a gilded monochrome, and a neo-Renaissance study with a paneled ceiling inset with Gien dinnerware.
Fortunately, this vessel made of stone has been preserved. Its heavy carved decoration is an excellent example of the pompous tastes of France's 19th-century merchant bourgeoisie.

ITINERANT COLUMNS

PARC MONCEAU
BOULEVARD DE COURCELLES / 8th
METRO: MONCEAU

The naumachia columns in Parc Monceau look like they came straight out of a wealthy Roman villa. While they are not archeological treasures, they certainly are curiosities of history. In fact, they are fragments of a mausoleum that was to be built just north of the Saint-Denis Basilica. Catherine de Médicis had ordered it for herself, her husband, and their children. In her opinion, however, it was not good enough for their sepulchers. Alas! This rotunda, 30 meters in diameter, designed like an ancient Roman tomb, was never finished, and the queen was laid to rest beside Henry II inside the basilica. The monument was dismantled in 1719 and the columns went into storage.
The Duke of Chartres acquired them in 1773 while redecorating his country house and gardens outside the Monceau hamlet. The landscaped grounds were designed by Louis Carrogis, also known as Carmontelle. He set up vantage points, undulating terrain, a stream, and other amusing inventions. Surviving, today, are the pyramid and the lovely colonnade with Corinthian capitals. The décor also received a centered obelisk as well as a gateway at the far end of the colonnade, which opened onto a small circular drive, now a sandbox. There, stood a fountain with marble and lead elements representing a bathing lady and her black domestic pouring water from a golden ewer.
The marble statue now belongs to New York's Metropolitan Museum of Art.
Parc Monceau was declared public property during the Revolution, and turned into a park. Later, in the 19th century, half of Parc Monceau was turned over to developers. The remainder of the grounds were relandscaped in 1861 by Alphand, who restored the naumachia.

DINNER IS SERVED!

NISSIM DE CAMONDO MUSEUM
63 RUE DE MONCEAU / 8th
METRO: VILLIERS AND MONCEAU
Tel: 01 53 89 06 50/06 40
www.lesartsdecoratifs.fr
Open Wednesday to Sunday
from 10:00 AM to 5:30 PM
METRO: VILLIERS AND MONCEAU

In 1911, architect René Sergent was commissioned by Count Moïse de Camondo, a collector of French 18th-century art, to design a charming pastiche of this period beside the Monceau city park. In 1935, upon the demise of this enlightened amateur of art and in memory of his son Nissim who died in action in 1917, the *Union Centrale des Arts Décoratifs* (now Les Arts Décoratifs) inherited the mansion and his entire collection.

Visitors can now enjoy a few recently and nicely restored areas in the servants' quarters, providing a good overview of early 20th-century working conditions and comforts. The large, soberly decorated third-floor bathrooms have hefty fixtures. Perhaps the most impressive fixtures, however, are in the kitchen on the ground-floor. Half-sunken, it was connected to the dining room by a serving hatch. The double ceiling gave added insulation between the domestics' quarters and the master's dining table. It is a perfect example of a bourgeois mansion's kitchen. It is tiled from top to bottom in no-nonsense white for ease of cleaning and maintenance, and equipped with the most modern appliances. The ingenious cast-iron ovens and rotisserie were manufactured by Cubain & Fils.

The domestics' mess hall might make you think of any pre-war movie set. Conveniently located next to the laundry room, the table there is set for the twelve servants' evening meal. The room is still equipped with their individual lockers.

Across the way is the well-lit pantry where the butler would receive suppliers and oversee kitchen operations. We learn for example that on June 2, 1934, dinner guests were served poached eggs in curry, roasted bass in Véron sauce, loin of lamb *à la Maintenon*, and strawberry granita followed by pastries. The wine selection included a Château Margaux 1878 and a Clos Vougeot 1928. Hôtel Camondo is a fine lesson in the art of savoir-vivre.

A ROYAL SMILE

CHAPEL OF ATONEMENT
SQUARE LOUIS XVI / 8th
METRO: SAINT-AUGUSTIN
Open on Thursdays, Fridays and Saturdays from 1 PM to 5 PM

In Square Louis XVI stands a chapel of atonement, erected on the site of the cemetery, where those guillotined at the Concorde were buried. The remains of Louis XVI and Marie-Antoinette were also laid to rest here. In 1794, the cemetery was closed and sold by lots at low prices. However, after spotting the royal tombs, a royalist neighbor bought back the site, and gave it to Louis XVIII. Excavations took place, and the king's remains were disinterred, as well as those of Marie-Antoinette, whose stockings worn on the day of her execution helped identify her. Chateaubriand made the macabre claim that she had been recognized because of her smile. The monarchs' ashes were transferred to the Saint-Denis Basilica where they remain today. Between 1816 and 1826, architect Fontaine erected this neoclassical edifice on the ground of the original cemetery. The chapel is ornamented with sculptures by J. B. Plantar and bas-relief sculptures by A. F. Gérard. A group by Bosio shows Louis XVI looking up at the sky, and Marie-Antoinette is by Cortot. The tombs in the courtyard are in memory of the Swiss Guards who fell when the Tuileries Palace was attacked on August 10th, 1792.

A CALL TO ARMS!

SIGN
1 RUE ROYALE / 8th
METRO: CONCORDE

One grim day in 1914, the mayor of the 8th arrondissement put up a general mobilization notice on one of the walls of the magnificent Hôtel de Coislin. War was breaking out, and tens of thousands of Parisians were to die on the front. After mobilization, the notice should have been taken down, but those who stayed behind were so busy that they did not pay any attention to it; "Maxim's" was always full, and omnibuses crossing Place de la Concorde were being driven by women. In 1919, an observant Parisian saw the notice – a little out-of-date to say the least – and had it framed. It has been there ever since, and may even have weathered the German occupation of Paris, although it was more likely to have been a facsimile, regularly supplied by the concierge of Hôtel Coislin (now head office of a private company). Today's photocopy probably dates back to the seventies. The very presence of this flimsy piece of paper serves as a reminder of one of the bloodiest wars of the 20th century.

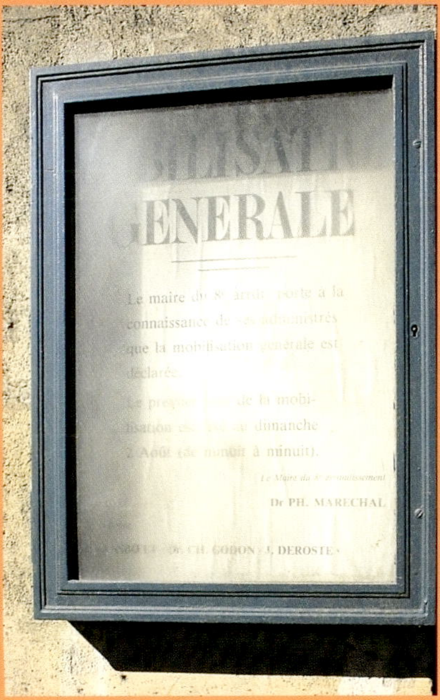

CHARMING CONVENIENCES

LA MADELEINE PUBLIC TOILETS
PLACE DE LA MADELEINE / 8th
METRO: MADELEINE
Open from 9:30 to 11:30 AM and 12:30 to 18:45 PM

To the left of the Madeleine, near the flower market, there are some steps leading down to the most amazing underground public lavatories in the city. Unlike the extraordinarily dull-looking, coin-operated public toilets in vogue at the end of the 20th century, this "convenience" was decorated by Porcher company in an Art Nouveau style, which even experts in the genre would not have failed to recognize. The stained-glass windows of the cubicle doors are decorated with floral designs, as are the walls, and the yellows and violets add a bright, cheerful note. Each cubicle has its own washbasin. Here, we are in the ladies' area, where there used to be another room opposite for men, no longer in use today.
For some strange reason, in his book on public conveniences in Paris, published in 1966, Jonathan Routh failed to mention the Madeleine toilets, which must rate at least four-star...

SUBTLE SCENTS

FRAGONARD PERFUME MUSEUM
9 RUE SCRIBE / 9th
METRO: OPÉRA
Tel: 01 47 42 04 56
Open daily from 9 AM to 5:30 PM

THÉÂTRE DES CAPUCINES MUSEUM
39 BOULEVARD DES CAPUCINES / 2nd
METRO: OPÉRA
Tel: 01 42 60 37 14
Open from Monday to Saturday
from 9 AM to 5:30 PM

Head to 9 Rue Scribe, a building built in 1860 by architect Lesoufacher, and enter the sweetest-smelling museum in Paris. The Fragonard Museum, opened in 1983, displays a splendid collection of practical and unusual objects that recount 3,000 years of perfume history. Delicate fragrances fill the air.
The world-famous perfume maker who began operations in Grasse in 1926, not only distills essences for discriminating noses, but also manufactures perfumes and a line of beauty products for large clientele.
The Fragonard Perfume Museum has a rich display. Over 2,500 pieces (a mere portion) from the vast collection of Jean-François Costa may be admired.
Both educational and pleasant, a visit to this Parisian museum will allow you to appreciate the astounding number of natural and synthetic raw materials used since antiquity in the elaboration of scents: jasmine, lavender, rose petals, sandalwood bark, benzoin resin, musk, and so many

more. Essence jars and alembics evoke extraction techniques used in the old days by glove-makers-cum-perfumers. Utilitarian items include: the charmingly named "*pisseuses à parfum*" (a type of perfume bottle), potpourri flasks, 17th- and 18th-century perfume bottles are displayed in the museum's exquisite salons. Some of these items are surprising to say the least. Take for example the curious bottle representing one child giving another child a leg up to dislodge a bird from its nest! Makeup cases and cases for beauty spots, and dainty perquisites recall the refined elegance of 18th-century Parisians salons.
The other part of the museum is located in the former Théâtre des Capucines whose pure art-deco style has been conserved. The ceiling is still decorated with amusing masks and musical instruments in relief which saw the stage debut of the Parisian star, Arletty. The visit continues with engravings, paintings, numerous works of art, and a highly instructive scale model of a perfume factory.
As you exit the museum, your head swimming after taking in so many lovely fragrances, the busy boulevard will jolt you back to reality. Fortunately, however, the magic of the alembics will continue to work its spell on you, making life a prettier and more pleasant place for us all.

STEAM DREAMS

OLD STEAM BATHS
18 RUE DES MATHURINS / 9th
METRO: HAVRE-CAUMARTIN

While this Moorish Revival façade may conjure up dreams of exotic lands, today's passersby cannot imagine how grand and stylish the old Alhambra-style bath house was. The façade was restored during the renovation of the entire block. It is the only remnant of the great steam baths of yesteryear, a veritable curiosity of Parisian life.
The *Guide du Baigneur* (the Bather's Guide) describe it in these terms, "[...] a huge vaulted room beneath a semicircular arch, a daring construction, lit by colored stain-glassed windows with stars.
The marble mosaic floor tells you are in the tepidarium. Its walls are lined with white marble divans half a meter high which cover wide heating vents. From the tepidarium, we move to the caldarium, the heated second level, then onwards to the massage room and the shower room. The lounge, a series of small rooms located off to each side of the central section, offers towel-wrapped bathers the luxury of stretching out on divans. A first-rate café-restaurant, a bookshop, a hair dresser, and a pedicurist, add an extra pleasant note to this oriental escapade."
Ladies could also reap the benefits of Turco-Romain baths, but only on certain days of the week, and providing they used the more discreet side door at number 47 Boulevard Hausmann.

A BANK'S CHARM

SOCIÉTÉ GÉNÉRALE
29 BOULEVARD HAUSSMANN / 9th
METRO: CHAUSSÉE-D'ANTIN-LA FAYETTE

In the years 1906 to 1911, Jacques Hermant, a talented architect of the School of Nancy, designed a block of seven buildings at this address. The imposing Haussmann-style structure was commissioned by the Société Générale bank. Esthetically pleasing and functional, it is a veritable manifesto of the elegant architecture of the early 20th century. The portion projecting onto the boulevard, copied from the original building, includes a pediment fitted with allegorical sculptures representing the City, the River, and Mercury. The fourth floor has six statues placed against the pilasters. They represent Commerce and Industry. Inside, the main hall is particularly noteworthy for its stupendous copula spanning over 23 meters in diameter. Hermant knew how to use the latest architectural ironwork techniques to create a majestic, luminous space. It includes arched moldings, green and orange stained-glass windows signed by glass master Jacques Galland, which presents the arms of France's main cities. The flooring is a splendid mosaic pavement, executed by Bourdet et Gentil. The design incorporates ornaments with interlacing plant-like patterns that wrap around openwork copper plates that disguised the ventilation ducts.

Even the safety-deposit room below is stunning. Particularly impressive is the 18-ton vault door, made to Jacques Hermant's order by the Fichet company, based on a model he had brought back from a trip to New York City. Built by Creusot, the vault door was transported by train, then carried through Paris on a trailer pulled by a team of nine horses.

PREY FOR THE HUNTED

ANIMAL FRIEZE ON THE OLD MAISON D'OR
20 BOULEVARD DES ITALIENS / 9th
METRO: RICHELIEU-DROUOT

The animals in this frieze seem poised to escape from the wall. The truth is that the masterpiece, created by the combined talents of Baptiste Lechesne and Pierre-Louis Rouillard, 19th-century sculptors of animals, narrowly escaped removal.
The Choiseul-Stainville mansion, which once stood on this site, was the home of Mrs. Tallien, the famous "Notre-Dame de Thermidor." After its demolition, it was replaced by the Café Hardy, frequented by wealthy romantics fond of gastronomy. The new building was erected in the 1830s and became home to Le Restaurant de la Cité. With its sumptuous décor, furniture, mirrors, and gilded molding, the establishment quickly became a fashionable place to be seen. Frequented by kept women and other "debris of the golden youth" to use Nerval's expression, the place soon became known as the *Maison d'Or* (literally: the house of gold), then later as the *Maison Dorée* (literally: the golden house).
By 1974, the dilapidated building was on the verge of collapse. It was restored and divided into spacious, functional cubicles. Thanks to a favorable press campaign launched by a group for the protection of historic sites, the façade was preserved and one of the far ends of the frieze was skillfully completed during the restoration.

HOUSING FOR ARTISTS

SQUARE D'ORLÉANS
80 RUE TAITBOUT / 9th
METRO: TRINITÉ

Square d'Orléans is one of the main highlights of the Nouvelle Athènes district, frequented by artists, musicians, actors, dancers, singers, and writers. To reach it, go down a high-ceilinged, heavily ornamented passage, cross one courtyard, and you will come into another, bigger courtyard with a fountain in the middle.

It was in 1830 that English architect Edward Crecy designed and built Square d'Orléans on the site of the former domain of *Comédie-Française* actress Mademoiselle Mars. Another Englishman, barrister Edward Richardson, whose great passion was ancient architecture, bought the Square, made a few alterations, and installed the fountain.

The British architects' preference for bricks, along with their style of building, endows the Square with a genre which distinguishes it from other 19th-century private housing developments in Paris.

Right from the start, it was a place of luxury, frequented by artistic and literary celebrities. Novelist George Sand moved into no. 85 in 1842, and Chopin lived at no. 9. Alexandre Dumas père, another resident here, gave a memorable party in his apartment decorated by Jadin, Delacroix, Boulanger, Grandville and Nanteuil. Many others decided to take up residence in this community of the Arts: opera singer Pauline Viardot, ballet dancer Marie Taglioni, painter and caricaturist Dantan Jeune, and pianist Zimmermann who used to entertain his neighbor, Chopin, as well as Liszt, Rossini and Berlioz, in his music room.

Silence reigns in Square d'Orléans today, but with a bit of imagination, you might hear a few notes of music wafting from the windows!

THÉRÈSE, QUEEN OF PARIS

DOSNE-THIERS LIBRARY AND HÔTEL DE LA PAÏVA
27 AND 28 PLACE SAINT-GEORGES / 9th
METRO: SAINT-GEORGES
Tel: 01 48 78 14 33 or 01 48 78 92 90
Guided visit

There is a lovely fountain in the middle of Place Saint-Georges, around which generations of motorists and bus drivers have circled. However, it looked quite different in 1840 when speculators of the Saint Georges Company decided to create a circular space designed to become the focal point of the "new Saint-Georges district". The Dosne-Thiers library with its sedate-looking façade stands at no. 27. Speculator Dosne's wife was the first to have a house built on this site. In 1833, she sold it to statesman and historian Adolphe Thiers, to whom she also offered her daughter's hand in marriage. Thiers lived here with his wife, his mother-in-law and his sister-in-law, and did most of his work in his study-cum-library on the second floor. His magnificent art collection, including his porcelain from China, was saved in extremis by the painter Courbet during the Paris Commune of 1871. However, he was unable to prevent the house from being burned down. The rebuilding of the house you see today was funded by the State in 1873.

Opposite, on the other side of the Place, at no. 28, you will notice a fine neo-Renaissance building, whose heavy decorations caused a scandal when it was erected in 1840. Architect Renaud's intention was to compensate the narrowness of the façade by lavishly ornamenting it with cherubs, griffins and lions. Above the ground floor, you will notice figures representing Architecture (with its ruler), Sculpture (with its hammer), Wisdom and Abundance. A certain Thérèse Lachmann took up residence on the ground floor, and her salon became a must for celebrities of Parisian elite society. A wealthy Portuguese, the Marquis de Païva, succeeded in attracting the pretty young woman's attention, and married her. She became known as *"La Païva"* and reigned over Parisian society. She had a manor house built on the Champs-Élysées, lived the good life, and became one of the most famous courtesans of the Second Empire.

Hôtel de la Païva

FROM BROTH TO BILLIARD BALLS

ACADÉMIE DE BILLARD
84 RUE DE CLICHY / 9th
METRO: PLACE-DE-CLICHY
Tel: 01 48 78 32 85
www.clichy-montmartre.com
Open from 1 PM to 5 AM

Three billiard balls above the door of 84 Rue de Clichy signal the entrance to the Billiards Academy, a veritable institution since its 1947 opening. Playing ball here is serious business. But people also come to have a drink or simply to admire the decor. This lovely hall and its vast skylight began as one of those numerous cheap *"bouillon"* (broths) diners. Billiard tables have since replaced the tables, but the walls have kept the wood panelling and framed mirrors from the time of Mr Duval's popular eatery.

Butcher Pierre Louis Duval, born in 1811, opened an establishment on Rue de la Monnaie that offered a startling new concept: *bouillon hollandais* (Dutch stew). Duval began by serving only this hearty dish to hungry customers. In response to increasing demand, the restaurant owner expanded his menu. An appreciative 19th century dictionary editor gave the *"bouillon"*-hall good publicity when he wrote: "You sit down at a carefully wiped white marble table, and immediately one of the ladies who serve comes to take your order. Often very sweet, the ladies always wear spotless attire: a woolen dress, either dark gray merino or alpaca, a white apron, a linen bonnet with ribbons fluttering down the back."

Other establishments soon opened in Paris, providing their promoter with good profits. Duval was an imaginative entrepreneur. He set up a wine warehouse in the Bercy district for some 3,000 barrels of wine to supply his numerous bouillon-halls in Paris. Next, in his Rue Montesquieu dining hall, he set up an ingenious (though costly) system that piped seltzer water directly to each table!

Duval had plans to apply the same successful business recipe to set up a model bakery and laundry, but he died before completing his work which outlined modern business practices.

A LEGENDARY PASSAGE

CITÉ MALESHERBES
59 RUE DES MARTYRS / 9th
METRO: PIGALLE

A stone's throw from bustling Pigalle, is a charming alley with a remarkable history. In the 18th century, it was the location of a mansion belonging to master surgeon Louis Raynal de Lescure. The property deed next went to Chrétien Guillaume Lamoignon de Malesherbes, a major political figure of his day. He was a knight, a State minister, the first honorary president of the Cour des Aides de Paris, and an honorary councilor in the parliament. The avid amateur botanist found the time to tend his garden himself. As a humanist, Malesherbes supported the encyclopedists and defended Louis XVI, resulting in a trip to the guillotine in 1794.

Nevertheless, the site continues to honor his name. In 1853, Adrien Abraham had the mansion razed to lay out a new street and housing development. The legendary Cité Malesherbes rose from the ground. Numerous residents and short-term guests have contributed to its fame.

The most notable of them belong to a decade of glory beginning in 1885. Writers, journalists, musicians, and painters pushed through the doors at 9 Cité Malesherbes to enjoy thrilling entertainment at Paris most extravagant cabaret – *Le Chat Noir*. Henri Rivière's shadow theatre played here, as did Erik Satie and Claude Debussy.

Another of the Cité's regulars was painter Pierre Jules Jollivet. At number 11, he left lovely terra cotta and enameled lava decors, exceptional pieces for Paris. *La Création d'Ève*, *Le Péché original*, and *Adam et Ève chassés du Paradis*, *L'Adoration des Mages*, *Le Baptême du Chris*, and *La Cène* belong to the group of religious scenes arranged beneath the windows. Originally painted for the Saint-Vincent-de-Paul church, these pieces were deemed to scandalous and were rejected. The painter reproduced them on this building, erected for him by Anatole Jal in 1856.

No less famous are the likes of Bernard Buffet, Johnny Hallyday, and even Françoise Hardy whose stays in the Cité Malesherbes was limited to the maternity ward (now closed) at number 3... But it was only to enter this world.

THE EAGLE-OWL'S NEST

VIOLLET-LE-DUC BUILDING
68 RUE CONDORCET / 9th
METRO: ANVERS

It is a mere detail, visible from the street, on the fourth floor of this rather ordinary Haussman-period building. As if high in its crow's-nest, staring down on us is an eagle-owl carved in stone positioned between twin neo-Gothic windows.
The signature is only obvious if you know that the French term for the bird is grand duc and that famed architect Eugène Viollet-le-Duc not only designed the building but lived here.
Often criticized, but immensely erudite, the man who restored Notre-Dame de Paris, the medieval city of Carcassonne, and the Basilica of Saint-Denis, actually designed several buildings in Paris.
This one was completed in 1862 to serve as home and office.
The ever assiduous Viollet-le-Duc would begin his day of work at dawn, preparing manuscripts, drawings for sculptors and various artisans. Every day at nine o'clock, his door opened to publishers, workers, artists, and architects.
He was equally courteous to everyone.
His lunch was invariably composed of two eggs, a slice of pâté, and tea.
Thereafter, he would return to his desk and work until 5 PM, then pause to eat.
At the end of the day, he would step out to visit construction sites dressed in his not so terribly new top hat and a strictly buttoned and fraying riding coat studded with his Légion d'Honneur medal.
The architect's Parisian career ended far from Rue Condorcet. He passed away in his chalet in Switzerland on September 17, 1879.

HOUSING FOR WORKERS

CITÉ NAPOLÉON
58 RUE ROCHECHOUART / 9th
METRO: ANVERS

An ordinary, Italian-style block of flats, seen from the street, belies the unexpected presence of an attractive, Louis Napoleon housing development. It is the sole evidence of what was originally a vast undertaking to build a cooperative with individual flats and communal areas for four hundred working families in each district. To this end, an association was formed, and Louis Napoleon donated 500,000 francs in order to convince the people of the social nature of his election.

Built between 1849 and 1853, the development was intended mainly for the neighboring gasworks employees. There were 86 apartments in the first building; rooms without heating cost 100 francs, those with heating, 150 francs. An inspector was appointed to keep an eye on the inhabitants' behavior, and the gates were closed at ten in the evening. A doctor visited the tenants free of charge, and there were communal wash houses, drying rooms and bathrooms. The Napoleon housing development, a veritable "*Cité radieuse*" – Le Corbusier's "living unit", built in Marseille (1947-52) – before its time, was typical of the fashion for Fourierist theories during the last century. However, such indulgence towards the underprivileged was not without ulterior motives. In 1857, on the eve of the elections, the estate manager put up the following notice: "Tenants, I would be failing in my duty if I did not remind you that it is owing to His Majesty the Emperor's great concern for the welfare of the working classes as a whole and of yours in particular, and thanks to immense sacrifices, that you have received such benefits. Thus, in view of the above-mentioned and because of the good relations I have always had with you, I hereby request you to go to the polls on Sunday and prove your gratitude to the Emperor by voting for the candidate he backs."

THE VANITIES AND THE VOLUPTUOUS

ART NOUVEAU FAÇADES
14-16 RUE D'ABBEVILLE / 10th
METRO: POISSONNIÈRE

Around the year 1900, strange new buildings in strange new styles started popping up around Paris. At the time Art Nouveau was still totally nouveau, it had its admirers and its critics, but, it left no one indifferent. Do not these two ultra-eclectic façades gracing Rue d'Abbeville still manage to surprise? The stone and brick corbelled building standing at number 14, designed by architects Autant Père & Fils, appears rather classic, and yet the façade is a swirl of thick vegetation with huge flowers and broad leaves. From out of this green fired-sandstone jungle (a capricious creation by the talented Alexandre Bigot), an owl and a bat seem poised to swoop down on passersby. Although easily understood in their time, today, the symbols' message about the vanities of this world is easily lost. The thistles running down the doorway and to the ground communicate an equally obscure message, a warning that not everyone may enter its doors.
Let us move up the street to number 16. Here, no fired-sandstone, but richly carved stone: cornices, garlands, grotesques, and much more animate the façade of this building erected in 1897 by Georges Mazza and decorated by Alexandre Dupuy.
This sample of Parisian architecture would be rather conventional if not for two disturbing caryatids higher up. These voluptuous female figures speak volumes of our grandfathers' preference for curvaceous women. While the façade may lack any semblance of refined taste, at least the subject matter isn't boring!

FROM CONVENT TO PRISON

THE OLD SAINT-LAZARE PRISON
107 BIS RUE DU FAUBOURG-SAINT-DENIS / 10th
METRO: GARE-DE-L'EST

A rather unremarkable square was laid out on the site of the old Saint-Lazare prison located off Rue du Faubourg-Saint-Denis. The façade of the old Saint-Lazare hospital could be seen at the end of the main drive. It was an odd, Louis XIII pastiche made from two single vestiges of the old lazaret located on this site: a doorway and a large baroque cartouche over it.

In 1630, when the Saint-Lazare convent, which had replaced the old lazaret, fell into disuse, Prior Adrien le Bon offered the buildings to Saint Vincent de Paul to house the Sisters of Charity. Besides serving as a convent, Saint-Lazare was used as a seminary, an asylum, and a prison. During the Revolution, once the nuns had been expelled and the buildings ransacked, it was used exclusively as a prison.
In its early days, at least, conditions in this penitentiary did not seem terribly harsh. Cells remained open and the detainees could gather in the hallways to converse. There, poet André Chénier met Aimée de Coigny for whom he penned *La Jeune Captive* (the young detainee).
O Death! You can wait. Stand back. Stand back.
Go console hearts filled with shame, fright, Pale despair devours.
In the mid 19th century, Saint-Lazare was turned into a women's prison. Inmates included Madame Stenheil (mistress of President Félix Faure), Mata Hari, Vera Galo, (who shot at Paul Deschanel), Thérèse Humbert, and Marthe Hanau (founder of the *Gazette du Franc*). Despite public outcry, the establishment was torn down between 1935 and 1940. All that remains are the chapel, erected in 1828 by Baltard who also designed the Halles, and the infirmary dating from the same period.

SUCH A TINY HOUSE!

39 RUE DU CHÂTEAU-D'EAU / 10th
METRO: RÉPUBLIQUE

Very little is known about the smallest house in Paris, barely noticeable, wedged between two tall buildings. This funny little place, about the size of a doll's house (approximately 1.20 meter wide and 5 meters high), comprises a ground-floor workshop and one upstairs room, and is alleged to have been built as the result of a family quarrel. The former site of the house used to be a passage linking Rue du Château-d'Eau and Rue du Faubourg-Saint-Martin. However, since the heirs to the land were unable to reach an agreement, the owner simply blocked up the tiny alley by erecting this tiny house, an unequivocal answer to the problem!

The city has some other "records" that deserve special mention. The shortest street in the capital, Rue des Degrés in the 2nd arrondissement, measures 5.75 meters long, and is, in fact, a set of fourteen steps between Rue Beauregard and Rue de Cléry. The longest street, Rue de Vaugirard (4.360 meters), starts at Boulevard Saint-Michel, goes through the 6th and 15th arrondissements, and ends at Boulevard Victor and Boulevard Lefebvre. The narrowest street, Rue de Venise (4th arrondissement), is 2 meters wide, with Rue du Chat-qui-Pêche (5th arrondissement), a close second, measuring 2.50 meters.

HIDDEN TREASURE

HÔTEL GOUTHIÈRE
CONSERVATOIRE HECTOR BERLIOZ
6 RUE PIERRE-BULLET / 10th
METRO: CHÂTEAU-D'EAU OR JACQUES-BONSERGENT

Who would expect to see a fine manor in the lower-class Faubourg Saint-Martin area? Yet, there it is, in all its splendor, a mere stone's throw from the 10th arrondissement's city hall building. This fine home first belonged to Pierre Gouthière, master carver and ornamentalist, purveyor to King Louis XVI and Madame Du Barry. Gouthière is particularly known for the jewelry box given to Marie-Antoinette for her wedding. The Gouthière mansion was built between 1772 and 1780 on a plot of land that extended all the way to the Faubourg-Saint-Martin. As is frequently the case, the property was sold off bit by bit, finally leaving the manor bereft of its former garden when the city laid out Rue Pierre-Bullet to create an isolated city block for the 10th arrondissement's city hall building. It became the arrondissement's municipal conservatory in 1981. The old mansion has preserved numerous items of its original décor. In the courtyard, we find a bacchanalian frieze gracing the front building. Over the main doorway is a niche with two sitting women crowning the bust of a divinity. Inside, visitors can admire murals in the main drawing room. They are Louis XVI in period, but were modified during the Empire. The antechamber has splendid inlaid woodwork. The library is fitted out with columns, fireplaces, gilded bronze window catches, and the marble floors add even more charm to this elegantly proportioned ensemble.

ATMOSPHERE...

HÔTEL DU NORD
102 QUAI DE JEMMAPES / 10th
METRO: GARE-DE-L'EST

Saint-Martin canal, built between 1822 and 1825, with nine locks, five bridges, five footbridges and three swing bridges, offers one of the most poetic strolls in Paris.
Hôtel du Nord on Quai de Jemmapes has come to symbolize both a mythical version of Paris and a film, and is a place of pilgrimage for cinema enthusiasts.
In 1929, Eugène Dabit, the hotel owners' son, published a collection of short stories depicting the lives of hotel-keepers and their clients. Shortly after his death in 1936, French film director Marcel Carné was inspired by the book to make his famous film, Hôtel du Nord. Film set designer Alexandre Trauner recreated the hotel surroundings in Boulogne-Billancourt studios. Only a few scenes were shot outside, near the footbridge, for the purpose of continuity. The film, released in December 1938, was a great success, and the general public became acquainted with the canal, already described by Marius Richard in 1935: "Who has never walked along these black and white banks, one for the coal which blackens men's faces and the other for the limestone which whitens them? Who has never strolled alongside, and run their fingers over, the tarred wooden barges, which, when unloaded, stand high in the water? [...] They form a floating village, and the sight of it waking up in the morning, preferably in the summer, as the keeper unhurriedly opens the gates of the Bassin de la Villette, should not be missed. A dog barks, a bargeman looks out of his cabin, the water laps along the brown hulls, seasoned like old pipes; pigeons coo, a woman chops wood, another stands with her arms folded while waiting for the water for the coffee to boil; the decks are being washed, breakfast is ready..."
In 1984, an association foiled part of a plan to demolish the hotel: Its president was the actress Arletty, who starred as a prostitute in Carné's film, and was famous for the catch phrase, "*Atmosphère, atmosphère...*". However, only the façade of the hotel was saved, an empty shell looking like a film set. The ground-floor restaurant, decorated by a film-set designer in the style of the period, serves traditional food, and a band plays music in the evenings.

IN QUARANTINE

SAINT-LOUIS HOSPITAL
2 PLACE DU DOCTEUR-ALFRED-FOURNIER / 10th
METRO: GONCOURT
Please note that the historic Saint-Louis quadrangle is only open Monday-Friday.

The central courtyard of Saint-Louis Hospital is very impressive, and, with its green lawns surrounded by tall stone and brick buildings, is somewhat reminiscent of Place des Vosges in the 3rd arrondissement (without the arcades, of course). This peaceful quadrangle, planted with trees, has hardly changed since the 17th century.
When there were widespread epidemics, it was the custom to isolate the sick outside the city to reduce the risk of contagion. In the 16th century, health inspectors assembled the plague victims in tents, away from the city center. Henry IV (known as Henry of Navarre), who had ambitious plans for the architecture of Paris, decided to create a royal nursing home in the early 17th century. This hospital, a veritable fortress designed to prevent the spread of disease, was surrounded by a wall. Vegetable gardens and orchards within the enclosure made it self-sufficient. An L-shaped group of four buildings, housing staff and administration, formed another barrier. The central quadrangle was reserved for patients only. Their rooms were over the vaulted ground floor areas used for grain storage. Only the chapel, still standing, was built in front of the walls to make it available to the congregation outside the hospital.

In 1818, Philippe Lebon built France's first gasworks next to the chapel. Gas pipes were made out of 1,500 gun tubes provided by the War Ministry, and, on December 25th, 1819, Parisians celebrated the first midnight Mass to take place in a chapel with such modern lighting.

METALWORKER MEMORIES

MAISON DES MÉTALLOS
94 RUE JEAN-PIERRE-TIMBAUD / 11th
METRO: COURONNES
Tel.: 01 48 05 88 27
Open Monday to Saturdays from 10 AM (2 PM on Saturdays) to 7 PM

The noble doorway graced by a lyre on the impost does not herald a 16th-century mansion, rather the *Maison des Métallos* (literally: the house of metalworkers), one of the hubs of the blue collar culture in Paris. Erected between 1881 and 1883, the six buildings are situated on both sides of an alley. At the end of this alley is a big metal Polonceau-type structure with a surface area of 680 square meters (7,320 sq. ft.). The building's structure is supported by two rows of eight cast-iron columns.
First owned first by Gautrot, then Couesnon, both firms were specialized in manufacturing high-quality wind instruments: flutes, oboes, horns, clarinets, bassoons, saxophones, etc. The company supplied the Garde Républicaine as well as music conservatories. The instruments were even appreciated by American jazz musicians. The showroom was on the first and second floors in the industrial building. Following the success of the *Front Populaire* and the subsequent purchase of the property by the metal workers' C.G.T. labor union, the site became home to metalworkers in 1937, and turned into the *Maison des Métallurgistes*.
The place ceased to hum with music, and began resonating with the chants of fervent activists who used the premises for rallies and meetings. When it was slated for demolition, a neighborhood association formed to defend it. As a result, the city of Paris purchased the property. It was then restored and refurbished by the Vincent Brossy architectural firm. This beautiful example of industrial architecture now houses a multidisciplinary cultural space, dedicated to live shows and other cultural events.

STAGE DOOR

CLOWN BAR
114 RUE AMELOT / 11th
METRO: FILLES-DU-CALVAIRE

In 1852, at the request of Champs-Élysées circus director Louis Dejean, Jacques Ignace Hittorf built the Cirque d'Hiver in a mere ten months. Recently restored to its original sheen, the columns of this temple of circus arts boast new crowns, the original bas-reliefs have been restored and the colors are brighter than ever. The Clown Bar, nearby, is another fine example of this period when architecture shone in every detail. The establishment, founded in 1902, served generations of lion tamers, acrobats, and artists of every stripe, who, once out of costume and their makeup removed, gathered here for a bit of fun and food after the show.
Their festive meals have been immortalized in a very amusing ceramic frieze entitled

La Grande Parade des clowns. In it, circus artists perform for an audience relegated to the background and reduced to Chinese shadows. The piece was painted in 1907 by Jean-Baptiste Memery and skillfully transposed to ceramic by a Sarreguemines porcelain factory. The restaurant's ceiling offers a splendid example of eludoric painting (painting under glass). It is yet another admirable aspect of the café's decor, which has been listed since 1995 on the registry of the *Inventaire des monuments historiques*.

BACK TO THE PAGODA

LE BATACLAN
50 BOULEVARD VOLTAIRE / 11th
METRO: OBERKAMPF

The Bataclan's façade has been restored to its original design. Garish (but authentic), the theatre's original colors are a bit of a surprise for 21st-century Parisians, unaccustomed to such exotic flourishes.
We owe the theater's design to Charles Duval, who, in 1864, erected here this famous pastiche, "based on an actual blueprint for a Chinese palace," as a brochure at that time claimed.
This establishment bearing the name *Grand Café Chinois Théâtre "Ba-Ta-Clan,"* an allusion to Offenbach's operetta of the same name, was a concert-café offering entertainment, dancing, drinks, and musical performances.
After being ravaged by a fire and partially demolished in 1950, it was turned into a cinema. The historic establishment lost its fan-shaped stage curtain that the public could admire up close for one franc.
The spacious hall with 2,000 seats was reduced and deprived of its big-busted Chimeras.
But the most important elements have survived. The Bataclan's famous stage that welcomed the likes of Dranem, Mayol, Aristide Bruant, Maurice Chevalier, and Buffalo Bill, has now returned to its roots. It's quite a revenge for the oldest pagoda in Paris.

A COCK AND SOME PRIMROSES

COUR DU COQ
60 RUE SAINT-SABIN / 11th
METRO: CHEMIN-VERT

Cour du Coq, near Rue du Faubourg-Saint-Antoine, is a quiet, obscure, paved cul-de-sac, preserved and very well looked after. It stretches out a long way behind a beautiful green gate decorated, not surprisingly, with a proud-looking cock, and has a gutter all the way down the middle to drain off rainwater not caught by the numerous pots of flowers dotted about.

The names of neighboring culs-de-sac at nos. 50 and 58 – *Impasse des Primevères* (Primrose Street) and *Allée Verte* (Green Street) – recall the district's rural past, when Rue Saint-Sabin ran alongside the counterscarp of the city's fortifications.

GOTHIC FACTORY

DUGAST, FORMER CABINETMAKER'S SHOP
5 CITÉ DE LA ROQUETTE / 11th
METRO: BASTILLE

Walk down this dead-end street and soon enough, you will be standing in front of an amusing Gothic-Revival, half-timbered structure, fitted with stained-glass windows.
It is the only one of its kind in the quarter. Erected in 1891 by architect Péchard and commissioned by a certain Mr. Louault, it once housed a small furniture factory.
In addition to the boss's accommodations, the building also comprised the accounting office, the paint and varnish workshops, and a showroom.
Dugast, a cabinetmaker whose sign still hangs over the premises, later rented the building in order to manufacture Japanese-inspired pieces, quite fashionable at the turn of the 20th century.

THE AROMA OF ROASTING COFFEE BEANS

COUR DAMOYE
12 PLACE DE LA BASTILLE / 11th
METRO: BASTILLE

It is easy to miss the entrance to Cour Damoye masked by the busy sidewalk cafés and the Bastille metro station exit. The grille – closed at night – of the 18th-century building protects one of the most charming passageways in the Faubourg Saint-Antoine. Cour Damoye narrowly escaped demolition when property promoters planned to preserve only the first building. Fortunately the passage was renovated with great care. Today this is a place with soul, a sure sign of a successful renovation.

In 1778, Antoine Pierre Damoye, a Parisian hardware dealer, purchased a house and garden where the arquebusiers of Paris trained. He wanted to turn a profit on the plot, and the creation of Rue Daval in 1780 gave his property transaction a golden opportunity. Most of the buildings (many now have added stories) in the courtyard date from this period. Lined by businesses and workshops with lodgings above, the Cour Damoye is the granddaddy of Parisian covered passageways. It was built in one go, whereas most similar courtyards in the Faubourg were added onto through the centuries.

The faithful renovation conserved numerous historic architectural elements. Thus, visitors can admire the odd frieze of a 1930s boutique on the right as one enters, the typical late 18th-century façades of business establishments, a simple assembly of beams inserted in masonry. Further along, the silhouette of a metal elevator (now disused) reminds us of the previous activities in Cour Damoye. Though calm today, the Cour used to team with artisans, rag-and-bone-men, scrap metal dealers, and constant clanking metal sounds. Fragrant wisteria now blooms where early 20th-century cart makers piled up their wheels.

The enticing aroma of roasting coffee beans has returned. Sometimes other pleasant and heady smells tickle visitors' nostrils, adding to the charm of this passageway where the soul of the Faubourg Saint-Antoine seems to have taken refuge.

JANUARY TO JUNE...

PASSAGE DU CHEVAL-BLANC
2 RUE DE LA ROQUETTE / 11th
METRO: BASTILLE

Passage du Cheval-Blanc is reached through a late 17th-century building. Originally devoted to the craft industry, this is one of those places that are being renovated and converted into "trendy" apartments. At the end of the passage, a bend leads to the building located Rue du Faubourg-Saint-Antoine (nos. 19-20), called Cité Parchappe after the Parchappe family who used to live here and who, in the 19th century, undertook a great deal of alteration work. In the early 20th century, the passage began to look as it does today. It will take you from January to June to walk along this passage – a succession of very dissimilar courtyards named after the first few months of the year!

Mid-19th-century buildings stand in Janvier courtyard. In Février and Mars courtyards, timbered workshops stretch out behind a more recent building. Avril is not a courtyard, but a three-storied building, while Mai courtyard was rebuilt by architect Sauger in 1910. Juin courtyard is lined with timbered buildings. Some artisans can still be seen at work in Passage du Cheval-Blanc, which, for a long time, was the site of numerous timber warehouses in the Faubourg, the district of cabinetmakers and furniture makers in general.

A PASSAGE IN THE FAUBOURG

PASSAGE LHOMME
26 RUE DE CHARONNE / 11th
METRO: LEDRU-ROLLIN

Before Avenue Ledru-Rollin was laid out, there used to be a network of dark, narrow little streets leading to Rue de Charonne. One of these, Passage Lhomme, is reminiscent of the bygone days of the Faubourg, where the workers were legion and hard at work in the busy workshops smelling of sawdust, glue and varnish. Today, after 150 years, the *Fle de gainerie* workshop still exists; the French polisher Hollard set up shop here in 1910, while the old workshops have since been turned into offices.
The paving stones are old and pitted, and there are lots of vines creeping up the walls of the three- and four-storied buildings lining Passage Lhomme, which, a little congested with cars, runs through an 18th-century building into Rue de Charonne.

IN PRAISE OF PEWTER COUNTERTOPS

BISTROT DU PEINTRE
116 AVENUE LEDRU-ROLLIN / 11th
METRO: LEDRU-ROLLIN

The wood façade shaded by the glass awning has not changed, nor has the plaque listing the café's goods and services. It reads, "Au Vrai Saumur, Beaujolais, coffee 10 centimes a cup, with a little shot 15 & 20 centimes, billiards, telephone." Opened in 1905, this café-restaurant miraculously weathered and resisted a century of changing fads, earning it much attention from advertisers. Credit for the 1902 building goes to Julien Galopin,

who built it at the height of the Art Nouveau movement with its whiplash lines.
Inside, behind the counter, a triptych of mirrors framed in wood carved with swirling lines, reflects the faces of café patrons sipping a *petit noir* or some other glass of red wine. In the main room, which has undergone few changes since it was built, two pretty ceramic pieces celebrate spring and summer. Winter and autumn have unfortunately vanished, unless, perhaps, these two seasons never found their way here.
A great many typically Parisian cafés have vanished, most sacrificed on the altar of fashion and Formica. It is regrettable, for the ambiance they offer is like no place else, and the espresso served with a "little shot of..." can't be beat anywhere!

ABOUNDING SOUL

SAINTE-MARGUERITE CHURCH
36 RUE SAINT-BERNARD / 11th
METRO: CHARONNE, FAIDHERBE-CHALIGNY OR LEDRU-ROLLIN

Set amid its green grounds, Sainte-Marguerite has managed to keep its original countryside church look. Originally, a simple chapel, it became a church in 1627. The edifice was enlarged numerous times to meet the needs of the growing Saint-Antoine Faubourg. Inside, the 17th-century nave is surprising large. But it is to the rear and the left, near the choir, that visitors will find an even bigger surprise, the funeral *Chapelle des Âmes du Purgatoire* (the souls in purgatory chapel).

Victor Louis drew up the plans and the chapel was built between 1760 and 1764 on land belonging to the cemetery. Despite the relatively tight budget he was working with, the architect refused to make any concessions on elegance, and so hired Paolo Antonio Brunetti, a trompe-l'œil master. Brunetti's stunning dove-colored piece perfectly imitates carved stone. The semi-circular vault is decorated with caissons, rosettes and other embellishments, all painted in varying shades of grays. Just beneath them are two low-relief friezes, and between the columns, placed here and there, we see allegorical statues recalling the brevity of life and vanity of this world. In the middle of this ensemble, behind the altar, is Gabriel Briard's 1761 painting depicting the passage of souls out of purgatory and into heaven.

Throughout the centuries, the church and its cemetery have taken in many souls. Numerous victims of the guillotine were buried here during the Reign of Terror. And, according to the engraving on a flagstone in the chapel, "the child who perished in the Temple's keep" in 1795. Digs carried out long ago proved that the child buried here was fifteen at his death and not ten, which would have been the age of the poor Louis XVII. But, then, legends die hard.

CONVENTS
IN THE COUNTRY

NOTRE-DAME-DE-BON-SECOURS AND LA MADELEINE DE TRESNEL
99-101 RUE DE CHARONNE (CITÉ DU COUVENT) AND 100 RUE DE CHARONNE / 11th
METRO: ALEXANDRE-DUMAS

Rue de Charonne follows the route of one of the oldest roads in Paris, which used to link Charonne village to the capital. It was here, in the country, that many religious orders were established during the 17th century. The Bon-Secours nuns settled Rue de Charonne in 1648. Despite the unfortunate demolition of the beautiful neoclassical convent chapel in 1937, and its portal in 1969, some of convent buildings have survived, and can be seen at no. 99. A large, rectangular courtyard leads to a smaller courtyard, both of which are surrounded by similar-looking buildings erected by Nicolas d'Orbay in 1739, and to which stories were added in the 19th century.
The religious calling of the Bon-Secours Convent suffered a great deal during the French Revolution, and the buildings were converted into a cotton spinning factory in the early 19th century. Later still, they housed a school of industrial arts and commerce, and then a hospice.
Opposite, at no. 10, in the early 18th century, another renowned convent, La Madeleine de Tresnel, had gardens stretching as far as present-day Rue Léon-Frot and Rue de Montreuil. The convent buildings were erected around two courtyards and a chapel with a round church tower. The remains of La Madeleine de Tresnel Convent – some of the arches on the side overlooking the street, the old church tower, and a few buildings – have been restored but can only be viewed from the exterior.

THE FLAGSTONES OF DEATH

SITE OF THE GUILLOTINE
16 RUE DE LA CROIX-FAUBIN / 11th
METRO: VOLTAIRE

Men sentenced to death were kept in the Grande-Roquette prison, built in 1836. It used to stand on the site of nos. 164-68 Rue de la Roquette, and was demolished in 1899. Five granite flagstones embedded in the ground on the corner of Rue de la Croix-Faubin serve as a reminder of the times when the guillotine was routinely set up in front of the prison; five regrettably famous flagstones, about which Aristide Bruant wrote songs, as did Pierre François Lacenaire, murderer and a man of letters:

Oh, I know you well,
footholds for a scaffold;
Immaculate white stones,
bearing no signs
of the executioner's bloody deeds.

The prison got its nickname – Abbey of the Five Stones – from the flagstones used by the executioner's assistants to securely wedge into place the sinister uprights of the guillotine, thus ensuring that the blade slid straight down to the lunette. Although executions took place at night only, they never failed to attract crowds of bystanders who were only too pleased to watch.
On the other side of Rue de la Roquette stood the Petite-Roquette prison, built between 1826 and 1830, which became a prison for women in 1835. In 1974, it was demolished, and public gardens, Square de la Petite-Roquette, were laid out on the site.
All that remains of the former prison is the porch, which is now the entrance to the gardens.

A PROSPEROUS NURSING HOME

DR. BELHOMME'S HOME
157-161 RUE DE CHARONNE / 11th
METRO: ALEXANDRE-DUMAS

Behind some tall buildings stand three attractive houses, looking out onto a pleasant garden. The middle most recently-built house is ornamented with garlands, cartouches, and lions' heads; the other two have a flight of steps each. This is all that remains of "*Pension Belhomme,*" a nursing home for the insane founded by former carpenter Jacques Belhomme in 1768; the rest was demolished in 1972.

Accommodation and treatment were not free. Only those from well-to-do families were accepted as inmates. The business really came into its own during the Reign of Terror, when the Jacobins' opponents were systematically executed during the French Revolution. The home not only provided the inmates with excellent treatment, it also protected those wishing to escape the Revolutionary Tribunal and the guillotine; the Duchess of Orleans spent a long time there.

Belhomme would appear to have had no qualms about profiting from such a situation! The Duchess of Choiseul, unable to pay her way, is alleged to have been thrown out – and guillotined shortly afterwards.

Imprisoned on January 28th, 1794, and condemned for misappropriation of public funds, Belhomme was reinstated a few months later as manager of his nursing home.

FLYING...

COURTYARDS
11-15 RUE TITON /11th
METRO: FAIDHERBE-CHALIGNY

Opposite an unusual-looking Lutheran church, at nos. 11, 13, and 15, out of sight behind a long, five-storied building are three attractive courtyards dating back to the late 19th century.
The building's wooden framework is reinforced with pieces of metal, decorated with strange-looking lions' heads.
Rue Titon extends over the site of an extravagantly majestic manor house built in 1673 by the son of a skilled, self-employed embroiderer from the Saint-Antoine faubourg, Maximilien Titon, who made a fortune selling arms. Mockingly nicknamed "Titonville", this splendid property comprised eight houses, built side by side, with five doors opening out onto Rue des Boulets and Rue de Montreuil.
A six-columned portico used to give access to a formal garden, ornamented with pools and statues. Maximilien's son, intensely loyal to Louis XIV, wished to erect an immense, sixty-foot-high statue in his honor. Sculptor Louis Garnier, pupil of Girardon (who created many of the sculptures at Versailles), worked ten years on the project which was never completed.
In 1763, Jean-Baptiste Réveillon set up his wallpaper factory on the site of Hôtel Titon's outbuildings. Twenty years later, in 1783, he lent the premises to physicist Pilâtre de Rozier who built the first hot air balloon there, out of canvas and paper. On October 15th, 1783, it rose 80 meters over the garden, tethered by ropes and piloted by Pilâtre, the first aeronaut in history. This marked the start of aeronautical exploits – already experienced by the tragic Greek mythic figure of Icarus – which were to make man's wildest dreams come true: flying.

WORKSHOPS AND DORMITORIES FOR CRAFTSMEN

RUE DES IMMEUBLES-INDUSTRIELS / 11th
METRO/RER: NATION

The tall buildings lining Rue des Immeubles-Industriels, between Boulevard Voltaire and Rue du Faubourg-Saint-Antoine, are rather unusual with their slender cast-iron columns, and are evidence of some of the industrial achievements of the 19th century. Industrialist Jean-François Cail, who instigated this project for the good of the community, had the inspired idea of providing the craftsmen and their families with modern workshops and decent accommodations under the same roof. Work on the nineteen buildings began in 1872 under the supervision of architect Émile Leménil, and was completed a year later. The workshops on the ground floor, the mezzanine, and the first floor were occupied by craftsmen mainly connected with the furniture trade, and the accommodations on the upper floors were fitted out with basic home comforts such as water, light, gas and space. Power was supplied by an enormous 200 hp steam engine, manufactured by Cail et Compagnie, and installed under the road.
In the late 19th century, two thousand people were working and living in Rue des Immeubles-Industriels.

THE STAR-SPANGLED BANNER FLYING AT PICPUS

PICPUS CEMETERY
35 RUE DE PICPUS / 12th
METRO/RER: NATION
Tel: 01 43 44 18 54
Group visits by appointment only.
From April to October, open daily from 2 PM to 4 PM, except Mondays and Sundays;
from November to March, open daily from 2 PM to 6 PM, except Mondays.

From June 14th to July 27th, 1794 (during the Reign of Terror when those brought before the Revolutionary Tribunal were systematically executed), bloodstained carts shuttled back and forth between the guillotine on Place de la Nation and a rectangular, hastily-dug grave in a field near the disused convent of Augustinian canonesses. These grim trips lasted seven weeks: 1,306 people were beheaded and "escorted" to Picpus, a place originally intended for a more light-hearted purpose.
A certain Mr. Coignard's plans to establish a convalescent home there came to halt when the garden was requisitioned and converted into a mass grave. Despite residents' protests, a wall was knocked down to enable the carts to get through more easily. The site was located at the far end of a plot of land so as to avoid attracting attention.
This was the final resting place of the cream of the aristocracy as well as of minor nobility and a great many commoners, 702 to be exact. The land fell into disuse, and, in 1802, was bought up by families of those who were guillotined. Even today, only descendants of the victims have the right to be buried at Picpus.
General de La Fayette was interred there next to his wife, Marie-Adrienne de Noailles, whose family was almost entirely wiped out during the Reign of Terror. The American national colors pay tribute to the heroes of the US War of Independence, undoubtedly the only American flag to fly in Paris without a break since 1834, including the years of the German occupation.

TIME STANDS STILL

RUE DE REUILLY / 12th
METRO: FAIDHERBE-CHALIGNY

Formerly a medieval path, Rue de Reuilly, now lined with unsightly buildings, has undergone many changes.
Who would have thought that attractive, picturesque culs-de-sac could be found here? And yet, they can!
At no. 18, a passage closed by metal gate leads to a delightful little courtyard.
Each house in this tiny cul-de-sac, built in the late 19th century, has its own stairway. Small zinc awnings and, above all, the house at the far end, topped by a lantern, give the place an indefinable appeal.
The clock is a trompe l'oeil painting, where time stands still at seven minutes past five.
The walls and part of the passage are overrun with vines.
As you come out, cross over to the other side of Rue de Reuilly. Thanks to a discerning property developer, the house at no. 29 was restored, and one-storied buildings erected to form a small cul-de-sac, which, decorated with a few flowers, has an atmosphere all of its own.
After the crossroads at Boulevard Diderot, Impasse Mousset starts at 83 Rue de Reuilly, and is surprisingly long.
Its workshops and small offices are still in business. Halfway down, an old rusty sign smothered in wisteria is a reminder that a hotel-cum-bar used to stand here.
Finally, no. 67 is the opulent-looking entrance to Cour Alsace-Lorraine.
No greenery here. The courtyard is divided into two culs-de-sac. The one on the left has a wooden stairway of a type rarely to be found in Paris today, while that on the right leads to a big garden surrounding a beautiful, mysterious-looking house.

NOTRE-DAME D'ALIGRE

ALIGRE-BEAUVAU MARKET
PLACE D'ALIGRE / 12th
METRO: LEDRU-ROLLIN

The stalls at the Aligre-Beauvau market on Sundays conjure up images of the big markets of long ago, with the hubbub and pressing of crowds of shoppers. This market building dates from the same period as the *ville nouvelle* (new town), which was a late 18th-century urban development plan carried out by Sanson-Nicolas Lenoir, a particularly dynamic Parisian speculator. He left his mark on the Ternes district as well as on the Faubourg du Temple area. Here, on land purchased from the Abbesses de Saint-Antoine, he planned the faubourg's grid of streets, had them laid out, and paved. He also equipped the area with two marketplaces for food and other wares. Unfortunately, the infrastructures attracted too few businesses, and during the Revolution, the market buildings were used to store fodder.

The rundown buildings were demolished in 1811, but rebuilt later. The "new" market building dates from 1843. The central building included the weight inspector's and the superintendent's offices. Once shorn of its two wings around 1880, the central structure, with its small belfry, oddly resembled a chapel, and locals jokingly nicknamed it *Notre-Dame-d'Aligre*.

THE LAST WASH HOUSE

THE LENOIR MARKET WASH HOUSE
3 RUE DE COTTE / 12th
METRO: LEDRU-ROLLIN

Place d'Aligre, generally rather dull and bleak, brightens up on Sundays thanks to a lively, bustling market. The outline of one of finest indoor markets in Paris – "Beauvau", built in 1843 by Marc-Gabriel Jolivet to replace an 18th-century building – can be made out at the far end.
Without the determination of residents in the district, the façade of the *"grand lavoir du marché Lenoir"* would have disappeared. This small, pedimented wash house used to stand at 9 Rue de Cotte [it has kept its number] before being moved 40 meters down the road to make room for the building of community facilities.
The Aligre wash house was built in 1830, and is the only one of its kind in Paris. There used to be around 300 of these establishments, whose friendly, rough and ready, quarrelsome clients created an atmosphere often described by novelist Émile Zola.

The Rue de Cotte wash house made its entry into literature on December 3rd, 1851, when Victor Hugo's cab tried to reach a barricade in Faubourg Saint-Antoine during the 1851 coup d'état. The writer recounts the scene in his book, *Histoire d'un crime* [Story of a Crime]:
"Which way do we go, sir?"
"Towards the sound of the guns firing."
We were in a narrow street; on my left I could see the words, Grand Lavoir, inscribed over the doorway, and on my right, a square with a building in the middle, resembling an indoor market. The square and the street were deserted; I asked the coachman:
"What street are we on?"
"Rue de Cotte."
"Where is the Roysin café?"
"Straight ahead."
"Let's go there."

THE BLACK MUSKETEERS' GAMING TABLE

COUR DU BEL-AIR
56 RUE DU FAUBOURG-SAINT-ANTOINE / 12th
METRO: BASTILLE

The furniture makers, cabinetmakers, upholsterers, French-polishers and japanners who used to occupy the courtyards and side streets of Rue du Faubourg-Saint-Antoine at the beginning of the century are not easy to find nowadays.
The entrance to Cour du Bel-Air is on the former site of a manor house of the same name. A long corridor, whose exposed beams hold up nothing but air, leads to two smaller courtyards, both surrounded by three-storied buildings. Here, as in many of the Faubourg's courtyards, there are vines everywhere, and grapes brush against the heads of passersby.
In the first courtyard, opposite an attractive, green-colored, Gothic Revival shop near the middle, one of the paving stones is bigger than the rest. Legend has it that the Black Musketeers from the neighboring barracks used it as a gaming table. In fact, there used to be some very old wooden steps here, known for a long time as the "musketeers' staircase."

HOUSES BY THE SEINE

RUE CRÉMIEUX / 12th
METRO/RER: GARE-DE-LYON

Rue Crémieux, near Gare de Lyon, is the picturesque site of a small, 19th-century housing development for workers. At first, it was called the Millaud development, which was marked out in 1857, and built almost as a single block. The merits of the houses – 35 in all and two-storied at the most – were praised in a newspaper article written at the time: "Each house comprises a basement kitchen, and a total of six rooms, with heating, on the ground floor and the two upper stories. There are no concierges, and you can be master in your own home for a yearly rent of seven hundred francs." The street was pedestrianized in 1993. Some of the façades have been renovated, and the road, repaved. Old-fashioned street lamps give this quiet little street an air reminiscent of bygone days. A small faience plaque at no. 8 indicates the level of the water – 1.75 meters – in Rue Crémieux when the Seine overflowed its banks on January 28 and 29th, 1910!

"BORNE BY THE WINE"

PARC DE BERCY
RUE PAUL-BELMONDO / 12th
METRO: COUR-SAINT-ÉMILION

Parc de Bercy is one of the most successful green spaces recently created in Paris. However, many Parisians regret the disappearance of the Bercy warehouses, whose romantic atmosphere, with their wine storehouses and wine barrels, was reminiscent of Paris in bygone days, dear to the heart of famed Paris photographer Robert Doisneau.
What delights were to be had in the shade of hundred-year-old trees, where thousands of birds nested, the paved streets, crisscrossed by railway tracks and lined with warehouses, large and small, and venerable old buildings... The smell of damp wood and corks, and the bouquet of a glass of wine sneaked from a broken old vat at the wine merchant's. Although difficult to imagine today, this place used to bustle with activity, as barges full of barrels unloaded their cargo onto the quays.
The wine merchants used to take their clients to an inn called "*L'Auberge de la Pomme d'Or*" (the Golden Apple Inn), where, after a meal washed down with plenty of wine, "juicy" contracts were signed.
In 1979, bulldozers put an end to more than one and a half centuries of wine trading, destroying many renowned wine stores such as "Joninon et Saillard" and "Badoc". The Sports Center with its lawns defying the laws of gravitation was built on the site, followed a few years later by the bulky new Finance Ministry building, a giant bar jutting out onto the riverbanks.
Parc de Bercy – a garden commemorating the past – has kept the old, paved warehouse roads. Preserved old buildings, some of them in ruins, and theme areas, shaded by centenarian trees, help recall Bercy's shattered past. A garden of aromatic plants enables young Parisians to become familiar with the different scents of herbs, and to discover vines and fruit trees trained on espaliers.
A few years back, these former wine storehouses were renovated, and the area was strikingly renamed "Bercy-village".
It offers a refreshing halt after a promenade through the park. These 19th-century warehouses, recently deprived of their veils of ivy and grime, have now recovered the sheen of their original white stonework, an unusual hue indeed for the old Bercy alleyway. On bright sunny days, you feel very far from Paris as you stroll past shops enticing enough to turn daytime-tourists into avid shoppers. After enjoying a few local specialties with a good glass of wine, you can trot away from Bercy completely satisfied. As poet Charles Baudelaire eloquently put it, "borne away by the wine toward an enchanting, divine sky."

POWERLESS PROTECTOR

NOTRE-DAME-DE-BERCY
PLACE LACHAMBAUDIE / 12th
METRO: BERCY OR COUR-SAINT-ÉMILION

The statuette of a black Virgin, forever darkened by the smoke of a fire, has not spared the little church on Place Lachambaudie its woes. Erected in 1823 on the plans of André-Marie Châtillon, Notre-Dame de la Nativité first suffered the ravages of flames during the Commune in 1871. It was rebuilt two years later by Antoine-Julien Hénard, who was also the architect of the new city hall of the 12th arrondissement. Despite its new name, Notre-Dame de Bercy, the church suffered severe damage in the great flood of 1910 and the air raids of 1944. It burned again in 1982. To end this martyrdom, which spiritual power must be invoked? One shudders to think of the consequences a new incident would have, for today, this humble church is home to some remarkable works of art: *L'Annonciation* by Daniel Hallé (1614-1675), *Jésus et la Samaritaine* by Jacques Stella (1596-1657), *The Martyrdom of Thomas Becket* by Jean-Baptiste Pierre in 1748, *The Resurrection of Jairus's Daughter* by Charles de La Fosse in 1690, and *Christ on the Cross* by Louis de Boulogne in 1708.

BASTION NUMBER 1

BOULEVARD PONIATOWSKI (NEAR RUE ROBERT-ETLIN) / 12th
METRO: PORTE DE CHARENTON

Over the centuries, walls have been built around Paris in order to protect the city. The last, the Thiers wall, was thus named because the decision to build new fortifications was made during Thiers' stint as Minister of War. Building work started in 1841, and lasted four years. The end result was a rampart – 34 kilometers long, 142 meters wide, with 94 bastions – surrounding not only the city of Paris itself but also its immediate suburbs. However, the actual strategic significance of these fortifications was never really established, and they were almost totally demolished in 1929. Apartment blocks were built on the site, including the area where building was prohibited, and a few – rare – green spaces were laid out.
Bastion numbers 1, 44, and 45 (Porte de Clichy, see page 217) are the last remaining vestiges of the wall. A paved avenue gently slopes from Boulevard Poniatowski towards bastion number 1, polygonal-shaped and a few hundred meters long, topped by a casemate with loopholes. From the top of the bastion, there is a good view over the Seine – and the incessant flow of traffic heading towards the motorway. Near the circular road, there are some remains of the curtain wall, 4 to 5 meters high, which used to run between the bastions.

PARIS
ENDS HERE

PARIS BOUNDARY MARKER
304 RUE DE CHARENTON / 12th
METRO: DUGOMMIER

The marble plaque on a wall bears the following inscription: "1726. Boundary markers. Under the reign of Louis XV. By order of the King. Building strictly prohibited between these boundary markers and the next village, a punishable offense according to His Majesty's declarations of 1724 (and) 1726." Louis XV was the great-grandson of Louis XIV, and was known as the "Well-Beloved".

This plaque, half of which has been restored, was a boundary marker demonstrating the King's intention to put a stop to the indiscriminate expansion of Paris, because of the city's problems with supplies, policing, and population increase. Within the city boundaries, landowners could build houses with the front walls overlooking existing streets, but under no circumstances could they build new roads. Only construction work currently under way on buildings in the faubourgs could be completed. Parisians, recalcitrant by nature, did not take much notice of these prohibitions.

The plaque in Rue de Charenton is one of the few plaques – 294 in all – to have survived until today. It was put up on December 27th, 1727, on the wall of the "last house in the street near the country", on the corner of Rue de Picpus and Rue de Lamblardie. In 1910, historian Lucien Lambeau discovered half of the plaque lying among some tiles on the floor of a room at the back of a hardware shop at 304-6 Rue de Charenton. The owner of the building agreed to the plaque being fixed on the façade – but charged one hundred francs! Another plaque similar to this one can be seen at 4 Rue de Laborde in the 8th arrondissement.

INSPIRED BY ISTANBUL

SAINT-ESPRIT CHURCH
186 AVENUE DAUMESNIL / 12th
METRO: DAUMESNIL

While this entrance to this religious structure is hardly appealing, visitors should not let that stop them from discovering the vast and majestic Saint-Esprit church. It is one of the most astounding places of worship in all of Paris. Paul Tournon, the architect of the cathedral in Casablanca, Morocco, and the church in Lubumbashi, Congo-Kinshasa, took inspiration from Istanbul's Byzantine basilica Hagia Sophia. Wishing "to glorify the Church through its roots and its history," Tournon designed a wide dome in reinforced concrete that is one solid piece, devoid of arch thrust, 33 meters high, which symbolizes the Holy Spirit. The iconography in each of its four pendentives celebrate the four great prophets and evangelists, and the twelve arches evoke the prophets and apostles.
The bas-reliefs on the outside, celebrating various trades and professions, were shaped in still wet cement by Gaudin and Carlo Sarrabezolles. Forty artists painted the stunning frescoes. In the apse, Maurice Denis and students executed the pictorial accounts of the Pentecost, Saint Paul, Saint Sophia guiding the fathers of the Greek Church, and Saint Peter overseeing those of the Roman Church. The fresco spans three walls. Raymon Subes, an ironsmith, created the choir enclosure, a masterpiece lit by truly admirable lamps.
Construction began in 1928 and ended in 1935. Although it needs refurbishing and lacks sufficient sunlight, it is a unique and somewhat exotic place of worship in the heart of the capital.

BUDDHA UNDER THE TREES

BOIS DE VINCENNES BUDDHIST CENTER
40 ROUTE DE CEINTURE DU LAC DAUMESNIL / 12th
METRO: PORTE DORÉE
Visit by appointment only. Tel: 01 43 41 54 48

A group sculpture by Japanese artist Torao Yazaki graces the entrance to the Bois de Vincennes Buddhist Center. The French Togo and Cameroun pavilions, where we are now, were designed by architects Louis-Hippolyte Boileau and Léon Carrière for the Colonial Exhibition in 1931. For a time, the bigger pavilion housed a museum devoted to the timber industries, and, as a result of this temporary occupancy, was fitted with pine wood roofing.
In 1977, it was decided to dedicate the place entirely to Buddha, which is confirmed by the presence of an imposing statue of "The Enlightened One" inside the building. The Tibetan Temple, built in 1985 according to spiritual leader Kalu Rinpoche's instructions, stands nearby. The symbolic elements of the edifice will probably mean little to those unfamiliar with the religion, but there can be no doubt that they convey infinite wisdom. For instance, the canopy above the porch would appear to express the primacy of spiritual matters over temporal ones... a truth which one cannot help but meditate upon throughout the visit.

URBAN FARMING

THE GEORGES-VILLE FARM
ROUTE DU PESAGE / 12th
METRO: CHÂTEAU-DE-VINCENNES
Tel: 01 43 28 47 63
Open weekends and bank holidays
1:30 to 6:30 PM April to September;
1:30 to 5:00 PM October to March;
Tuesday to Sunday from 1:30 to 6:30 PM
July, August, and during spring vacations

The Georges-Ville farm, still called the *la ferme de Paris*, was named after a pharmacist, physician and chemist who carried out experiments here with chemical fertilizers. For educational purposes, Georges-Ville advocated setting up farms near French schools that would be tended by schoolteachers.
Their observations were read and discussed in their classrooms, then carefully noted in reports sent to the professor and advocate of intensive farming.
Today's farm caters to youngsters generally unfamiliar with life on a the farm from the greater metropolitan area. Twelve acres have been set aside to give them the chance to see cows, pigs, geese, rabbits, sheep, goats, chickens, and ewes. The farm also introduces youngsters to crops characteristic of the Ile-de-France region such as wheat, barley, oat, flax, sunflower, etc. They can also discover an orchard and a vegetable patch. Children, and sometimes parents, can take part in the harvesting and gathering, and animal husbandry. They can also discover how wheat is turned into bread, and how butter and jams are made.

POINTING NORTH

PYRAMID IN THE BOIS DE VINCENNES
ROUTE DE LA PYRAMIDE / 12th
METRO: CHÂTEAU-DE-VINCENNES

The pyramid, or obelisk to be more precise, in the Bois de Vincennes was erected to mark the crossroads formed by Route de la Pyramide, Route du Champ-de-Manœuvres, Route de Bourbon, Route de La Faluère, and Route Royale-de-Beauté. In 1731, Louis XV ordered the ancient Vilcena forest to be restructured. Over one million pounds were spent planting oaks and laying out rectilinear roads, roundabouts, and wide open spaces for royal hunting parties.
The obelisk, carved by brothers Sébastien-Antoine Slodtz and Paul-Ambroise Slodtz, was placed here to commemorate the reforestation program. A stone globe fitted out with a gilded compass needle tops the structure.

A TOWNHOUSE

VILLA PLANEIX
24-BIS BOULEVARD MASSÉNA / 13th
METRO: PORTE-D'IVRY

In this part of the 13th arrondissement of Paris, where little attracts the eye, the sober façade of the Villa Planeix constrasts sharply with its surroundings, which resemble the rather unremarkable homes so common in the suburbs of Paris. Le Corbusier and Pierre Jeanneret designed the house for Antonin Planeix, a tombstone sculptor by trade. Their dream was an avant-garde townhouse. Planeix was an amateur painter and very interested in modern architecture. He knew what he wanted and kept a close eye on the construction project. Le Corbusier applied the principles of his Modulor system, designed to create living spaces in harmony and scaled to the proportions of the human body. To make the operation financially viable, Planeix planned two separate ground-floor workshops that were to be rented out. It was a wise move, as once the house was completed in 1928, he had problems paying the 350,000 francs due.

A BREATH OF FRESH AIR!

PITIÉ-SALPÊTRIÈRE HOSPITAL
47 BOULEVARD DE L'HÔPITAL / 13th
METRO: SAINT-MARCEL

A former explosives factory, Salpêtrière became a hospital in the 17th century. Louis XIV's intention was to cram in all the vagabonds and beggars of Paris. In 1684, it became a women's prison. Go through the main entrance, turn left and walk down the arched passage (Division Mazarin), and then down another passage leading to Division Montyon. Once through the porchway, you will see on your left the former prison buildings where prostitutes and common law criminals were locked up. Rue Saint-Félix, an 18th-century alley, runs alongside the prison, and a low building on the other side served as lodgings for the archers who rounded up the prostitutes. As Rue Saint-Félix bends to the right, you will see the former explosives' factory straight ahead, a magnificent restored building. If you go round it on the right-hand side, you will find some steps leading up to three one-storied buildings, the remains of the mentally handicapped women's quarters created in 1789. Each of the 600 inmates was locked up in a very small cell, a few meters square. Semicircular benches can still be seen securely fixed to the outside wall of the middle building. The guards used to chain the women to them so that the latter might benefit from the fresh air, a theory dear to the hearts of late 18th-century hygienists.

THE FUTURE OF MANKIND

TEMPLE DU DROIT HUMAIN
5 RUE JULES-BRETON / 13th
METRO: SAINT-MARCEL

"In humanity, women have the same obligations as men. They must have the same rights both within the family and society." So reads a Masonic lodge's motto engraved on a strange Neo-Egyptian façade.

This lodge, or to be more accurate, this *grande Loge symbolique écossaise mixte de France* (Grand Lodge of Mixed Scottish Rite Freemasonry of France), was founded in 1893 by Maria Deraisme, a pioneer of women's rights in France.

She threw her support behind a movement begun in the 1880s by several brothers who felt that the exclusion of women from the *Grande Loge Centrale de France* was wrong. Maria Deraisme died the year after the creation of *Droit Humain* (Order of Mixed Freemasonry), and never saw the worldwide growth of this Masonic offshoot. But times have changed. Today, the French federation, created by 17 women, boasts a membership of over 15,000.

AN ORANGERY FOR WATTEAU

3 BIS RUE DES GOBELINS / 13th
METRO: LES GOBELINS

At the far end of this courtyard, you will find a very old, two-storied building on the right-hand side. Sometimes wrongly called Hôtel Mascarini, it first belonged to a very famous family in the Gobelins district. Then, in 1686, the manor house was bought by wealthy dyer Jean Gluck, who made some radical alterations. His nephew and heir, Jean de Jullienne, took up residence there, and added to the magnificence of the house with his collection of carefully selected paintings, rare pieces of furniture and bronze statues. Despite the ravages of time, the building is still a fine sight. If you go up the front steps, at the top of which there is an attractive mascaron, you can see the house's straight staircase, originally fitted with a beautiful, wooden balustrade.

A stroll down the passage on the right will lead you to the wing built at right angles – remains of an orangery facing north, laid out by Jean de Jullienne, a great art collector and patron of rococo painter Watteau. The former used to hold lavish painting exhibitions in this orangery, almost 20 meters long, supported by tall Tuscan columns, and very tastefully restored by its current occupants.

THE "WHITE QUEEN'S" CASTLE

17 AND 19 RUE DES GOBELINS / 13th
METRO: LES GOBELINS

Near Boulevard Arago, the tiny street called Rue des Gobelins, formerly Rue de Bièvre, seems to have escaped the attention of city planners.
At no. 17, at the far end of a factory courtyard surrounded by unsightly brick workshops, stands an ancient, gabled residence: the legendary White Queen's castle. Books about Paris, written in the 19th century, never fail to mention this strange building, giving detailed, colorful – though invariably untrue – accounts of the house's history.
Today, everyone knows that no White Queen – not even Blanche de Navarre, Blanche de Castille or Blanche de Bourgogne – ever set foot in the house at 17 Rue des Gobelins.
It was not so much a private house as a dyeing workshop, built by the Gobelin family in the 16th century. Long neglected, it has been totally renovated and transformed into private upscale apartments. With the listing of the building as a heritage site, funds were made available to restore the elegant timbered gallery adjoining the cart archway.
The impressive three-storied building was in very bad condition. It deserved, and thankfully is getting, better treatment after a legal battle between the City of Paris and its owners.
Joris-Karl Huysmans described the building – a tannery at the time – in very vivid terms when he visited it in 1900: "It comprises vast, beamed rooms and spacious workshops where leather is cut and curried, for this little castle is, in fact, a tannery. Down below, along the length of an enormous room, whose slippery paved floor stretches out like a quagmire smelling of latrines and hot vinegar, stands a gigantic tank, parallel to the River Bièvre. And in the courtyard, it looks as if colossal cauldrons, dug into the ground, are boiling away; these are the tons and vats where the skins lie soaking."
Next door, at no. 19, there is another house dating from the same period and which was used for a similar purpose. Both houses used to overlook the River Bièvre which is covered today by Rue Berbier-du-Mets.

A MERE SHADOW OF THE CORDELIÈRES CONVENT

CORNER OF RUE PASCAL AND RUE DE JULIENNE AND THE GROUNDS OF THE BROCA HOSPITAL / 13th
METRO: LES GOBELINS

Some ruins – the remains of the Cordelières Convent – next to Broca Hospital, are a rather unexpected sight. The nuns of the order of Saint Clare, François d'Assise's sister, came here in 1289; the buildings were extended and improved by Marguerite de Provence, widow of Louis IX, known as Saint Louis, who led the Sixth Crusade. The nuns lived for years in this peaceful convent in Saint Marcel, a village in the country. During the French Revolution, the abbey was parceled out, and the church and two sides of the cloisters were destroyed. In 1836, the former convent was converted into a hospital.
In 1974, the tall structures with traces of ribbed vaults and medieval buttresses had become old and dilapidated, and were replaced by today's modern buildings.
In the wards inside, rows of columns with capitals represented more tangible evidence of a bygone age. Even some of the original framework, a masterpiece by journeymen, had survived.
There are still some remains in the hospital garden – former dormitory windows, shafts of columns and capitals dating back to the 13th and 14th centuries. These ancient stones are a final reminder of the existence of the Cordelières Convent.

WORKSHOPS IN THE CLOISTER

THE FORMER CONVENT OF THE ENGLISH NUNS

28 RUE DES TANNERIES / 13th

METRO: GLACIÈRE

There are some modest workshops under the arches of a 17th-century cloister at the far end of a beautiful, paved courtyard. The cloister used to be part of the English Nuns' Convent, named after the English Benedictine nuns who took refuge here in 1664 when fleeing persecution. The first Mother Superior was no other than Sister Brigitte More, granddaughter of Sir Thomas More, former Lord Chancellor of England.

The courtyard was converted into a cloister in 1693, and the chapel, which used to stand on the present site of the concierge's office, was restored in 1784. After a first escaping Catholic persecution in England, the English nuns, along with their French counterparts, suffered further persecution during the French Revolution. Sequestered in their convent, stripped of their belongings, they were finally deported back to their own country in 1794. England – rarely daunted by paradoxical situations – welcomed back with open arms its fellow citizens who had suffered at the hands of its barbaric neighbors on the Continent!

THE BIÈVRE POPLAR TREES

SQUARE RENÉ-LE-GALL
43 RUE CORVISART /13th
METRO: CORVISART

The River Bièvre no longer runs through Paris – the main Pascal-branch sewer captured its last flow at Parc Kellermann. When it was covered over at the beginning of the century, it was nothing more than a repulsive, muddy stream, whose fetid water washed along the foul-smelling waste from the numerous tanneries on its banks.

Not far from Rue Croulebarbe, the river divided into two arms which joined up again a little further on, thus forming a tree-planted island. A century ago, it had small gardens which the Gobelins' tapestry factory put at the disposal of its employees.

Square René-Le-Gall was opened to the public in 1938, and its oldest section covers most of the island. Old poplar trees, now replaced by hornbeams, were planted along the former bed of the river after the Bièvre was covered.

Architect Jean-Charles Moreux took into account the layout of the island's former paths when he designed this country-style garden, prettily decorated with an obelisk, wide rose arbors, and rockery.

Below Rue Berbier-du-Mets, a chestnut tree, more than a hundred years old, towers over younger specimens from other countries: chestnut trees from the Balkans, locust trees from North America, sophoras from Japan, walnut trees from the Caucasus, pine trees from the Himalayas, etc.

HEALING THROUGH BELIEVING

ANTOINIST TEMPLE
34 RUE VERGNIAUD / 13th
METRO: GLACIÈRE

With its copper-green steeple, this house of worship sits on an acute angle formed by Rue Wurtz and Rue Vergniaud. Members of the Antoinist church belong to a religious movement that sprang up in Belgium in 1910, initiated by a man named Louis Antoine.
Born in 1846 in a coal mining family near Liège, Antoine became a metal worker then later took interest in Allan Kardec's Spiritism movement. He set up an association called *Les Vignerons du Seigneur* (the Lord's wine growers) to provide a framework for his work as a healer. At one point, he received up to sixty people per day at no charge. Persuaded he had a genuine gift of healing, he began treating more and more people suffering from various ailments. In 1901, his treatments, mostly in the form of herbal teas and magnetized sheets of paper, got him into trouble for the "illegal exercise of the art of healing." Five years later, he moved to another level of faith healing by donning the "revealed robe" and founding the "New Spiritualism" movement. The sect grew rapidly, and by August 15, 1910, the Antoinists had consecrated their very own temple at Jemeppe-sur-Meuse.
After the death of the movement's "father," two years later, Antoine's wife took over and led the congregation until her own death in 1940. It was under her leadership that the temple on Rue Vergniaud was consecrated on October 26, 1913. Today, there are thirty-one Antoinist temples in France, with two others in Paris, one near Place des Ternes and the other on Rue du Pré-Saint-Gervais.

MEADOWS, MILLS AND POPLARS

SQUARE DES PEUPLIERS AND RUE DIEULAFOY
74 RUE DU MOULIN-DES-PRÉS / 13th
METRO: TOLBIAC

In the 18th century, fields and arable land stretched out along the River Bièvre, and a path lined with poplar trees crossed the plain. The trees have long since disappeared, but the names on blue and green plaques on every street corner bear witness to them. Near the crossroads at Rue du Moulin-des-Prés (whose name Windmill-in-the-Fields speaks for itself) there is a curious, triangular-shaped cul-de-sac called Square des Peupliers (poplars). To anyone enjoying a quiet walk round this tiny square, with its little houses nestling behind their railings, the hustle and bustle of city life seems a long way off. It was built in 1926, as was most of the district between Rue Ernest-et-Henri-Rousselle and Place de l'Abbé-Georges-Hénocque. This area used to be wasteland with just a few ragmen's sheds dotted here and there.

Rue Dieulafoy is easily reached via Place de l'Abbé-Georges-Hénocque. The houses with their attractive, pointed roofs all look alike, and are similar to those in Rue Santos-Dumont in the 15th arrondissement.

Gable-roofed houses along Rue Dieulafoy.

STREETS WHERE CATS MAY MEDITATE

CITÉ FLORALE (OR FLORÉALE)
36-8 AND 50-4 RUE BRILLAT-SAVARIN / 13th
RER: CITÉ-UNIVERSITAIRE

Although the 13th arrondissement did not, for the most part, escape the onslaught of excavators, particularly active during the big city-planning developments of the 1960s and 1970s, some delightful spots did manage to survive.
One of these is Cité Florale – next to Place de Rungis, a stone's throw from Boulevard Jourdan and Boulevard Kellermann – built towards the end of the 1920s. Its site, a pond that had been filled in during the 19th century, could not support the weight of tall buildings. Consequently, detached houses in all sorts of architectural styles were built, and they make a very pretty sight for anyone who cares to stroll down here. Wisteria, morning glory, orchids, and mimosa are the names of these tranquil, barely congested streets. Hush, lest we disturb the cats meditating in the sun!

ALSACE IN PARIS

VILLA AND CITÉ DAVIEL ("LITTLE ALSACE")
10 AND 7 RUE DAVIEL / 13th
METRO: GLACIÈRE OR CORVISART

With the withdrawal of the renown "Little Russia" from the public eye – now protected by a door code – one can find solace in discovering its neighbor, the *Petite Alsace*. The wide entrance at 10, rue Daviel opens into a rectangular courtyard lined with gabled, brick houses, designed by architect Jean Walter in 1912 for a company called "*Habitation familial*." There are a total of forty houses which can accommodate up to 302 people. The architect was awarded a silver medal by the Seine Regional Council Sponsor Committee. These attractive houses, built around a 550-square-meter central square, were recently renovated. The Cité Daviel has been officially listed among Paris' most picturesque sites since 1979.

Just as pretty as Cité Daviel is Villa Daviel, a cul-de-sac located at No. 7 on the opposite side of the street, with its unpretentious yellow and red brick houses and their small gardens, where the fuchsia, roses and wisteria reflect the owners' taste in flowers. A unique place, it is hoped it will remain visible to the public for a long time to come.

MERIDIAN MARKER

PARC MONTSOURIS
BOULEVARD JOURDAN ENTRANCE / 14th
RER: CITÉ-UNIVERSITAIRE

Parc Montsouris, a charming landscape garden, and the nearby Cité Universitaire are the great green lungs of south Paris. The park was designed by expert landscape gardener and engineer Alphand, who worked closely with Baron Haussmann, city planner under Napoleon III. Near the exit on Boulevard Jourdan stands a curious stone stele with a round hole though the top. Dated 1806, it bears the inscription: "*Du règne de...*" (in the reign of). Napoleon's name was removed, probably during the French Restoration (1814-30).

It is a common error to consider that this stone marker indicates the Paris meridian (long the prime meridian used by sailors until supplanted by the Greenwich meridian in 1884). This is not its purpose, however. The marker was used by astronomers at the Paris Observatory to set one of their instruments called a quarter-circle. It was located in an outbuilding which no longer exists. The Paris meridian links up Dunkerque with Perpignan on the map of France. In the north of Paris, another marker, older than its southern counterpart, is unfortunately under lock and key on private property near the Moulin de la Galette in Montmartre.
In 1806, while still a student at École Polytechnique (the prestigious engineering school), François Arago was given the task of extending the meridian as far as the Balearic Islands. As a tribute to him, France asked Dutch sculptor Jan Dibbets to create a "virtual" monument: 135 medallions in copper, zinc and tin, embedded in the ground within the city limits, all along the Paris meridian. The first of these medallions can be seen a few meters away from the stone marker, the only visible trace of the Paris meridian in the Parc Montsouris.

THE WORLD AT OUR DOOR

CITÉ UNIVERSITAIRE INTERNATIONALE
19, BOULEVARD JOURDAN / 14th
RER: CITÉ-UNIVERSITAIRE

This quiet campus provides a real change of scenery in the Paris cityscape, and is a mere stone's throw from the equally peaceful Parc Montsouris, across Boulevard Jourdan. The vast grounds, beside the busy Paris "beltway,"contains 37 student houses of varying architectural styles.
Over 124 nationalities are represented on the Cité Universitaire campus, commonly referred to as the "Cité U" by its inhabitants. Students of all stripes and ages reside in this verdant oasis often ignored by Parisians. The campus was the brainchild of Paris university superintendent Paul Appell. A few years after the First World War had swept away one third of the student population, the day for reconciliation of nations had come. French industrialist Deutsch de la Meurthe, who wanted to promote a social project in memory of his beloved wife, seized the opportunity and financed the construction of the first buildings by donating ten million gold francs. Education Minister André Honnorat had an even bigger vision for the project.

On July 9th, 1925, the *Deutsch de la Meurthe Foundation* was set up. The campus went up on land previously occupied by the, then demolished, Thiers city walls. Neo-Oxford style was the order of the day under the direction of architect Lucien Bechmann. Bartizans, turrets, and mullioned windows gave the first buildings a neo-medieval style. Next, architects from foreign countries designed student housing in line with traditional styles from their respective nations. Japan's student house incorporated several panels by the painter Fujita. Sweden built a charming blue and white pavilion. These were but the first of a long series, each

house taking inspiration from a particular artistic or architectural repertoire. Other areas were later financed by John D. Rockefeller.
Europe's first self-service cafeteria opened here in 1936. Since then, the campus has been enriched with other amenities (a theater, a library, an orchestra, a swimming pool, a gym, etc.) to make life more pleasant for over 5,000 students who also enjoy the colorful festivals given in honor of each nationality represented.

COUNTRY STREETS IN PARIS

SQUARE DE MONTSOURIS
(AND AREA STREETS)
ALONGSIDE PARC MONTSOURIS / 14th
RER: CITÉ-UNIVERSITAIRE

All along Rue Nansouty and Rue Émile-Deutsch-de-la-Meurthe, bordering Parc Montsouris, there are some delightful little alleys, a veritable paradise on the fringes of the 14th arrondissement, best visited in spring when the lilac is in bloom.
The first of these side streets, as you come from Avenue René-Coty, is Square de Montsouris. The house at the far end was designed by Le Corbusier. As you come into Avenue Reille, notice the elegant, glass-fronted buildings of the Montsouris reservoir. In order to reach the next street, go back down Square de Montsouris. Rue Georges-Braque is a cul-de-sac built in 1927, called Rue du Douanier until 1976, when it was named after painter Georges Braque. He lived at no. 6 in a brick and concrete house-cum-atelier designed by architect Auguste Perret. The atelier on the second floor has a very big window. Continue up Rue Nansouty towards Boulevard Jourdan and stroll down the other alleys and culs-de-sac bordering the park: Rue du Parc-de-Montsouris, Villa du Parc-Montsouris (a real headache for those delivering mail!), Impasse Nansouty. Each one is appealing in its own way, demonstrating, not for the first time, how Paris can sometimes resemble a sleepy country town.

Square de Montsouris

19 Rue du Parc-de-Montsouris

12 Rue du Parc-de-Montsouris

53 Avenue Reille

THE ARTISTS' RESIDENCE

VILLA SEURAT
101 RUE DE LA TOMBE-ISSOIRE / 14th
METRO: ALÉSIA

Villa Seurat – a charming cul-de-sac – was created at the instigation of architect André Lurçat who spotted some land in 1919, and persuaded its owner to divide it up into lots. A solution had to be found to the serious housing crisis facing the "Montparnos" (artists and writers working and living in the Montparnasse district between the two World Wars), who had to leave their base and move to this district, not far from the city fortifications. The place was to become a veritable laboratory for experiments in architecture.
The first order came from Jean Lurçat, the architect's brother, renowned for his revival of the art of tapestry. In July 1924, André Lurçat built him an L-shaped house with a square courtyard at no. 4. This order was followed by others from painters Marcel Gromaire and Édouard Goerg; the striking feature of both these ateliers at nos. 3 and 3 bis is their slightly rounded façades, somewhat reminiscent of Villa La Roche in the 16th arrondissement (see p. 202). André Lurçat continued to receive orders from painters, sculptors, and writers (nos. 1, 5, 8, 9, 11), and famous architect Auguste Perret designed a building (no. 7) for sculptress Chana Orloff.
Part of the cul-de-sac's attraction is that the avant-garde façades of the ateliers and houses are singularly alike. It can also pride itself on having been home to Expressionist painter Soutine and, at no. 18, writer Henry Miller, who wrote his famous books, Tropic of Cancer and Tropic of Capricorn, while he was here.

The harmonious curved façade at 3bis

QUIET TIMES
IN ALÉSIA

VILLA D'ALÉSIA
111 RUE D'ALÉSIA/39 BIS RUE DES PLANTES / 14th
METRO: ALÉSIA

Built in 1897, Villa d'Alésia, formerly called Villa Parquet, is a tiny right-angled street linking Rue d'Alésia with Rue des Plantes. Its greenery and its small buildings, some of which are surrounded by vast gardens, make a pleasant change from the noise of the traffic nearby.
Large workshops are still to be found here, a reminder that craft industries continue to operate, albeit less actively, in the 14th arrondissement. In fact, around 1910, there used to be a print shop, where only deaf-mutes were employed. Now, there is very little industrial activity here, except for handicrafts: a potter, on request, will create all sorts of shapes imaginable. It offers the peace and quiet of a street in the country, just a stone's throw from the heart of the capital.

ORLÉANS VILLAGE

RUE HALLÉ AND VILLA HALLÉ
36 RUE HALLÉ / 14th
METRO: MOUTON-DUVERNET

The architectural styles of the buildings erected along a curve in Rue Hallé, not far from Avenue du Général-Leclerc, are amazingly different. Rue Hallé – along with Rue Ducouédic and Rue Rémy-Dumoncel – was part of a housing development, known as the "*Village d'Orléans*", built around 1830 on parcels of land, which had been put up for sale for this purpose. The original plan was to build houses in similar styles, but this was never to be! However, the results of the city-planning operation along Rue Hallé add to the charm of this quiet neighborhood. Villa Hallé – a small, curved cul-de-sac – starts at no. 36, behind the remains of a gate topped with spikes. There is something about this cul-de-sac which is reminiscent of villages on the outskirts of Paris with their small houses in contrasting styles and their tiny back gardens. It was undoubtedly because of the atmosphere here that one of the houses was used as the home of the heroine – played by Catherine Deneuve – in Francis Girod's film, *Le Bon Plaisir*.

ROYAL HOSPICE

LA ROCHEFOUCAULD HOSPICE
19 AVENUE DU GÉNÉRAL-LECLERC / 14th
METRO/RER: DENFERT-ROCHEREAU

Just a few steps from the Villa Adrienne, the La Rochefoucauld retirement home provides strollers with a peaceful respite. This elegant group of buildings with prominent linear features, was originally the Royal Nursing Home. Built near the former "*barrière d'Enfer*" (Enfer tollgate), it took in old and ailing clergy and indigent soldiers. The home's first occupants must have had no shortage of room as there were a mere 23 boarders at the start of the French Revolution!
There is a good view of the rear façade from Avenue René-Coty.
Just in front of the wall, there is a small, curious-looking structure – actually a former "manhole cover" – that allowed inspection of the pipes that conveyed water to the nursing home from the Arcueil aqueduct. (see also p. 177).

THE LAST ONE

THE LAST OF PARIS' OLD-FASHIONED PUBLIC URINALS
BOULEVARD ARAGO / 14th
METRO:/RER DENFERT-ROCHEREAU

A much-talked-about urinal stands near the Santé prison's north wall, opposite no. 86 Boulevard Arago. It is the city's last *vespasienne* (double-booth, free-of-charge public urinal). Such conveniences placed on the city streets caused an uproar, and inspired Second Empire newspaper cartoonists to satirize users standing ridiculously immobile in a rounded niche of the columnar form. Urinating in a structure specifically designed for this seemed utterly grotesque to 19th-century men, as filthy, muddy city streets offered plenty of darkened corners to relieve oneself.

However, the origin of the outhouse goes back to ancient Rome. Emperor Vespasian had the idea of placing sections of barrels in the streets of Rome for the comfort of his contemporaries. In early 19th-century Paris, a few pay urinals were set up in public gardens. In 1841, the "Rambuteau column" made its appearance. It provided room for one occupant, and was topped with a spherical calotte. This version gained instant popularity. Two years later, the city had some 468. In 1877, the columns were replaced with dual-occupant urinals with a large slate divider to separate the compartments. Other models were introduced. Once covered with advertising bills, these vespasiennes turned a pretty profit. Moralistic campaigns demanding their removal spelled their demise. In 1930, there were 1,200 vespasiennes. By 1966, the number had dwindled to 329. "Chalets" for women were always far less numerous. This discrimination remained until automated, self-cleaning, pay toilettes appeared.

Abandoned on the dreariest bank of Boulevard Arago, this last urinal, much like the well-maintained benches, trees, and sidewalks, is a strange sight beside the high prison wall and the high walls of the convent across the busy boulevard. The last vespasienne in Paris is frequented by taxi drivers, who complain bitterly of the scarcity of free conveniences.

Until rather recently, the Right Bank also boasted its last vespasienne, Place de Barcelone, in the chic 16th arrondissement. But, as residents of this quarter found the smell a great inconvenience, it too was demolished.

A "MOBILE" MANOR HOUSE

HÔTEL DE MASSA
38 RUE DU FAUBOURG-SAINT-JACQUES / 14th
METRO: SAINT-JACQUES OR RER: PORT-ROYAL
To visit the garden, telephone 01 43 07 09 69

Hôtel de Massa, a strictly private establishment, stands in a shady garden next to the Observatory park, and is the home of the "*Société des Gens de Lettres*" (Literary Society). The most unusual feature concerning this beautiful manor house is that it used to stand elsewhere – on the corner of Rue La Boétie and the Champs-Elysées – before being moved to this quiet spot in the 14th arrondissement in 1927.
It was built in 1784 in the middle of a large park, and was the scene of lavish parties, elegant receptions and romantic encounters. Seized as national property during the French Revolution, the manor house was later allotted to the Italian ambassador who invited Napoleon and Joséphine to the brilliant receptions he gave there.
Many years later, in 1926, when the Champs-Elysées became more popular again, two property developers – Théophile Bader, director of department store Galeries Lafayette, and André Lévy – bought the manor house and its parkland with the intention of building a vast complex on its site. Unfortunately for them, the edifice was listed. In order to get round this difficulty, they offered to finance the dismantling and reassembling of the house elsewhere, which they did. The harmonious dimensions of Hôtel de Massa were noted on a plan, each stone numbered, and the pieces carried across Paris to the present site. The job took two years to complete, and required sixty workers possessing a variety of skills.
In April 1929, the Literary Society held its first session at Hôtel de Massa, on the very site where a resident from Rue Cassini nearby (see p. 174) used to stroll a century earlier: his name was Honoré de Balzac... the first president of the "*Société des Gens de Lettres*".

THREE VERY DISSIMILAR HOUSES

3 BIS, 5 AND 7 RUE CASSINI / 14th
METRO: SAINT-JACQUES OR RER: PORT-ROYAL

Rue Cassini can pride itself on having been the home of some very important people, beginning with the famous family of astronomers – four generations – who lived here and gave the street its name. From 1828 to 1835, writer Honoré de Balzac lived in a house which used to be no. 1. This was where he started planning his masterpiece, *La Comédie Humaine* (The Human Comedy), and he had his first work published while he was still living there. At the end of his garden, a small door communicated with the Observatory gardens, enabling the writer to converse with the pupils of that establishment. Astronomer, physicist and politician François Arago, his neighbor, liked to reminisce about that time: "[...] from this window on the terrace, I could see his candles flickering: we both used to work late into the night, my eyes were riveted to the sky, his head was bent over a sheet of paper. And perhaps the astronomer was not the one who saw the furthest!"
The exact site of Balzac's house, no longer standing, has never been known with any certainty; it probably stood on the south side of Rue Cassini.
On the other hand, three beautiful, big houses, built between 1903 and 1906, are quite visible.
Bricks have been used to fill in the reinforced concrete structure of the house at no. 3, undoubtedly the most refined and the most elegant of the three houses. It was built for painter Lucien Simon who was responsible for some of the ceilings of the Senate.
The house at no. 5 is an austere, brick, medieval-looking building, erected for painter Jean-Paul Laurens, whose paintings still grace one of the City Hall's reception rooms.
The building at no. 7 is in a freely-inspired, neoclassical style, and was designed for painter Czernikowski.
Three different styles were all created by one man, painter and architect Louis Süe, who was not averse to a certain degree of eclecticism. He was also responsible for the artists' ateliers at 126 Boulevard du Montparnasse (see p. 179).

PORT-LIBRE

PORT-ROYAL CLOISTER, BAUDELOCQUE HOSPITAL
123-25 BOULEVARD DE PORT-ROYAL
2-22 RUE DU FAUBOURG-SAINT-JACQUES / 14th
RER: PORT-ROYAL
Chapel open on Sunday at 10:30 AM (for Mass)

Most of Paris' cloisters have disappeared, and many people are unaware of the existence of those that have survived. Such is the case of the Port-Royal Convent cloister on Boulevard Port-Royal.

In 1204, Mathieu de Montmorency and his wife, Mathilde de Garlande, founded Port-Royal-des-Champs Abbey in the Chevreuse valley. In 1603, Mother Angélique Arnauld bought the former Hôtel de Clagny – on Rue de la Bourbe near Rue Saint-Jacques – and the surrounding land.

In 1626, the nuns of the order of the Blessed Sacrament, won over by Jansenist ideas, moved in. Mother Angélique had more convent buildings erected.

Port-Royal-de-Paris became a leading center for religious thinking, and served as a retreat for scholars such as Lemaître de Sacy, Nicole, Abbot de Saint-Cyran, and sometimes Blaise Pascal, French philosopher, mathematician and physicist.

The convent's history is marked by persecution, and the eventual disappearance of the Jansenists; during the French Revolution it was closed down, and, in 1793, converted into a prison – known as the "Port-Libre Prison".

The prisoners set up a phalanstery, whereby the rich financed the poor, and an internal organization to ensure that prison management was under their control. However, many of its inmates – politician Malesherbes and chemist Lavoisier among others – ended up on the scaffold during the Reign of Terror.

In 1795, the Convention decided to use the convent for accommodating foundlings and their wet nurses along with women about to give birth.

Arrows indicating "chapelle" at the entrance will lead you to the ancient buildings.

The cloister is three-sided, and, on the north side, there is a small door opening into the chapel, whose nave has just one row of benches. The chapel was designed by architect Lepautre (1646-48), and used to be decorated with Philippe de Champaigne's extraordinary paintings, now hanging in provincial museums as well as in the Louvre. The metal screen separating the chancel from the nave serves as a reminder of the austere lives the nuns led here.

THE KING'S TURNCOCK

THE TURNCOCK'S HOUSE
42 AVENUE DE L'OBSERVATOIRE / 14th
METRO: DENFERT-ROCHEREAU OR RER: PORT-ROYAL
Open to public on National Heritage Days.
A monthly visit is organized by a non-profit historical site preservation group.
For information, call: 01 48 87 74 31

Thanks to the perseverance of volunteers of the Association for the preservation and enhancement of historical Paris, the basement of the oldest house in the 14th arrondissement has been preserved and restored.
This small, sand-colored stone structure with its flat-tiled roof played a major role in the history of water in Paris, and was listed in 1994.
Between 1613 and 1623, Queen Marie de Médicis had the famous Arcueil aqueduct built to supply water to her gardens at Luxembourg Palace. This superb structure was erected on the site of a similar construction dating back to the Gallo-Roman era.
Between 1619 and 1623, the "Main Inspection Chamber of the Observatory", or more simply the "turncock's house," built on the aqueduct, which diverted water from Rungis, was surrounded by fields, a few farms and two windmills. Thomas Francini, General Manager of the King's water supply and fountains, worked and lived here with his family. His descendants occupied the premises until 1784. This small building comprises a ground floor, an upper floor, and a converted loft.
The basement is divided into three rooms equipped with decanting reservoirs, one for the King, one for the city, and one for the Carmelites. Water from the aqueduct poured into each of the reservoirs, and was then conveyed by three lead pipes of different diameters to the Luxembourg gardens, the religious communities of the area, and several fountains in Paris. In the presence of the city aldermen, these water mains were inaugurated on May 19th, 1623; they continued to supply water to the Medicis fountain in Luxembourg Gardens until 1904.
Today, water from the aqueduct no longer passes through the turncock's house.
An enormous control reservoir with a capacity of 1,030 cubic meters, designed to reprocess water at night, was closed down in 1874 when the Montsouris reservoir came on line.

Opposite page: Point of departure of the three water pipes destined for "the King", "the Carmélites," and "the city."

The control reservoir

RENDEZVOUS IN HELL

PASSAGE D'ENFER
RUE CAMPAGNE-PREMIÈRE/249 BOULEVARD RASPAIL / 14th
METRO: RASPAIL OR EDGAR-QUINET

Passage d'Enfer, an L-shaped, private road, owes its name to the area around Boulevard d'Enfer (Hell), renamed Boulevard Raspail in 1887. The rear façade at nos. 24-7 is that of a superb building at nos. 31-4 Rue Campagne-Première, decorated with ceramics and well worth a visit (architect André Arfvidson, 1911). There is also a faded façade of a former dry cleaner's. The cul-de-sac, which runs into Boulevard Raspail, is a haven of peace amid the hustle and bustle of Montparnasse.

TO EACH HIS OWN

MONTPARNASSE ARTISTS' STUDIOS
126 BOULEVARD DU MONTPARNASSE / 14th
METRO: VAVIN

A fine, freestone façade decorated with a string course of floral motifs has two entrances, the right-hand one leading to a staircase, and the left-hand, to a courtyard. There is a majestic, luxurious air about this extraordinary complex, comprising apartments and ateliers. They are privately-owned and rented apartment blocks, designed by architect Louis Süe, and built of concrete covered with mortar. Couples of young artists were given priority to rent the six- and eight-storied apartment units, and Mr. Moreau, a dormant partner, had one of the privately-owned blocks. Privacy is an important feature. The windows are tiered, letting in a maximum amount of light, while hiding the big gardens at the back. Socialist Party statesman Léon Blum once lived on the first floor of the building overlooking the street.

LIGHT FROM DARKNESS

MONTPARNASSE CEMETERY, DIVISION 22, SECTION 22
ACCÈS PAR LE 3, BOULEVARD EDGAR-QUINET / 14th
METRO: RASPAIL

The bronze couple reclining on this tombstone strikes a highly unusual pose, unusual at least for a cemetery. The wife is stretched out on the marriage bed while her husband, leaning on his elbow, appears to be daydreaming.
Is he contemplating the passage he has just read in the book he is holding or has he suddenly had an ingenious idea?
An angel hovering over the bed's headboard brandishes a flame symbolizing the source of the couple's wealth, light!
Charles-Joseph Pigeon (1838-1915) began his career as a salesman at the Bon Marché department store. He left to open his own light fixture shop on Rue du Cherche-Midi. He became interested in improving the particularly dangerous gasoline lamp and patented his own invention in 1884. Pigeon's massed-produced lamp had an instantly recognizable shape and was etched with a pigeon on a globe.
The immensely popular item made its inventor a fortune. Humanity also owes a debt to Mr. Pigeon for his "unsinkable mattress," with which the great man himself saved two bathers in Trouville, his "speculum chair," and his night table billed as "healthy and odorless." He was awarded the Légion d'honneur in 1915 for his many contributions to society.

THE WINDMILL OF CHARITY

MONTPARNASSE CEMETERY
3 BOULEVARD EDGAR-QUINET
CIMETIÈRE DU MONTPARNASSE, 9TH DIVISION
ENTRY: PORTE FROIDEVAUX, RUE FROIDEVAUX / 14th
METRO: GAÎTÉ

Clearly visible from the streets around Montparnasse cemetery, a tower-like structure looking rather lonely and out of place among the graves, is none other than the remains of "*Moulin de la Charité*," used today to store gravediggers' equipment. This windmill is the last of many that used to exist around "Mont Parnasse" in the 18th century.
Strictly speaking, it is probably a 14th- or 15th-century tower mill whose roof – originally mobile and fitted with vanes – used to rotate on a revolving shaft.
As was often the case in those days, the windmill served both as a tavern and a flour mill. The miller would serve some *galettes* (a round, flat cake) and a small glass of wine. Students from Clermont College (now Louis-le-Grand High School) frequented Moulin de la Charité. As they were pro-Jesuits, they steered clear of nearby Moulin des Trois-Cornets, a favorite haunt of Jansenists.

FROM ONE EXHIBITION TO ANOTHER

NOTRE-DAME-DU-TRAVAIL CHURCH
36 RUE GUILLEMINOT / 14th
METRO: PERNETY

This church's stone façade is very misleading as it hides the building's entirely metal structure. Built by Jules Astruc in 1899, Notre-Dame-du-Travail was commissioned by Abbot Soulange-Bodin, who was actively involved in social and charity projects for the working class. This man of God aimed to give the many workers on the construction site of the 1900 Universal Exhibition a place of prayer and a place to feel at home. The architect cleverly took advantage of the dismantling of the *Palais de l'Industrie*, the flagship of the 1855 Exhibition, which was designed to be even more audacious than London's Crystal Palace, and recycled building materials, including stones and metal beams, needed for the new church.

In 2002, the city of Paris restored this "sanctuary of union and concord." It added four paintings of patron saints who represent labor: Saint Luke (artistic professions), Saint Francis of Assisi (poetry and ecology), Saint Eligius (metal workers and goldsmiths), and Saint Fiacre (farmers and gardeners). Lucien Simon's *La Messe du Soldat* and *Le Sacrifice* (1920) were placed in the chapel for the deceased to commemorate the heavy toll World War I took on workers.

Beside the entrance to the church on Rue Vercingétorix is the half-ton Sebastopol bell. It was captured by French troops during the Crimean War. It was a gift from Emperor Napoleon III to the parish of the Plaisance neighborhood.

WORKINGMAN'S CHÂTEAU

RENTAL PROPERTY
71 RUE RAYMOND-LOSSERAND / 14th
METRO: PERNETY

The workingman's château off Rue Raymond Losserand rises proudly at the far end of a driveway. It is a broad sidewalk, lined with low-rise homes. Who today would have ever suspected that this building, which belongs to the Didot urban development zone (or "ZAC" in French), might be slated for demolition? It is a neighborhood landmark. For today's residents of the Pernety area, it serves as a reminder of their quarter's activist history, a period when several advocacy groups and determined tenants mobilized to save number 71. Now, pleasantly restored by architect Pierre Colboc, the building has never looked lovelier. It is a remote, very remote evocation of the 18th-century Château du Maine that stood not too far away. While the building off Rue Raymond-Losserand may have never had any aristocratic trappings, its two wings have always impressed residents of this popular district. It was erected by architect Louis Gauche in 1891 on a plot of land purchased from the Villemain family who had already built a portion of the low-rise dwellings on the alley. Gauche made consistency his rule of thumb, and put eight identical, but small, one-bedroom apartments on each floor. Each apartment was even equipped with its own toilet, a veritable luxury.

ATTRACTING THE BLUE-COLLARS

THE PLAISANCE DISTRICT
RUE DES THERMOPYLES, CITÉ BAUER, VILLA JAMOT, VILLA DUTHY, VILLA MALLEBAY, VILLA DESHAYES, AND VILLA COLLET / 14th
METRO: PERNETY OR PLAISANCE

If you stroll through the pleasant Square du Chanoine-Viollet, exit through the western gate on Rue Didot. Cross the street there, and go straight ahead to Cité Bauer, a charming street lined with two- and three-story houses. You will soon reach a narrow passage at the end on the right. This is Rue des Thermopyles. The old village of Plaisance has many twists and turns. Plaisance... the name conjures up images of pleasure cruises and yet it was built on nearly deserted land. Victor Hugo fondly described the village's *"mélancolie pénétrante"* (penetrating melancholy). By 1832, land developers were eying these isolated plots of land outside of the town of Vaugirard (not yet incorporated in Paris). They carved out narrow streets and lined them with new homes on both sides. Buyers of these tiny parcels, blue-collar workers for the most part, became proud owners of humble homes. They flocked here and the population quickly swelled. By 1845, Chauvelot had created the village of Les Thermopyles as well as the street of the same name and Passage Léonidas. Residents in Vaugirard protested, arguing that the new development would attract noisy people. Their protests were in vain. The population of busy beavers stuck to their guns and moved in to claim their new lands. There is a fishbone-like layout to the series of dead-ends named Villa Jamot, Villa Duthy, Villa Mallebay, Villa Deshayes, and Villa Collet – all named for the neighborhood's persevering builders.

Rue des Thermopyles

A LEMON TREE IN A TELEPHONE BOOTH

RUE AND VILLA SANTOS-DUMONT / 15th
METRO: CONVENTION

Villa Santos-Dumont is a hidden paradise, which only the well-informed explorer will find easily accessible. If you come from Rue de Vouillé, you will find Villa Santos-Dumont – a leafy cul-de-sac with vines growing through the paving stones – about halfway down Rue Santos-Dumont, also a very peaceful street. Many famous people have lived at Villa Santos-Dumont: sculptor Ossip Zadkine at no. 3, painter Victor Brauner at no. 10 bis, mosaicist Gatti at no. 15, and, two numbers further down, writer Jeanne Champion.
The most well-known area resident was without doubt singer and composer Georges Brassens, renowned for his songs about friendship, love and death; he also set to music poems by Hugo and Villon.
Brassens actually resided on Impasse Florimont in the 14th arrondissement where kindhearted Jeanne le Bonniec from Brittany had put him up since the dark days of World War II. On her death one sad day in 1968, Brassens decided to move to 42 Rue Santos-Dumont, almost in exile, even though it was only a stone's throw from the 14th arrondissement. Here in this garden home, the man nicknamed "*le Gros*" (Fatty) divided his time between working and entertaining lifelong friends such as René Fallet, André Vers, Pierre Maguelon, to mention but a few in his beloved "*bande des cons*" (the gang of jerks).
One day, while resting in Saint-Gély-du-Fesc, between Sète and Montpellier in southwestern France, Brassens fell in love with a lemon tree. He wanted to take a cutting of it back to "Santos-Dumont", and when somebody objected that the poor plant would not survive the climate in Paris, he said he would buy a telephone booth for it.
However, his death on October 29th, 1981 did not leave Brassens time to carry out his plan.

A HIVE OF ACTIVITY

LA RUCHE
PASSAGE DE DANTZIG / 15th
METRO: CONVENTION
Open to the public on National Heritage Days

There is a gigantic, rusty key at La Ruche's entrance; getting through the gate is easier for cats than it is for mere mortals.
La Ruche (the beehive) – its name comes from the layout of ateliers around the central staircase, resembling cells in a beehive – was a wine pavilion at the 1900 World Fair. Erected by the team working for Gustave Eiffel, designer of the Eiffel Tower, the building was later auctioned, and bought by Boucher, a sculptor in vogue at the time, who wished to provide accommodations for artists less fortunate than himself.
Once reassembled on some wasteland near Rue de Vaugirard, and fitted with the gates originating from the "*Palais de la Femme*" (a hostel for women in the 11th arrondissement), La Ruche was officially inaugurated in 1902.
Boucher, who affectionately referred to his protégés as bees, took in Fernand Léger as early as 1905. Later, many artists from central Europe and elsewhere came to "gather nectar" at *La Ruche*. Chagall, Soutine, Modigliani, Archipenko, Zadkine, poet Apollinaire and writer Blaise Cendrars, all came to work in this center of the School of Paris.

In the 60s, *La Ruche* was saved from demolition, thanks to action taken by Chagall and other artists, and to the then Minister for Arts, André Malraux, and was subsequently listed. *La Ruche* is still a hive of activity, where numerous painters and sculptors continue to dedicate themselves to art.

MASTER GLASSWORKER IN A SECLUDED SQUARE

SQUARE VERGENNES
279 RUE DE VAUGIRARD / 15th
METRO: VAUGIRARD
Open Tuesday to Saturday from 12 to 7 PM (closed August and bank holidays)

Master glassworker Barillet's house, listed a historic monument since 1991, stands at the far end of Square Vergennes, a quiet, attractive cul-de-sac. Mallet-Stevens designed the building in 1932 for Barillet, whom he regarded as his friend and colleague, and who often accepted orders from the architect, and supplied him with glass on many occasions.

Mallet-Stevens put the living quarters on the fourth floor and the workshops for cutting glass and creating mosaics on the three floors below, and placed the entire weight of the building on a single, central, load-bearing post – an astonishing feat of engineering. The features of the façade make it possible to distinguish the workshops on the left – behind big glass windows – from the offices on the right – in the narrow, rounded part of the building. An awning over the front entrance is surmounted by a narrow, stained-glass window by Barillet, extending up to the top of the building. The building, which had undergone many alterations, has since been carefully restored by its current owners. Both the interior and the façade were restored to their former glory. Today, it houses a foundation dedicated to the works of the sculptor Yonel Lebovici, temporary exhibition rooms for art and design, and a collection of architectural materials to showcase innovative trends.

THE SCIENTIST AND HIS HOME

THE PASTEUR MUSEUM AND MAUSOLEUM
25 RUE DU DOCTEUR-ROUX / 15th
METRO: PASTEUR
Tel: 01 45 68 82 83
Open Monday to Friday from 2 PM to 5:30 PM; closed in August

© INSTITUT PASTEUR

Everybody knows and uses the term "pasteurized" nowadays, but ask who the man behind the name is, and you may get a blank stare. At best, the question may bring to mind the world-famous scientific research institute. The man was Louis Pasteur. On July 6th, 1885, Pasteur vaccinated a shepherd boy named Jupille who had been bitten by a rabid dog. After the child's spectacular recovery, the ill flocked to the Paris university where the scientist worked (l'École normale, located Rue d'Ulm). "Give me a laboratory, and I will rock the world!" Pasteur obstinately petitioned government officials to provide better conditions for researchers. The first building of the Pasteur Institute was inaugurated on November 14th, 1888.
Located on two floors of this neo-Louis XIII building, a reconstructed apartment-museum gives visitors a wealth of information. Appointed in gracious late 19th-century furnishings, the museum holdings include Pasteur's personal belongings, clothes, knickknacks, family portraits, plush furniture, and works of art collected by Pasteur and his wife. The great scientist's laboratory equipment occupies a converted linen room. Note the simple magnifying glass used in most of his observations. Numerous items displayed in glass cabinets bear witness to the gratitude of the entire world: wine makers, beer brewers, silk worm farmers, and others who benefited from Pasteur's breakthroughs.
Louis Pasteur died at his home in Marnes-la-Coquette on September 28th, 1895.
His widow requested a crypt for his remains be built in the basement of the Institute. The impressive and sumptuously decorated Latin cross chamber was the work of architect Charles-Louis Girault. The mosaics were the work of Auguste Guilbert-Martin and painter Luc-Olivier Merson. In 1896, Pasteur's remains were placed in a sarcophagus made of Swedish porphyry, set in the center of the crypt. Angels watch from overhead. The mosaic panels feature animals (sheep, diseased dogs, rabbits, chickens) as well as plants such as hops and grape vines, all tributes to the deceased's accomplishments. Engraved in the marble is a chronology of the major discoveries made by this benefactor of humanity. In the Institute which still bears his name, researchers in the fields of immunology and biology pursue Pasteur's battle against contagious diseases.

ART ALLEY

CHEMIN DU MONTPARNASSE / 15th
21 AVENUE DU MAINE
METRO: MONTPARNASSE-BIENVENÜE
Tel: 01.42.22.91.96.
Museum open daily (except Mondays and Tuesdays) from 12:30 PM to 7 PM

This alley is practically the only survivor of the Montparnasse artist colonies. As fate would have it, the artist studios here were not transformed into luxurious lofts for well-heeled Parisians. Part of the area was taken over by a museum whose scope includes not only the artistic past of Montparnasse, but also modern-day and future creations. How can you not fall for the charm of this area tucked beneath the most invasive skyscraper in Paris?
The alley is lined with glass and wood studio-homes covered in the summer greenery of Virginia creepers. Nevertheless, this enchanting place nearly disappeared forever, battered by deadly property promoters' projects. A high-spirited preservation association formed and successfully petitioned for the cancellation of the building permit – much to great pleasure of today's strollers.
It was in 1901 that lawyer Joseph Roux ordered the construction of some thirty artists' studios to be built from discarded materials from the previous Universal Exposition. As rents were low, artists and craftsmen wasted no time to set up here. Eleven years later, at the far end of this cul-de-sac, the *Académie du Montparnasse* opened. Gromaire and Despierre taught here. Next came "the two Maries of painting and dire straits," namely Marie Blanchard and Marie Vassilieff. The latter opened an "artists' cantina" in the alleyway. For a pittance, food for the body and food for the soul could be had by the likes of Modigliani, Léger, Picasso, Cocteau, Matisse, and several others. It is even said that a visit by Trotsky got Marie Vassilieff a war tribunal hearing and a few months in jail.
Many artisans set up shop in the alley, lending added charm to Chemin du Montparnasse. Here also, great architects trained in the offices of Gromort & Arretche. Parade floats for the school of fine arts were assembled here, in an easily-imagined festive setting, and student groups prepared their disguises for the famous *Bal des Quat'z Arts* (a costumed ball) as amused workmen from the passageway looked on. During the German Occupation in the 1940s, the discreet Chemin du Montparnasse was a hideout for members of the resistance. After American troops freed France, art reclaimed its rights in this passageway. Thanks to today's painters, sculptors, and photographers, art is alive and well in this quaint alley.

MILD WOMEN, WILD MUSIC

LE BAL NÈGRE
33 RUE BLOMET / 15th
METRO: VOLONTAIRES

© AKG-IMAGES/DANIEL FRASNAY

The Bal Nègre in 1955

Located on a long, quiet street cutting through the Convention district, this 18th-century building is one of the rare vestiges of the old Vaugirard village. But its real claim to fame was as an exotic nightclub during the interwar years.
In 1924, it was a simple café and tobacco shop located mere steps away from studios of Masson and Miró (at number 45, now torn down, on the present-day Square Blomet). That year, Jean Rézard des Wouves, a politician from the French Caribbean running for a seat as deputy in Parliament, decided to set up his campaign offices in the back room. Campaign meetings held here were often followed by dances. This launched the famed *bal colonial*, also called the *bal nègre*.
Ernest Léardée and his small orchestra of black musicians played in this venue frequented by the surrealists and night-owls keen on rubbing elbows with the lower classes in a colorful ambiance. On any given night, Joséphine Baker, Foujita, Robert Desnos, or Kiki might slip away from riotous Montparnasse nightlife and pop in here. It was a hangout for Cocteau, Fitzgerald, and Miller.
The place is still dedicated to French Caribbean music. Far from fancy, the simple public house is celebrated in literature. "At that time," wrote Simone de Beauvoir in *La Force de l'Âge* (*The Prime of Life*, 1960), "very few white women would mix with a black crowd, even fewer could hold their own on the dance floor against supple Africans, shimmying Caribbeans. Pitifully stiff. Those who tried to shed their stiffness looked more like hysterical women in a trance. [...] The noise, the smoke, the alcohol in the air, the band's thumping rhythms would numb me; through the fog, I could see beautiful, happy faces gliding by."

A TREE IN A CHURCH

SAINT-SÉRAPHIN-DE-SARROW CHURCH
91 RUE LECOURBE / 15th
METRO: VOLONTAIRES

Streets like Rue Lecourbe are hard to find these days. Its many, varied stalls take us back to the happy times when markets were lively and cheerful, with crowds of light-hearted Parisians jostling one another on their way to buy bread, poultry, and vegetables on Sundays. Some of the vendors call out to the customers, recommending the "extra fresh" peas or the "extraordinary" cherries. This busy shopping street is one of the oldest roads in the capital, and villages Meudon and Sèvres, just south of Paris, could be reached by it.

Such hustle and bustle in the street makes it difficult to imagine that behind one of its doors there is an incredibly peaceful place, with a timeless quality about it. The entrance of the nondescript, 19th-century building at no. 91 gives access to a passage leading to two small courtyards lined with attractive houses built in the same century. At the far end of the second one, there is a wooden chalet, housing the Saint-Séraphin Church, topped with a sky-blue, onion-shaped dome. In 1933, the building – erected around a tree – was even smaller; today's church dates from 1974. The bottom part of the tree was preserved, and is still on view in this orthodox chapel, whose congregation is composed of members of the Russian community – descendants of "White Russian" immigrants – living in the 15th arrondissement. Many of them took up residence here, as well as in the 16th arrondissement, because of the proximity of the Citroën and Renault automobile plants.

For a long time, the "White Russians" in this district had their own shops, restaurants, pharmacies, and school. Parties and receptions – the most well-known of these being the "Russian drivers' party" – enabled exiles to get together, thanks to the efforts of a large number of associations.

BLESSED FRIENDS

SAINTE-RITA CHURCH
27 RUE FRANÇOIS-BONVIN / 15th
METRO: SÈVRES-LECOURBE AND VOLONTAIRES

This late 19th-century church in English neo-Gothic style is actually of little artistic interest. While it cannot claim to be the most beautiful Gallican church in Paris, it is among the most important, as it is the cathedral of the Gallican Church in the Île-de-France. The primate is Monsignor Dominique Philippe.
A singular ambiance prevails inside centered on the patron saint. Behind a wrought iron grille, lit in the glow of numerous candles, is the casket containing the earthly remains of Saint Rita, defender of lost causes. Beside her casket, a glass case holds relics of Saint Peter the apostle, Saint Geneviève, and a few others. Visitors will also notice a plethora of mawkish statues of saints, flags, press clippings, and flyers decorating the walls. Every first Sunday in November, the faithful line up for a special occasion honoring Saint Francis of Assisi. This is the day for the blessing of the animals. From gold fish to dogs, camels to zebras, on this day, the church welcomes all God's creatures, though no other day of the year is necessarily to be ruled out. Did not Saint Rita save the souls of all who invoked her?

CHÂTEAU VIOLET

SQUARE VIOLET
PLACE VIOLET / 15th
METRO: FÉLIX-FAURE

There are some very old trees in Square Violet, a garden not far from Rue du Commerce, and in particular a cottonwood tree, 25 meters high. Château Violet, the rather tall building in the enclosure of the neighboring fire station, partly concealed by the wall in the garden, used to be the residence of speculator Léonard Violet, who created the district. The Square itself was built on his property.
In 1824, Léonard Violet, along with Alphonse Letellier, bought some vast pieces of land which were part of the Grenelle agricultural plains. Instead of using it as arable land, he built a new town called "Beaugrenelle", complete with shops, a place of worship, a theater, a river port, and an industrial site. The streets were planned from scratch, and right-angled intersections were created, still a rare sight on this scale in Paris today. The building work was completed very rapidly; it took only a few years to transform the rural area into a town.
The house, still called *Château de Grenelle*, which first belonged to Léonard Violet, had to be sold, as the latter suffered a reversal of fortune around 1927. He was compelled to live in small house in the street named after him. However, he continued to follow up the development of what was to become a town in its own right, and was even a member of the town council for 36 years. The "château" changed hands several times before being made into a fire station in 1860.

Château Violet, partly visible from Square Violet

NOTRE-DAME OF AUTOMOBILES

SAINT-CHRISTOPHE-DE-JAVEL CHURCH
28 RUE DE LA CONVENTION / 15th
METRO: JAVEL-ANDRÉ-CITROËN

In the years between the two World wars, Grenelle became home to the many automobile and aviation industries. Citroën's factories made up the largest single presence. It was hardly surprising, then, that the new neighborhood church should be dedicated to Saint Christopher, the patron saint of travelers. On the façade, the saint's right hand blesses a race car while his left hand touches the steering wheel to keep the car from veering off the road.
Designed by Charles-Henri Besnard, construction on the church began in 1926. For this workers' district, the goal was to build "a church pretty enough for them to want to frequent it." Besnard used many prefabricated concrete elements.
The technique allowed for astonishingly thin pillars.
From one end of the nave to the other, the work of Jacques-Martin Ferrières recounting Saint Christopher's life is admirable. In painting these glue-on scenes in light, sandy tones, the artist resorted to a very old and very delicate procedure, hot wax. However, the most astonishing scene has to be Henri-Marcel Magne's fresco in the choir with its host of cyclists, aviators, motorists, and skiers. The same artist executed the colorful stained-glass windows in the tympanum over the presbytery's main entrance. The composition is the crucifixion with three blue-collar workers symbolizing the ages of life. Over the confessionals, one may also admire the famous virtues and vices bas-reliefs based on a drawing by Auguste Roubille, an early 20th-century artist known for his humoristic drawings.

MARITIME ARCHITECTURE

THE PIERRE PATOUT OCEAN LINER "LE PAQUEBOT"
3 BOULEVARD VICTOR / 15th
METRO: BALARD

Pierre Patout (1879-1965), the architect of this concrete "ship," set up his workshop and his apartment in the prow. Numerous buildings signed by Patout dot the Paris cityscape. From pavilions for universal exhibitions to the modern façade of the Galeries Lafayette department store on Boulevard Haussmann, the list even includes Nicolas wine shops.

Patout was also active in equipping two ocean liners: the Île-de-France and the Normandie, both commissioned by the Compagnie Générale Transatlantique. In 1929, he purchased a plot of land just 2,4 to 10 meters deep, on the south side of the city's *Petite Ceinture* railway tracks. There, he built an apartment building comprising 70 units and ample ground-floor space for businesses. It has pure international style: a white façade scored by dark bands, all-metal doors and windows, light-weight concrete panels for cladding. Viewed from the exterior, it looks just like an ocean liner, complete with gangway and smokestacks. Overhanging the entrance is a bas-relief by Alfred Janniot entitled: *L'Architecture, clef de voûte des arts* (Architecture, the keystone of the arts).

PROLETARIANS IN THE 16TH ARRONDISSEMENT...

VILLA MULHOUSE
86 RUE BOILEAU / 16th
METRO: EXELMANS

Of all the "villages" in the 16th arrondissement, Villa Mulhouse – a humble, working-class version of Hameau Boileau nearby – is the one whose history is the most moving.
It comprises Villas Dietz-Monin, Émile-Meyer, Cheysson, and Avenue Georges-Rissler, and adjoins Auteuil cemetery.
Villa Cheysson is a surprisingly narrow road. Since they were first built, some of the one-storied houses have had an additional floor added or their basement converted. Each house has a tiny front garden, the walls are overgrown with ivy, and fragrant flowers scent the air.
In 1835, Jean Dollfus, a spinning mill owner in Mulhouse, had some small, modest houses built for his employees; fifty years later, there were more than a thousand such houses. This inspired Émile Cacheux – author of a work praising the merits of workers' housing developments "where hygiene and moral standards go hand in hand" – to create the Passy-Auteuil Society for workers' housing developments in 1882. It was responsible for the building of Villa Mulhouse with its 67 houses, which were both practical and inexpensive, and provided several generations of workers with a minimum of space and comfort.
Nowadays, it is difficult to imagine the Point-du-Jour district as a working class area. As for Villa Mulhouse, the residents there do not appear to be very representative of the working classes these days!

Villa Dietz-Monin

BIRDSONG IN THE TREES

HAMEAU BOILEAU
38 RUE BOILEAU / 16th
METRO: CHARDON-LAGACHE

Hameau Boileau is a housing development built on part of the former property of Nicolas Despréaux, known as Boileau, poet and critic. As you go in, you will see a gilded medallion, which calls to memory the poet's house, later to be occupied by painter Hubert Robert.
Printer and lithographer Rose-Joseph Lemercier bought the land in 1838 and divided it into lots with the help of architect L. C. T. Charpentier. Financial speculation in Auteuil was a fairly risky business, but there was a regular omnibus service between Paris and this outlying countryside, and the talents of 19th-century property developers were not to be underestimated. They knew how to promote their product, particularly when it "combined the convenience of city life with the pleasure of living in the country."
Whether neoclassical or rustic in style, the houses all looked very luxurious.
The gothic-style country house at 24 Avenue Despréaux is the most striking example of the original buildings.
The architect, Jean-Charles Danjoy, who also restored cathedrals, designed a charming edifice whose most salient feature – a turret – emphasizes the medieval appearance of this imitation half-timbered house.
Other buildings are more reminiscent of the countryside around Auteuil in the past, such as the one at no. 21, opposite a house whose style is typical of architecture in the thirties. Two roads meet to form a tiny square from which radiate leafy culs-de-sac where birds can be heard singing in the foliage on bright, sunny days.

LITERATI IN THE ATTIC

THE GONCOURT BROTHERS' HOME
67 BOULEVARD DE MONTMORENCY / 16th
METRO: PORTE-D'AUTEUIL
Maison des Écrivains et de la Littérature
Tel: 01 55 74 60 90
www.m-e-l.fr

This 19th-century bourgeois mansion was purchased in 1868 by brothers Jules and Edmond de Goncourt. Since its renovation in 2007, it has been home to the *Maison des Écrivains et de la Littérature*, an association devoted to defending and advising writers. The group holds meetings and literary-related events, thus, respecting the spirit of the home to the letter, for it was here that Edmond de Goncourt finished his last will and testament and founded the academy bearing his name.

Jules de Goncourt enjoyed but a brief stay in this house. He died in 1870 before reaching his fortieth birthday. Edmond survived him by twenty-six years and amassed the majority of what he called the *"jolités"* (niceties) of the house. An avid collector of Oriental art and a booklover, Edmond was an aesthete who assembled the marvels presented here.

The most touching room is the famous attic. Its initial dimensions were sacrificed to dividing walls in 1884 by architect Frantz Jourdain, who, at the same time, demolished the bedroom where Jules had died.

On Sundays, Edmond would meet in the attic with France's literary giants for friendly conversations. Regulars included Zola, Barbey d'Aurevilly, Daudet, Maupassant, Mallarmé, as well as Pierre Loti, José Maria de Heredia, Anatole France, and François Coppée, to name but a few.

GREENHOUSE STROLLS

JARDIN DES SERRES D'AUTEUIL
1 AVENUE GORDON-BENNETT, 3 AVENUE DE LA PORTE-D'AUTEUIL / 16th
METRO: PORTE-D'AUTEUIL
Tel: 01 40 71 74 00
Open every day from 10 AM to 5 PM in winter, from 10 AM to 6 PM in summer

This 15-acre park is located just off Porte d'Auteuil, on the way to Roland-Garros stadium, and a short drive from the Bois de Boulogne. Inaugurated in 1898, it has been home to a conservatory of prized plants and a nursery that supplies plants to municipal gardens all over Paris. That activity was transferred to the suburbs after the park lost one third of its total surface area at the end of the 1970s to make way for the Auteuil freeway interchange.
Jean-Camille Formigé (1845-1926), head architect of the Paris' park's service, spearheaded the creation of this garden, all the more remarkable as the vast Auteuil greenhouses (99 meters long) are the last remaining examples of France's 19th-century greenhouses. Formigé wanted to build a useful tool for horticulturalists all while preserving the monument's artistic features. He managed to eliminate the intermediate supports, thus facilitating circulation while increasing transparency. Renovated in 1999, the palm tree hothouse reproduced tropical and subtropical climates essential for papaya trees, banana trees, mango trees, coffee bushes, and achiote shrubs. Near the Canary Island date palms, koi carp swim in unending circles. Farther ahead, a bird cage is home to budgies and zebra finch.
The park also boasts a few sculptures. The fourteen grotesques on the terrace come from the old Trocadéro palace. Rodin oversaw their creation. As for the *Triomphe de Bacchus* fountain, at the end of the green strip of the central lawn, it is graced by a highly erotic sculpture by Dalou.

A VISIT TO THE GREAT ARCHITECT

LE CORBUSIER FOUNDATION (VILLAS JEANNERET AND LA ROCHE)
8 AND 10 SQUARE DU DOCTEUR-BLANCHE / 16th
METRO: JASMIN
Tel: 01 42 88 41 53
www.fondationlecorbusier.asso.fr

Between 1924 and 1925, Charles-Édouard Jeanneret, best known as Le Corbusier, built two houses (nos. 8 and 10) at the far end of Square du Docteur-Blanche, on rue du Docteur-Blanche (no. 55). The first one was for his brother, Albert Jeanneret, and the second for a Swiss banker from Basel, Raoul La Roche. The Jeanneret house was a family house complete with a music room. The structure of the La Roche house, on the other hand, is more complex since a gallery was required to house La Roche's extraordinary collection of works of art by Braque, Picasso, Léger, and many other artists. Since the plot of land was small, and windows could not overlook neighboring properties, Le Corbusier built a large hall extending to the top of the house.
A staircase leads up to the main room, the gallery, where there is a ramp giving access to the library.
From the outside, the two buildings look very different, and yet there is an underlying connection between the convex volumes of the La Roche house and the flat façade of the house next door.
In 1968, the Le Corbusier Foundation moved into the two buildings. It looks after the architect's estate, and is devoted to acquainting the general public with his work. To this end, the architect's files are kept here, a public library has been opened, and exhibitions are regularly held in the La Roche house.

PEACEFULLY GEOMETRIC

RUE MALLET-STEVENS / 16th
METRO: RANELAGH

It is highly unusual for an entire street to be the exclusive work of one architect. Such is the case, however, of this small street in the 16th arrondissement, inaugurated on July 20, 1927. The entire development was designed by Robert Mallet-Stevens (1886-1945).
Mallet-Stevens, first a furniture and movie set designer, didn't switch career paths to architecture until the 1920s. His work integrated new materials into audacious shapes. The idea for the street germinated after he met Daniel Dreyfus, a wealthy landowner, who wanted a block of houses for friends and relatives who were musicians, sculptors, and artists. Mallet-Stevens designed a block of five fine homes of varying sizes and a superintendent's house.

The ensemble gains its unity from the homogenous cubes and cylinders arranged with a remarkable sense of space. Wide windows and doorways allow light to pour in, and the use of reinforced concrete allowed for spacious interiors. The stained-glass windows in the stairwells were the work of Louis Barillet and the ironwork of the doors was carried out by Jean Prouvé. The architect moved into no. 12.
He describes his street in these terms, "It will be open to no business. It is exclusively for peaceful, residential use; it must remain truly calm and removed from any hubbub or noise. By its very appearance, its overall structure, it must elicit placidity without the slightest hint of sadness. A street may be cheery, even joyous, yet tranquil."

"ECCENTRIC HOUSE"

CASTEL BÉRANGER
14 RUE LA FONTAINE / 16th
METRO: MICHEL-ANGE-AUTEUIL

Before creating the most unusual Metro entrances in the world, architect Hector Guimard designed Castel Béranger in Rue La Fontaine. His idea was as unconventional as it was successful, a combination of advanced technology and unbridled imagination.
When the house was built in 1897, Parisians were fascinated, amused or disgusted by its design. It brought the young, thirty-year-old architect to the notice of the general public, and became his hallmark. Although not much care was taken to preserve many of Guimard's works, his building on Rue La Fontaine continues to bear witness to the architect's unique talent. Everything about its atypical façade, from its strange sea horses, clinging to the corners of the brick walls, to the caricature of the architect's face set in the wrought-iron balconies, is a source of astonishment. Straight lines appear to have been banished.

You can go into the courtyard where you will see a fountain and the stained glass decorating small windows on all floors. The fact that the City of Paris awarded a prize to Guimard in the first competition for the best façade in 1898 did not alter the local residents' disapproval of what they called the "Devil's House" (because of the grimaces on the faces dotted all over the façade), also nicknamed "*Castel Dérangé*" (Crazy Castle).
In 1897, painter Paul Signac moved into one of the ateliers on the sixth floor. He called the house "Eccentric House," and thought it was badly designed. Nevertheless, it was practical, light, and had a telephone, an uncommon feature in those days. Guimard thought of everything.
He left his mark in every apartment, and the decorations – curtains and wall coverings, furniture, doorknobs, locks – all bore his hallmark. He was able to do this thanks to highly skilled artisans, experts in wrought iron, brickwork, ceramics and ironwork.
Guimard was also responsible for another block of apartments a little further on, where Rues Gros and Agar come into Rue La Fontaine. The design of the monochrome building, erected about fifteen years after Castel Béranger, is much more restrained. This was one of the architect's biggest undertakings. The small Guimard bar on the corner of Rue La Fontaine and Rue Gros has been preserved.
Hôtel Mezzara at 6 Rue La Fontaine, built in 1911 for a textile manufacturer, is now state property. The wrought-iron and ironwork staircase and, above all, the dining room entirely furnished by Guimard, may be seen on appointment (Tel: 01 55 74 69 20).

LOUIS ROUSSEL'S LADS

AUTEUIL FOUNDATION
40 RUE LA FONTAINE / 16th
METRO: JASMIN
Tel: 01 45 24 70 04
www.fondation-auteuil.org
Chapelle Sainte-Thérèse open Monday to Friday from 7 AM to 7:15 PM, Saturdays from 8:30 AM to 7:15 PM and Sundays from 8:30 AM to 7:00 PM;
Espace Muséographique Louis-Roussel open Tuesday, Thursday, and Saturday from 2 to 5 PM;
park open to the public from 8 AM to 8 PM

The *Fondation d'Auteuil*, previously known as the *Orphelins Apprentis d'Auteuil* (the apprentice orphans of Auteuil), is a registered charity organization. Every year, it takes in some 10,000 underprivileged youngsters to provide them with vocational training in 170 establishments. It all began in 1866 when Father Louis Roussel founded *l'Œuvre de la première communion*. He set up his outreach in a rundown house. His aim was to evangelize young, homeless orphans, most often vagabonds and victims of industrialization. A few years later, he completed their spiritual training with apprenticeships in shoe repair, woodworking, the locksmith trade, horticulture, and printing.
The garden at the foundation's headquarters on Rue La Fontaine is appreciated by neighborhood residents. On the left side as you enter, an odd brick building houses a small amusing cloister. Straight ahead, the Saint-Thérèse chapel, built by Father Daniel Brottier in 1924, founder of the *Union Nationale des Combattants*, who had taken over the reigns of the foundation's the preceding year.
The cloister's main attraction is the capitals where all the trades the lads were being taught are depicted. Lastly, off to the right, beyond the garden, is a small building erected in 1867, the Louis-Roussel chapel, followed by the old *masure* (a humble home) once occupied by the abbot himself. It is now a museum dedicated to the history of the foundation.

Saint-Thérèse chapel

FROM PASSY WITH LOVE

RUSSIAN-STYLE COUNTRY COTTAGES IN VILLA BEAUSÉJOUR

7 BOULEVARD BEAUSÉJOUR / 16th

METRO: LA MUETTE

Boulevard Beauséjour follows the route of an old avenue in the former Beauséjour park, and runs alongside what is left of the Auteuil railway line, no longer used today. Villa Beauséjour is a cul-de-sac which starts at 7 Boulevard Beauséjour, between a pale pink house and a series of small, 19th-century buildings. Adolphe Alphand, creator of so many squares and parks in Paris, had a beautiful, neoclassical residence built here, and lived in it until his death in 1891.
However, the cul-de-sac is really more well-known for its charming Russian-style country cottages at the far end (nos. 3 ter, 4 and 6). Built out of brick and stone, and covered in wood, the four houses come from the Russian stand at the 1867 World Fair. Only one of them originated from Saint Petersburg, and was sent to Paris in kit form. The other three were built by French architect Paul Bénard, according to plans drawn up by the Russians. In 1872, landowner Alphonse Lasnier bought the cottages in order to create this unusual setting, just a stone's throw from La Muette metro station.

"PLUMS ARE IN SEASON"

BALZAC'S HOUSE
47 RUE RAYNOUARD AND RUE BERTON / 16th
METRO: PASSY
Open every day except Mondays and public holidays from 10 AM to 6 PM

Rue Berton, with its street lamps and zigzags, still looks like a street in the country, similar to those in the village of Passy in the mid-19th century. It runs alongside the former property of Madame de Lamballe, now the Turkish embassy. Opposite, a 1793 boundary stone against the wall of Balzac's house still marks the dividing line between the Passy and Auteuil domains.

In 1840, Honoré de Balzac, author of *Le Père Goriot* (Father Goriot), was up to his eyes in debt, and moved from Ville-d'Avray to Rue Basse. The house, fairly isolated and surrounded by leafy trees, had a back door onto Rue Berton, which enabled Balzac to elude his creditors. He opened his door only to those who knew the passwords: "Plums are in season," or "I am bringing lace from Belgium."

In 1960, Balzac's house (entrance on Rue Raynouard) was opened as a museum, and the public can now visit the writer's study where he wrote several of the novels making up his masterpiece, *La Comédie Humaine* (The Human Comedy). The tiny garden adjoining the museum is a good place for reading the novels of this highly creative writer, described rather unkindly by a contemporary as a "fat boy, with sharp eyes, dressed in a white waistcoat, with the bearing of a herbalist, the face of a butcher, and the look of gilder."

Rue Berton

SPRING WATER... AND WINE

WINE MUSEUM (CAVEAU DES ÉCHANSONS)
RUE DES EAUX/5 SQUARE CHARLES-DICKENS / 16th
METRO: PASSY
Open every day except Monday from 10 AM to 6 PM.
Tel: 01 45 25 63 26

Some steps below Passy metro station lead to the secluded Rue des Eaux. The name of the street is a reminder of the numerous chalybeate springs which used to rise here and a little further up, towards Rue Raynouard.
The museum – a small house several stories high – looks lost amidst a veritable forest of tall buildings. It is devoted to wine, wine making and the history of wine, and is the only one of its kind, because of both its site and its wine collection. Let's push open the door... In summer, this museum is a pleasantly cool place to visit.
Inside, there are galleries which have been dug out of the rock and converted into exhibition rooms. They used to be quarries, discovered in the 1950s by a restaurant owner, who first of all made them into a wine cellar for the Eiffel Tower restaurants, and then had the excellent idea of opening to the public.
Chaillot Hill was still covered by a vast forest – the Rouvray Forest – in the 6th century, when some monks decided to clear a few acres of ground in order to settle there. The Nigeon manor house was to expand and prosper. Simply dressed in long, hooded frocks with cord girdles knotted in five places, the monks, nicknamed the "*bonshommes*" (good-hearted men), converted most of the hill into an enormous vineyard (the name of Rue Vineuse – literally, vine-covered street – serves as a reminder). Later, when they discovered the existence of Chaillot limestone, they built a cellar, still here today, and visitors are invited to taste a glass of wine before returning to city life in the 20th century.

IN THE TIGER'S DEN

CLEMENCEAU MUSEUM
8 RUE BENJAMIN-FRANKLIN / 16th
METRO: PASSY
Tel: 01 45 20 53 41
www.musee-clemenceau.fr
Open Tuesday to Saturday from 2 PM to 5:30 PM; closed August and bank holidays

Georges Clemenceau was born in the Vendée in 1841. While still in medical school, he cut his teeth as a journalist. In his political career, he was mayor of the 18th district of Paris, then deputy of the department of the Seine. He went from the position of president of the Paris municipal council to senator, then interior minister, and was twice president of the Conseil d'État.
Various stages in this statesman's rich life are presented in his Paris apartment, now a museum. Photos, manuscripts, and other mementos shed light on the man's character. On display are the pistols he used in numerous duels and the famous 1898 front page of *L'Aurore* with Zola's "*J'accuse*" (Clemenceau himself came up with the title), a newspaper editorial written in defense of Dreyfus.
France's "head cop" owned a Browning 7.65, used by the *brigades du Tigre* (tiger brigades), and Bertillon system measuring instruments, dating from the earliest days of scientific police investigations.
The bedroom on the ground floor looks the same as it did on November 24, 1929, the day that Georges Clemenceau died. The Tiger (as he was nicknamed), was an amateur of Oriental arts, and his bed was decorated with a menacing dragon. The study has a few original plasters by Rodin, a painting by his friend Claude Monet (a copy actually), several boxes of incense, a painting of his dog, and several thousand yellowing books befitting of a man whose motto was "serve others and become well acquainted with human knowledge."

Georges Clemenceau in his office in the late 1920s

HEALING WATERS

SQUARE LAMARTINE / 16th
METRO: RUE-DE-LA-POMPE

A curious ballet of water jugs has been performed for unending years at Square Lamartine. Area residents stop here, then carry away a transparent, colorless liquid: mineral water! While rather high in iron content, this water has a unique quality. It is the only water to flow from a Parisian park and out of a limestone cube. Originally meant to supply the rivers and ponds in the Bois de Boulogne, this water flows from an artesian well dug from 1855 to 1861 under the supervision of an Englishman named Kind. The well taps the Albien, which runs 550 to 750 meters underground. This great depth explains why the water remains unpolluted by dirty runoff or urban waste. Residents of the area as well as people from nearby suburbs regularly come to fill bottles and jugs with the precious liquid. The water of Passy is reputedly therapeutic. Passy was one of the best known Paris-area spas from as early as the 17th century. The estate of the Abbot Le Ragois, once chaplain to Madame de Maintenon, was known in the 18th century for its healing waters. Entertainment attractions included gaming pavilions and salons. The very fashionable Passy water was even a theme in one opéra-comique production. Madame de Tencin came to recover here after her release from the Bastille prison. Jean-Jacques Rousseau made it his "retreat from the crush of city life."
The last estate boasting its one fountain disappeared around 1900. Up to that time, the area between Rue Raynouard and the River Seine still had 18th century "water pavilions" equipped with decanting jars. Historian Georges Cain visited these sites around the year 1912, and wrote: "The softer soil here already indicates we are nearing the springs... This long path, with its mossy stone stairs and frame of centenary trees, leads to the mouth of the caves from which the mineral water flows. We descend a few dozen steps, and reach the ruddy stream, which has healed weary stomachs for so long."

ZEN

PANTHÉON BOUDDHIQUE
19 AVENUE D'IÉNA / 16th
METRO: IÉNA
Tel: 01 40 73 88 00
Closed Tuesdays. Galleries open from 10 AM to 5:45 PM, the park from 1 to 5 PM
Tea ceremony upon reservation

Despite being the Musée Guimet's free annex, the Panthéon Bouddhique (Buddhist Pantheon) is not nearly as busy. This unusual venue is located in the mansion that banker Alfred Heidelbach commissioned architect René Sergent to build in 1913. It was renovated in 1991. The Panthéon Bouddhique's collection contains 250 Japanese pieces brought to France in 1876 by the museum's founder, a Lyon industrialist named Émile Guimet. The collection also includes Chinese Buddhist pieces, all presented in a very didactic manner. Paintings, reliquaries, and divinities offer a glimpse of the progression of the religion throughout Asia well as in terms of ideology and art. The Bouddha Amida facing the windows on the garden reportedly "opened the path" for Alexandra David-Néel when it was placed in the Émile Guimet Library.
The Japanese garden is graced by a genuine *chashitsu* (tea house) built in 2001 by master builders from the Land of the Rising Sun. Initiations into the Japanese tea ceremony are held here regularly.

REMEMBER... FOR THE SAKE OF PEACE

THE ARC DE TRIOMPHE FLAME
PLACE CHARLES-DE-GAULLE / 16th
METRO/RER: CHARLES-DE-GAULLE-ÉTOILE

In 1923, Gabriel Boissy, a journalist for the daily *L'Intransigeant*, launched the idea of a perpetual flame in honor of the Unknown Soldier, fallen in the battle of Verdun and interred three years previously beneath the Arc de Triomphe. The timeless symbol revived the ancient image of the light guiding our path, a warming, protecting, and unifying flame. The symbol won public approval and lifted spirits in a France barely recuperating from the horrific ravages of World War I. Edgar Brandt, master ironworker and weapons manufacturer, created an ingenious system so that the flame would never (or almost never) go out. Every evening, since November 11, 1923, the flame is relit at 6:30 by representatives of the various war veteran's associations. The immutable ritual includes the salute to the flag, a bugle rendition of *La Flamme* and *Aux Morts*, then the hymn *Honneur au soldat inconnu* and *La Marseillaise* are sung. This daily remembrance of the past is closely connected to the future; today's younger generations actively participate in the homage, a peaceful salute addressed to all humanity.

A CHÂTEAU WITH A ROAD THROUGH THE MIDDLE

THE FORMER CHÂTEAU DES TERNES

17-9 RUE PIERRE-DEMOURS, RUE BAYEN / 17th

METRO: TERNES

"Château des Ternes" has the unusual feature of a pedestrian area – part of Rue Bayen – running through it. A portal, some relics in the grass, and two 18th-century façades are all that remain of the vast property. 15th-century plans and records show that a fortified farm existed here, surrounded by wide expanses of countryside. The domain expanded over the years, and a great deal of land was added to it. One of the owners, protégé of Richelieu, statesman and cardinal under Louis XIII and virtual ruler of France, succeeded in raising it to the status of a seigneury in 1634.

The château often changed hands, either through inheritance or sale, and was always being converted, but it was undoubtedly in the mid-18th century that it reached the height of its fame, when it became a magnificent, exquisitely furnished residence, decorated with tapestries from Flanders. The domain included a vegetable garden, an orangery, a dovecote... and afforded a beautiful view over the surrounding parkland.

However, architect Samson-Nicolas Lenoir, who became the new owner of the domain in 1778, was also a speculator. He sold all the furniture, including the park ornaments, and built a new road right through the main building (Rue Bayen). He parceled out the parkland, and set up his own irons factory on one of the plots of land.

Swamped by city development in the 19th century, the domain became the "village" of Ternes, with a population of 8,000 in 1840.

A "MOVING" CHAPEL

NOTRE-DAME-DE-LA-COMPASSION CHAPEL
2 BOULEVARD D'AURELLE-DE-PALADINES / 17th
METRO: PORTE MAILLOT
Tel: 01 45 74 83 31
Open the 2nd Saturday of each month at 4 PM.
Open to the public on National Heritage Days

Saint-Ferdinand chapel on Place de la Porte des Ternes – not far from the roaring traffic on the nearby circular road – appears somewhat of an anachronism.

The chapel commemorates the death of Louis-Philippe's son, Duke Ferdinand d'Orléans, on July 13th, 1842, following an accident, when his carriage swerved and he was flung to the ground. The prince was immediately carried into grocer Cordier's house nearby, but to no avail.

An exact replica of the room in which he died was created at Neuilly château, and fitted out with the grocer's own furniture. Cordier was given an annuity from the Civil List, and made warden at Versailles Château museum.

It was also decided that a chapel – a small, hybrid building in the form of a Greek cross – be erected on the site of the grocer's shop. It was consecrated on July 11th, 1843.

Inside, the monument is a very expressive representation of the duke dying on the grocer's mattress, dressed in his army inspector general's uniform. The angel, a creation of Princess Marie, Ferdinand's sister, has been placed above the head of the deceased.

The Sèvres glass factory made the fourteen stained-glass windows, based on cartoons by Ingres. Royal features can be recognized on most of the saints' faces; to the left of the altar, Louis-Philippe wearing the frock of his patron saint, Saint Louis, and on the right, Queen Marie-Aurélie's long face. Christ's face is represented by that of Ferdinand d'Orléans, the deceased.

When alterations were made at Porte Maillot in 1970, the chapel was dismantled and reassembled, stone by stone, and moved 150 meters away.

CELEBRATING LIGHT

SAINTE-ODILE CHURCH
2 AVENUE STÉPHANE-MALLARMÉ / 17th
METRO: PORTE-DE-CHAMPERRET

This curious church with its minaret-like tower (at 72 meters high, it's very probably the capital's tallest bell tower), is one of the most representative monuments of sacred art built in the first half the 20th century.
Sainte-Odile church, one of Cardinal Verdier's construction projects, was erected between the years 1934 and 1946 on old fortification walls. As the lot in the new neighborhood beside Porte de Champerret was deep and narrow, architect Jacques Barge took his inspiration from early Christian architecture and designed a relatively low but long nave that faced west. Each of the three sections was covered with a dome and enlarged on the left side by a vaulted semi-circular apsidiole.
The kingpin for this construction project was Monsignor Loutil, better known under his penname Pierre l'Ermite, then the priest at Saint François de Sales. This patron of the arts who was actively involved in getting Saint-Jean-de-Montmartre built, hired extraordinary talent for the decoration of Sainte-Odile. Master glassworker François Décorchemont executed the stained-glass homage to Odile, the saint of light, cured of her blindness by baptism.

His composition is a veritable fireworks of color and includes the master himself, in beggar's garb. It also includes Father Loutil carrying the scale model of the church, a reminder of the years of hard work to see the church rise from the ground. Loutil received his reward on November 18, 1956, when his church was at long last consecrated.

FLOWER POWER

HAUTS-DE-MALESHERBES GARDENS
70-72 BOULEVARD BERTHIER / 17th
METRO: PORTE-DE-CLICHY
Open from 8 AM to 7:30 PM

Just off the Paris *périphérique* (beltway), this 1.5-acre green space was planted atop old railway tracks. Design credit goes to the Christian de Portzamparc architectural firm. The special ambiance here springs from the original plant species scattered throughout the park such as the medlar, catalpa, dove tree, blue bean shrub, silverbell tree, and the katsura tree. A few steps away, huge potted bamboos planted by the Flower Tower building by Édouard François further reinforces the natural look of this new neighborhood.

The place offers visitors yet another curiosity. The park's back wall is a vestige of the Thiers fortifications, at least this section marked bastion no. 45 is. An engraving informs us it was built between 1842 and 1843.
Walking on Boulevard Berthier towards the Porte de Clichy, we can see no. 44, one of three other bastions. It is situated adjacent to the Opéra Comique's impressive warehouses (see page 145).

SARAH'S RATS

35 RUE FORTUNY / 17th
METRO: MALESHERBES

Despite a few bungled alterations, Rue Fortuny remains one of the most characteristic streets of the Plaine Monceau, a neighborhood that rose out of a turnip field during the Second Empire. The façade at no. 35, an odd mixture of neo-Gothic and neo-Renaissance, offers a real curiosity: two rats in bas-relief near the corner have nibbled a hole in the wall, and appear to be entering the house.
Is it a parable of the vanity of this world and of all things ephemeral?
The great actress Sarah Bernhardt chose this corner lot bordering Avenue de Villiers for her mansion. In 1876, she commissioned Félix Escalier to build her home here with its front door on the avenue while the grounds behind the house were for her garden, her sculpture workshop, and her winter garden. But by 1885, she was deep in dept and was forced to sell her property.
The buyer was Adolphe Dervillé, a marble quarry operator. He kept the main house but replaced the workshop with the present-day building, integrating various elements of the demolished structure, built a mere nineteen years previously. The house on the corner was razed to make way for a high-rise of no stylistic merit. The only bits remaining of the tragedian's mansion are these rodent-nibbled stones.

A CHÂTEAU FOR THE BANK OF FRANCE

HÔTEL GAILLARD
1 PLACE DU GÉNÉRAL-CATROUX / 17th
METRO: MALESHERBES

Hôtel Gaillard, prestige branch office of the Bank of France, has a certain elegance. Its architect, Jules Février, drew his inspiration from a wing of Blois château to build this manor house for the manager of the Bank of France, Émile Gaillard. Building work was completed in 1844, and the house was decorated with original, 16th-century wainscoting and sculptures, and fitted out with magnificent furniture from Issogne château in the Aoste valley. The banker's vast art collection included a Murillo portraying Saint Anthony of Padua, a portrait of Henry II, King of France and husband of Catherine de Médicis, along with some fine, 17th-century Flemish works. A sumptuous, costumed ball, to which 2,000 people were invited, was held on April 11th, 1885 to inaugurate the building.
The banker died on May 5th, 1904, and his valuable collections were rapidly broken up. It was not until 1919 that a new owner – the Bank of France – was found for the manor house, whose character was not affected by the alterations that had to be made. For instance, the basement was used as a safety-deposit room, protected by a water-filled ditch. This original safety device gave rise to a fantastic rumor according to which crocodiles were let into the moat at night to better protect the valuables deposited in the safes!
The façade overlooking the street looks particularly opulent. The letter "G" appears on the dormers in the roof, and there are grotesque figures above the small entrance; the one carrying the coin purse looks like banker Gaillard, and the other, holding a square, resembles architect Février.

PARIS BY THE SEA

CITÉ DES FLEURS
154 AVENUE DE CLICHY/59 RUE DE LA JONQUIÈRE / 17th
METRO: BROCHANT

A historical guide to Paris, published in 1910, affirmed that when walking down here, "you suddenly feel as if you had been transported to a quiet, attractive street in a seaside resort".
This bumpy road with its pillars and cast-iron oriental vases certainly has a provincial air about it. In the mid-19th century, Mr. Lhenry and Mr. Bacqueville divided their land into lots, and imposed restrictive conditions on the builders – the height of the houses, three trees in the front gardens, the design of the cast-iron vases – and even stipulated the variety of flowers to be planted in the vases!
No. 17, built in 1852, has a double stairway. A monogram, "C.S.", and some oak-leaf motifs are the only embellishment on the otherwise plain façade at no. 21.
No. 25, a one-storied building, has some cabled columns. No. 29, typical of most of the houses in this street, has a neo-Renaissance façade, an entrance topped with grotesque figures, and black and white marble inlays at the level of the floor above. Above the window on the left, there is a relief of a small elephant. The pink and white façade at no. 31 has two medallions.
No. 33, similar in style to no. 25, is better preserved, and cabled columns ornament its picturesque façade.

THE THUNDER OF HOOVES

COUR SAINT-PIERRE
47 AVENUE DE CLICHY / 17th
METRO: LA FOURCHE
Association Cour Saint-Pierre
Tel: 01 43 87 18 72,
http://fest.courstpierre.free.fr

Once you pass through the iron gates at 47 Avenue de Clichy, the noise of the traffic gradually fades as you walk down this delightful alley. It is said that many years ago, race horses from the Gaumont race track raised a thunderous noise as they took the passageway. Stand still, and you might hear an echo...
This charming impasse narrowly escaped demolition in the 1990s. Lobbying and swift action taken by the *Association de défense du village de la Fourche* saved it.

Today, the courtyard, restored and decorated with flower pots, has recovered its former beauty. The Association Cour Saint-Pierre holds art exhibits and cultural events, contributing to the neighborhoods' vibrant cultural life.

STAIRWAY C

VILLA DES ARTS
15 RUE HÉGÉSIPPE-MOREAU / 18th
METRO: PLACE-DE-CLICHY

Access to Villa des Arts is through a fine wrought-iron gate, and the name of the street is cut out in the curved metal arc above the entrance.

When Desmichel and Gueret decided to restructure the entire block in 1888, this cul-de-sac was already in existence. Henri Cambon was responsible for its elegant buildings. He salvaged building materials to first of all erect the houses lining the courtyard. The amazing stairway on the right is said to have come from a pavilion built for the 1900 World Fair.

Opposite the cemetery in Rue Ganneron, an ingenious cascading structure comprising about sixty ateliers provides artists with excellent lighting conditions.

There was a continuous flow of celebrities through the doors of these ateliers, including, between 1899 and 1901, Eugène Carrière, Paul Signac, and Paul Cézanne who painted his famous portrait of gallery owner Ambroise Vollard, which required more than a hundred sittings! Louis Marcoussis, Jean and Raoul Dufy also contributed to the renown of the place.

It was here that Nicolas Schöffer created his very first cybernetic sculpture and a spatio-, luminodynamic work, still exhibited in his atelier which is now a private museum.

This charming area, so characteristic of the atmosphere of 19th-century Montmartre with its artists' ateliers, has often been used as a film set, for instance by Fellini for The *Clowns*, and by Jean-Charles Tacchella for *Escalier C* (Stairway C).

DEMIMONDE
IN HIGH SOCIETY

TOMB OF ALPHONSINE PLESSIS
MONTMARTRE CEMETERY, 15TH DIVISION, 4TH ROW, NO. 12
20 AVENUE RACHEL / 18th
METRO: PLACE-DE-CLICHY OR BLANCHE

The tombstone is engraved quite simply with "here lies Alphonsine Plessis, born January 15, 1824, died February 3, 1847." It is a sober epitaph for one of the most famous courtesans of the 19th century. Her white grave is often covered with flowers, just as in Alexandre Dumas fils' novel *The Lady of the Camellias*. She was the inspiration for the main character in the novel as well as in the opera *La Traviata* by Verdi. "Quite slender, black-haired, with a pink and white complexion, she had a small head and wide sparkling eyes, like those of a Japanese, bright and delicate, her lips were cherry red, and her teeth were the loveliest the world had seen." So the author described his muse. Indeed, he was madly in love with her, as were Liszt and numerous others.
The little peasant girl from Normandy arrived in Paris at age 15 and went to work in a dress shop in Palais-Royal. Young and ravishing, the girl attracted many suitors and was introduced to Paris socialites by the Comte de Guiche. A spendthrift, she appreciated refined accommodations. Alphonsine soon changed her name to Marie Duplessis, traveled, lived in a constant whirlwind of excitement, and frequented the most respected writers and artists of her time. She engraved her carriage and dishes with an aristocratic emblem, and went by the name "Madame la Comtesse du Plessis."
Unfortunately, her dazzling life ended far too soon. At the tender age of 23, the lady of the camellias was swept away by tuberculosis.

WHOSE STREET IS THIS?

CITÉ VÉRON
94 BOULEVARD DE CLICHY / 18th
METRO: BLANCHE

A blue and white enamel sign announces a long cul-de-sac, next door to the Moulin-Rouge, threading its way between the buildings. Though the alley's measurements may be modest (80 x 3 meters), its residents were held in high esteem, with the exception, however, of those who lived there before World War II, when Cité Véron was a haunt for delinquents from seedy Pigalle with its nightclubs and its prostitutes' hotels.

In 1953, poet Jacques Prévert moved into no. 6 bis Cité Véron, where he lived for twenty years. Writer Boris Vian, who also spent much of his time playing jazz, lived in the apartment opposite, where, surrounded by a few books and very little furniture, he wrote *L'Arrache-Cœur* (*Heartsnatcher*) and many of his songs, including *Le Déserteur* (*The Deserter*) for which he was also famous. Writer Raymond Queneau, dramatist Ionesco, and many others would meet on the communal terrace, site of the French cancan dancers' dressing rooms in the early 20th century.

Life in the cul-de-sac these past few years was disrupted by the arrondissement council's decision to rename the street after humorist Pierre Dac. This was not all to the liking of the residents, particularly Prévert's and Vian's descendants, who pointed out that Pierre Dac had never set foot in the place! After the usual preliminary excitement, vigorous protests, and a search for influential support, this delightful

cul-de-sac in the heart of old Pigalle officially retrieved its former name.

Incidentally, who was Véron? A local resident, mayor of Montmartre from 1830 to 1841, and an honest citizen, who certainly never imagined that his name would continue to be so heroically defended at the end of the 20th century!

NUTMEG, VANILLA AND THEOLOGY...

7 IMPASSE MARIE-BLANCHE / 18th
METRO: BLANCHE

The attractive, medieval-looking building in Impasse Marie-Blanche is an unusual sight. It belonged to antique dealer Eymonaud, and provides us with an excuse for mentioning the house that Count Charles de l'Escalopier had built nearby on Rue Joseph-de-Maistre in 1835. The 1837 yearbook on the surroundings of Paris contains a glowing description of this very strange house, characteristic of its owner's tastes. It had steam-heated greenhouses decorated with rocks and pools, and was open to the public. Exotic trees, particularly banana trees, were the main attraction, not to mention sandalwood, nutmeg, coconut, vanilla, mangosteen and copaiba trees.
In 1840, Count de l'Escalopier applied for and obtained the post of librarian at the Arsenal Library (public library in the 4th arrondissement). He subsequently devoted himself entirely to his passion for research, and razed the greenhouses to make way for a library containing around 6,000 volumes, of which nearly 2,000 were works on theology!
A small museum devoted entirely to the Middle Ages adjoined the library. Charles de l'Escalopier, an eccentric typical of the last century (reminiscent of Bouvard and Pécuchet, characters in an unfinished, satirical work by Flaubert who criticized amateurish dabbling in science), died in Liancourt in 1861. The charming Gothic Revival castle was demolished in 1882.

THE DEAR OLD MAQUIS

MONTMARTRE "MAQUIS"
65 RUE LEPIC / 18th
METRO: ABBESSES

An inconspicuous entrance at 65 Rue Lepic gives access to a steep stairway. The passage, which has never been given a name, leads to what remains of the Montmartre "*maquis.*" Halfway up, there is a platform bearing an enormous rock, fragment of some rockery garden. An abandoned house on the right emphasizes the romantic air of the place. Just before this picturesque little alley comes into Avenue Junot, there is a piece of land on the right, where there is always a game of bowls going on. This is the last remnant of the *maquis*, which, but for the perseverance of the local residents who put up a fierce fight a few years ago to save the place from the hands of a property developer who wanted to build a car park, would have disappeared altogether.
Before the lovely Avenue Junot was built in 1909, this used to be an immense wasteland, the famous *maquis*. It was dotted with miserable shacks full of penniless daubers and destitute Montmartre locals, whose presence there was undoubtedly one of the reasons why the picture of the good-natured tramp – a "quaint" Montmartre souvenir – became so popular.
At the end of the passage, turn left into Avenue Junot and go along to no. 23–bis where there is a delightful cul-de-sac, Villa Léandre, whose brick houses look very British in style.

SCALLYWAGS' SQUARE

OUTDOOR STAIRCASE
40 RUE DURANTIN / 18th
METRO: ABBESSES

A stroke of luck may get you past the gate guarding this block of buildings. A courtyard framed by 19th-century buildings is graced by a staircase with double flights of steps lit by an amusing street lamp. Oozing with charm, it has been used as an outdoors location in numerous films, for instance Philippe Fourastié's *La Bande à Bonnot* (*Bonnot's Gang*, 1969) starring Jacques Brel.

"Surrounded by yellowed buildings, the rather unattractive courtyard off Rue Durantin, a wide terraced space, was where neighborhood kids from Les Abbesses would gather. Just about any afternoon that Madame Frisepoulet, the concierge, was out shopping, the gang would hold council on the steps of the stairs. Clinging to the street lamp, Anatole would preside over the councils and mete out harsh justice. The last time, Marcel had to hand over his slingshot for the odious reason that he hadn't 'smashed' enough windows! Not assertive enough, Marcel! It cost the gang valuable revenue as the glazier would tip them for each window pane he had to replace. Another time, little Pierre was congratulated for managing to pocket a fortune by walking the horrible mutts belonging to the old countess on Rue d'Orchampt. The boy complained that the stupid, nasty, four-legged monsters had ripped his socks to shreds. By a show of hands, it was unanimously decided to give him the cash needed to replace his damaged reekers. A paternal scolding was thus avoided thanks to the little scallywags' sense of solidarity." (Amédée Lauriot, *Loustics et compagnie*, 1934.)

SAINT JOHN OF THE BRICKS

SAINT-JEAN-DE-MONTMARTRE CHURCH
19 RUE DES ABBESSES / 18th
METRO: ABBESSES

Begun in 1897, this church, dedicated to Saint John the Evangelist on June 13, 1904, would never have been built were it not for Father Sobaux's fierce defense of the project and that of Architect Anatole Baudot.
De Baudot called upon engineer Paul Cottancin, who employed a revolutionary technique. The façades, dressed in brick and fired sandstone signed by Alexandre Bigot, are not load-bearing walls. The structure is rather held up by a monolithic floor-pillar-roof system held together by a concrete-encased iron frame. The astonishingly slender pillars so alarmed building inspectors that they halted the construction and issued a demolition order, which, fortunately, was never carried out.
Inside, the impressive stained-glass windows offer a kaleidoscopic display. Figures include the four horsemen of the Apocalypse and the fourth gospel. The last series designed by Pascal Blanchard during World War I, was crafted by Jac Galland between 1918 and 1920. The main altar, designed by Anatole de Baudot, is graced by surprising sandstone pieces by the sculptor Roche. The head of Christ and the four evangelists are central to the iconography. The baptismal basin, a humble caldron, was recently replaced by a work designed by the goldsmith Goudji. The basins' shape mirrors the mitered arches and the octagonal dome. The silver basin has inlays of rock crystal, jasper, and aventurine, and the eight-legged pedestal is made of wrought iron. The basin is truly a gem in a church full of surprises.

THE LOST CRYPT

THE CRYPT OF THE MARTYRIUM
11 RUE YVONNE-LE TAC / 18th
METRO: ABBESSES
Tel: 01 45 44 65 53
Open Fridays from 2:30 PM to 6 PM

It is believed that in the year 250, Denis, Bishop of Lutetia, was decapitated on the hill then known as Mons Mercurius and now as Montmartre (literally: martyr's hill). A chapel was soon erected on the site. The pilgrimage to the Saint-Denis Abbey north of Paris stopped there every seven years. On August 15, 1534, Ignatius of Loyola and six other students from the University of Paris founded the Society of Jesus. Assigned to the care of the royal abbey of thc Montmartre Benedictines, in 1611, the chapel was restored by the Abbess Marie de Beauvilliers with funding from Marie de' Medici and other benefactors. During the renovation, workers stumbled upon the crypt carved in the bedrock. Some felt sure this had to be Saint Denis's final resting place. The discovery spurred the construction of a "downhill abbey" with the result that the "uphill abbey" was abandoned. All that remains is the Saint-Pierre church. The abbey was dismantled during the Reign of Terror and all trace of the martyrium was lost. In 1854, however, a Jesuit priest named Tournesac calculated the crypt's "probable" location. Abbot Le Rebours had a small oratory built over it in 1870. It was subsequently maintained by the sisters from the Society of the Helpers of the Holy Souls, charged with promoting the veneration of Saint Denis. The present-day chapel was consecrated on August 15, 1887. There remains but one antiquity at the site, a bas-relief dated 1252 depicting the martyrdom of Saint Denis.

FOR SO LITTLE

THE CHEVALIER DE LA BARRE STATUE
SQUARE NADAR / 18th
METRO: ANVERS, THEN THE FUNICULAR

For over half-century, the pedestal where the statue of Sir de La Barre had stood remained empty. Only an engraving paid homage to the young man executed for failure to salute a procession. The statue by Armand Bloch, melted down in 1941 by occupying German forces, was inaugurated in 1905 before some 25,000 people in front of the Sacré-Cœur.
In 1765, François-Jean Lefebvre de La Barre was a young man of 19. First accused of vandalizing a crucifix on a bridge in Abbeville (it was later discovered that the damage had been caused by a passing cart), some of the townsfolk then recalled that the young chevalier had neither knelt nor removed his hat as a procession went by. They immediately assumed that he was guilty of the vandalism. A search of his home turned up banned books such as Voltaire's *Philosophical Dictionary*. Damning evidence. Despite notable talents of the day rushing to his defense and widespread support, the Chevalier de la Barre was sentenced to be tortured, mutilated, decapitated, and ultimately, burned upon a pyre.
The case of this young man, a victim of rampant rumor, was taken up by free-thinkers of his day, and the public deemed that a statue to honor him would be a fitting monument to tolerance. With its air of an 18th-century Gavroche, hands thrust in his pockets, the new 2001 version by sculptor Emmanuel Ball is not to everyone's liking. The knights last words were, "I had no idea that a gentleman could be put to death for so little."

A MEDIEVAL LETTER

SAINT-PIERRE-DE-MONTMARTRE CHURCH
2 RUE DU MONT-CENIS / 18th
METRO: ANVERS THEN FUNICULAR

In the early 20th century, after the construction of the new Sacré-Cœur cathedral in Montmartre, the dilapidated Saint-Pierre-de-Montmartre church was slated for demolition. A preservation group stepped in and prevented the demolition of one of Paris's oldest churches. Dating as far back as the 12th century, it is also the sole vestige of the great Dames-de-Montmartre abbey.
In 1899, Sauvageot, an architect, launched efforts to save the crumbling structure.
In 1905, a worker made a marvelous discovery. Slipping his hand into a putlog hole, he felt several small objects. He pulled out a few broken pieces of glass, a dried out twig of boxwood, and a parchment leaf folded in four and covered with eight lines written in Gothic. Here is the translation: "Jehan of Gisors sends greetings to damsel Aelis of Lisle, as the woman whom he loves most in the word although it is not right [for him to have these feelings]. But know that truly he does love you, as one loves a sister, that you may trust him as one trusts one, or even two brothers, for the love of Sir Philip and for yours. And know that, truly, he would wish you no ill or would ever speak ill of you, any more than he would his own mother. Know that this letter was written in Belvaiz and that he who wrote it never received any favor whatsoever of you; he swears it before God. May God's grace be upon you."

Purists claimed it was a fraud. Newspapers derided it. And yet... A search through the archives confirms the existence of a certain Jean of Gisors, and we find further written evidence in the *Livres des Tailles*, dated 1293. The manuscript, a courtesy letter, was addressed to a Montmartre nun, and is now in the manuscript collection at the Bibliothèque Historique de la Ville de Paris.

APPROPRIATELY NAMED

FOLIE SANDRIN
22 RUE NORVINS / 18th
METRO: LAMARCK-CAULAINCOURT OR ANVERS THEN FUNICULAR

The word *folie* in French not only has all the meanings of folly in English, but also indicates a charming home generally immersed in greenery, like this 18th-century edifice built for Sir Sandrin. But here, the word is doubly appropriate as in 1805, Dr. Pierre-Antoine Prost turned the property into an insane asylum.
The avant-garde physician was an admirer of Pinel. Prost's therapeutic approach was based on a search for the real underlying causes of his patients' mental illness, causes "which must be tackled not by medicine alone, as moral treatment is often more efficacious than mere reliance on the medical arts."
Dr. Esprit Sylvestre Blanche, an asylum doctor, took over in 1820. Under his administration, the Montmartre mental hospital admitted rich and poor patients alike. His most famous pensioner was poet Gérard de Nerval, committed in 1841 after a fit of dementia. "The place I stayed at was located on a hill. It had large grounds, graced by precious trees. The pure air on the hilltop, the first wisps of springtime, and the sweetness of caring people, gave me many long, calm days... The view extending over the plain, offered delightful vistas from morning to evening, its graduated hues most pleasing to my imagination."

THE PLANTER'S SQUARE

SQUARE SUZANNE-BUISSON
7-BIS RUE GIRARDON / 18th
METRO: LAMARCK-CAULAINCOURT

This terraced city square, laid out in 1930, located behind the famous Château des Brouillards, is loved by neighborhood residents and tourists alike. A fountain offers us a reminder that, according to the hagiography, as Saint Denis headed out to the plain, he stopped here to wash his head which had been cut off on Montmartre. The original fountain, believed to be a spring of miraculously healing waters for "believers stricken by fever who come to stand at this fountain and drink of its waters," sank into a quarry pit.
In the early 20th century, this plot of land was tended to by an extraordinary man, a horticulturist named Godefroy-Lebeuf. In his greenhouses, he hardened a variety of exotic species to the local climate: coffee trees, tea shrubs, cacao trees, guava trees, palm trees, and rubber trees which he lovingly raised and shipped around the world. Some people even claim that Brazil's rubber trees actually originated in Montmartre.

MISTY ALLEY

CHÂTEAU DES BROUILLARDS
ALLÉE DES BROUILLARDS (RUE GIRARDON) / 18th
METRO: LAMARCK-CAULAINCOURT

The romantic Allée des Brouillards – a narrow street off Place des Quatre-Frères-Casadesus, giving access to Rue Girardon – is the focal point of the history of Montmartre. On the right-hand side, at the far end of a lawn, stands the delightful façade of the famous *Château des Brouillards* (Château of the Mist), in front of which countless artists have set up their easels.

In the 17th century, a small farm and a mill used to stand here, shrouded in mist on stormy days, hence the name. In 1764, a large, walled piece of land, including the dilapidated farmhouse and mill, was sold to a high judicial court advocate, who ordered the building of a fine residence, the *Maison des Brouillards* (House of the Mist). It used to be a pleasant country house complete with farmyard, orchard, cellars and wells. After a visit to this romantic château, poet Gerard de Nerval described it as "such a light structure! A small house in the style of Pompeii, something like the house of the ill-fated poet."

In 1850, after the outbuildings were demolished to make way for some small houses, one of which was occupied by painter Renoir, the château and its surroundings deteriorated considerably. Tramps and delinquents invaded the house, and shabby-looking shacks gradually encroached on its parkland, which eventually became the famous "*maquis*", so dear to the hearts of nostalgic Montmartre locals.

It was twenty years before the owner of the château – a fine name for what was not much more than a ruin – began to restore it, and took steps towards preserving it. In fact, at one point, the City of Paris was planning to do away with the alley and demolish the old house in order to establish a link between Rue Girardon and Rue Simon-Dereure. Fortunately, the *Château of the Mist* was saved from demolition, and is visited every year by people in love with Montmartre and in search of its rural, picturesque past.

THE OLDEST HOUSE IN MONTMARTRE

MONTMARTRE MUSEUM
12 RUE CORTOT / 18th
METRO: LAMARCK-CAULAINCOURT
Tel: 01 49 25 89 37
Open every day except Mondays from 11 AM to 6 PM

Montmartre museum has found shelter in the oldest house in Montmartre, at the top of the hill. The house escaped demolition thanks to architect Claude Charpentier, and restoration work began in 1958. Beyond the small shop overlooking Rue Cortot, a tree-lined road leads up to the entrance of the museum, a living shrine to the history of Montmartre. Located on the hillside, tradition has it that this pretty white house was bought by Claude de la Rose, also known as both Rosimond and Jean-Baptiste Dumesnil, in 1680. He was an actor in Molière's troupe, and, like the playwright, died on stage during a performance of *Le Malade Imaginaire* (The Imaginary Invalid).

In the 19th century, many artists lived and worked in the old house on Rue Cortot. In 1875, Auguste Renoir, in search of an atelier near the Moulin de la Galette, moved into two rooms under the roof and a lean-to on the ground floor. It was here that he painted some of his most famous paintings, such as *The Swing* or *Dance at the Moulin de la Galette*. Suzanne Valadon and her son, Maurice Utrillo, lived in the atelier, annex to the museum, on the second floor on the Rue Cortot side of the building.

Here, amid quarrels, broken dishes, and tears, Utrillo found the energy to paint when he was not under the influence of alcohol. Sketch artist Poulbot, painter Raoul Dufy, painter and engraver Démitrius Galanis, actor and theater director Antoine, and poet Pierre Reverdy were also occupants of the house on Rue Cortot.

Here, the fine collections of the Historical Society for Old Montmartre have found the home they deserve. Temporary exhibitions are held regularly, whereas some superb pieces of Clignancourt porcelain, together with historical reconstructions such as musician Gustave Charpentier's study, are permanently on view.

From the museum windows, there is an exceptionally beautiful view of the gardens and the vineyard, and, further down appears Paris shrouded in mist.

MOTHER NATURE IN PARIS

SAINT-VINCENT NATURE GARDEN
OPPOSITE 14 RUE SAINT-VINCENT / 18th
METRO: LAMARCK-CAULAINCOURT
Open Saturdays from 10 AM to 12:30 PM
and from 1:30 PM to 6:30 PM from April to October (6 PM in October)
For more information call: 01 71 28 50 56 (service Paris-Nature)

Overlooking Rue Saint-Vincent, the nature garden is all that remains of the forest of Montmartre. This little enclosure was laid out in 1985 by the City of Paris Parks and Gardens Department, which periodically opens the garden to the public, while making sure it retains its natural state. In order to recreate an area of natural parkland on a small scale, the Department had to consolidate the sloping land, lay out a path, and dig a pool.
This garden really is just as Mother Nature created it: not one tree nor bush has been planted by a gardener. The vegetation runs wild, and is untouched by human hand, except when it becomes necessary to protect it from the city environment. Annuals and plants which cannot grow in the shade or are unable to survive competition, gradually give way to the more resistant, woody or perennial species.
A large number of insects, small animals and birds find shelter in this miniature forest, and are barely disturbed by the garden's rare visitors. Naturalists are on hand to answer any questions the public may have about the garden's plant and animal life, offering a veritable lesson on the environment in the middle of Paris.

STOLEN ROSES

SAINT-VINCENT CEMETERY
6 RUE LUCIEN-GAULARD / 18th
METRO: LAMARCK-CAULAINCOURT
Open Monday to Friday from 8:00 AM to 5:30 from November 6 to March 15, and every day from 8:00 AM to 6 PM from March 16 to November 5

In addition to the cemetery on Avenue Rachel, Montmartre has another two lesser-known, but nevertheless very interesting, graveyards. The first, Calvaire Cemetery, adjoining Saint-Pierre de Montmartre Church, is open on All Saints' Day only, whereas the second, the little Saint-Vincent Cemetery, is much more accessible, and affords a superb view of the *Lapin Agile* cabaret, the vineyard, Montmartre Museum and, of course, the dome of the Sacré-Cœur, which you cannot fail to notice.
This modest enclosure is the final resting place – a kind of promised land – for the souls of Montmartre locals, after a life of sadness or happiness, more or less in the public eye. You will find the names of well-known Montmartre families, after whom streets have been named – Tourlaque, Labat, Muller, Lavigne, etc. A large number of celebrities are buried here: Émile Goudeau, founder and president of the Society of Hydropathy, writer Marcel Aymé, cabaret singer Gabriello, painters Maurice Utrillo, Gen Paul, Jules Adler, Eugène Boudin, actor Harry Baur, musicians Arthur Honegger and Désiré Inghelbrecht. Théophile Alexandre Steinlen, author of eloquent depictions of cats and human suffering, was laid to rest under a tree in the south-east corner of the cemetery.

Roland Dorgelès, a fine writer who became strongly attached to Montmartre, is also buried here. "Often," he wrote, "when a friend couldn't afford to buy a bunch of flowers for his girlfriend on her name day, he would slip into the old cemetery and filch a few roses from the flowers of a recent funeral." Those no longer in the land of the living could not really begrudge him this, since Montmartre, as everybody knows, is a favorite haunt for lovers.

FULL STEAM AHEAD

SQUARE LÉON-SERPOLLET
IMPASSE DES CLOŸS / 18th
METRO: JULES-JOFFRIN

This terraced square of over three and a half acres is framed by Rue du Ruisseau, Rue Marcadet, Rue Achille-Martinet, Rue Montcalm, Rue des Cloÿs and Impasse des Cloÿs. The series of construction phases kicked off in 1981 and was completed in 1996. The landscape artists planted the slope with alders, hornbeams, and crabapple trees. Aquatic plants, water lilies, and irises give the pond an old-fashioned grace. Curious white silhouettes advertise the presence of a neighborhood gym. In 1881, at number 25 Rue des Cloÿs, Léon Serpollet perfected his newly invented flash boiler. Six years later, a steam-powered three wheeler, an ancestor of the modern automobile, rolled out of his workshop. In 1890, Serpollet set out from Paris, making the first automobile trip ever, and reached Lyon fourteen days later. The following year, city officials issued him the first driver's license.

ARTISTS' QUARTERS

MONTMARTRE AUX ARTISTES
187-93 RUE ORDENER / 18th
METRO: JULES-JOFFRIN
Open to the public on National Heritage Site Days

Inside the beautiful brick building, a big entrance hall, whose walls are covered with brightly colored ceramics, leads to a complex of artists' ateliers. Sculptor Louis-Aimé Lejeune, along with a few friends, created a real-estate company, whose main objective was to provide decent accommodations for artists. At that time, the availability of housing of this nature was not sufficient to meet the enormous demand.
Adolphe Thiers drew the plans of the future complex, which was built in 1930.
It comprises three buildings containing 187 ateliers with very big windows, all facing north. There was something very attractive about the atmosphere in the courtyards, despite the plainness of the white walls dotted with rusty balconies. This was undoubtedly due to that special feeling of living on the outskirts of the city, while nevertheless remaining in close contact with it.
Adolphe Thiers accomplished a great deal in Montmartre, notably the ateliers at 36 Avenue Junot (very similar in layout to those in Rue Ordener), a house at 22 Rue Simon-Dereure, and two hotels at 24 and 26 Avenue Junot.

SWIMMING POOL OR CINEMA?

PISCINE DES AMIRAUX
13 RUE DES AMIRAUX / 18th
METRO: SIMPLON

What street could be more aptly named than *Rue des Amiraux* (Admirals' Street), where an imposing, white-tiled building, built by Henri Sauvage (1922-1927), stands like some majestic liner lying at anchor?
Built for the City of Paris, and originally intended as low-income housing, the structure is based on criteria already adopted by the architect at 26 Rue Vavin in the 6th arrondissement. The apartments are tiered, have terraces, and are extremely light. The outside walls are covered entirely with white tiles like those you see in the Metro.
The main issue concerned the decision on how the building's interior space, created by the unusual, tiered layout of its structure, could be usefully employed. Sauvage thought of turning it into a cinema, whereas the City of Paris wanted a swimming pool. Those who control the purse strings generally win... and the swimming pool is still open today.

AN AIR OF RUSSIA

SAINT-SERGE CHURCH
93 RUE DE CRIMÉE / 19th
METRO: LAUMIÈRE

A path – where an old vine creeps up the walls – leads to a small, colorful house, decorated with a fresco representing Saint Serge de Radogène. Turn right, and walk past some apartment buildings and a dilapidated wooden construction – formerly a Protestant dispensary and now a workshop for making church candles – until you see, at the top of some steps, Saint-Serge Church with its amazing wooden porch.

Built in 1861, this chapel was Protestant with an active congregation of Prussian immigrants until 1914, when it became Orthodox. The property belonged to the Germans, was requisitioned after World War I, and then sold by auction. In 1924, the Orthodox Church announced plans to buy it on July 18th, Saint Serge's day according to the Julian calendar. The influx of Russian emigrants fleeing the October Revolution had made it necessary to open a new religious center.

Between 1925 and 1927, Dimitri S. Stelletsky supervised the decoration work. The wooden porch and the outside stairway were added in 1925. Some representations of the defenders of the Orthodox faith before Russia was converted can be seen on the walls alongside the stairs leading into the church on the first floor.

The interior is splendid. Scenes from the Old Testament can be seen on the walls of the narthex: Noah's Ark, the Burning Bush, and the three adolescent boys in the blazing fire. Pictures of twelve saints, symbolizing Orthodox feast days, are painted on the walls of the nave. On the icon wall at the far end, Christ in majesty is represented, surrounded by the animal symbols of the Evangelists.

A VIEW
OVER PARIS

BUTTE BERGEYRE
RUE GEORGES-LARDENNOIS, RUE RÉMY-DE-GOURMONT, RUE EDGAR-POË, RUE PHILIPPE-HECHT / 19th
METRO: BOLIVAR

Before World War I, an amusement park with merry-go-rounds and sideshows stood on the spot where Rue Georges-Lardennois begins. "*Les Folles Buttes*", the name of the fair, has vanished, but Butte Bergeyre (Bergeyre Hill) with its attractive houses built in the 1920s and 1930s still flourishes.
The most charming feature of this unusual site, wedged between Avenue Simon-Bolivar and Avenue Mathurin-Moreau, is its atmosphere of a timeless, sleepy village in the country a long way out of the city, or perhaps it would be more accurate to say, a long way above the city, as anyone who has climbed the steps in Rue Barrelet-de-Ricou or clambered up winding Rue Georges-Lardennois will confirm! The character of the place certainly stems from its high altitude, and if you stand at the junction of Rue Georges-Lardennois and Rue Rémy-de-Gourmont, you will find yourself looking out over a beautiful panorama of the city of Paris, including an unusual view of the Sacré-Cœur.
Before coming down to earth in the busy avenues on either side, linger a while up here on the hill, and take a leisurely stroll along the tiny streets.

At right: rue Rémy-de-Gourmont
Below: rue Edgar-Poe

QUARRY GATES

BUTTES-CHAUMONT PARK / 19th
METRO: BUTTES-CHAUMONT

In 1862, Napoleon III commissioned an engineer named Alphand to create a landscaped city park on the site of old Buttes Chaumont gypsum quarries. While Davioud designed the park's conveniences and attractions, including the famous Temple of the Sibyl perched atop its rocky hillock, Alphand laid out five kilometers of walkways and a meandering stream. Once the technically difficult exploit of bringing in adult trees was accomplished, the new park gave the illusion of a venerable, old country estate. A lake was dug, and tons of soil were carted in to cover the bare, rocky, and clayey site.
Inaugurated during the 1867 universal exhibition, the new park was an instant

success with Parisians. It is still hugely popular. At the base of the waterfall beside the lake, are two wide cavities that create the illusion of a grotto. In fact, they are entrances to the old quarry galleries, cleverly disguised by Alphand.
After obstructing the entrance, he graced the ceiling with impressive (and entirely artificial) stalactites.

A PARADISE FOR LITTLE BOYS

THE FORMER MECCANO FACTORY
78-80 RUE RÉBEVAL / 19th
METRO: PYRÉNÉES

Rue Rébeval was once a country road leading to the Saint-Laurent district via Chemin de la Chopinette.
For the best view of this street, start at the Rue de Belleville end, and slowly walk down towards Boulevard de la Villette.
Before it became what was until recently the Paris-Belleville School of Architecture, the building on the left-hand side at nos. 78-80, with its extraordinary rounded, brick and freestone façade, used to house the Meccano factory workshops. Millions of little pieces of metal which inspired generations of budding mechanics were manufactured here.
In former times, Rue Rébeval had lots of small side streets giving access to Chaumont hill with its quarries and windmills. Cité Jandelle, which turns off at 55 Rue Rébeval, no doubt follows the track of one of those country paths.
The cul-de-sac itself is not very inviting; however, at the far end there are some old Belleville country houses, surrounded by greenery, which have been restored and painted in bright colors.

PHANTOM OF THE ADOUR

VILLA DE L'ADOUR
13-A RUE DE LA VILLETTE / 19th
METRO: JOURDAIN

Until 1877, Villa de l'Adour, a private street created in 1817, was called Villa Berthélemy, but it now bears the name of a river in southwestern France. This lovely, narrow passage offers a delightful stroll through greenery. It is one of a few magical spots in Paris that still exudes an air of village life near Paris in the old days. Old Belleville suddenly springs up here with its tiny individual homes, yards, and adventurous alley cats. Two architects restored an old industrial washhouse at number 3, preserving the tall, brick chimney. The painter Jérôme Mesnager added one of his ghostly silhouettes to it.

Villa Claude-Monet

"QUARRIES OF AMERICA"

THE MOUZAÏA DISTRICT
AREA SURROUNDING RUE DE MOUZAÏA AND RUE MIGUEL-HIDALGO / 19th
METRO: DANUBE

The picturesque area around Rue Miguel-Hidalgo and Rue de Mouzaïa, between Buttes-Chaumont Park and Square de la Butte-du-Chapeau-Rouge, makes a welcome change of scenery.
You can feel the atmosphere of the place as soon as you exit Danube metro station. Here, there are no high-rises, just buildings with one or two stories at the most. It looks as if a quiet corner of suburbia has been transplanted to the city. The light structure of the buildings is explained by the nature of the substratum: gypsum was quarried here from the Middle Ages right up to the 19th century.
It was long claimed that *Rue des Carrières-d'Amérique* (literally, the "Quarries of America", and now Rue Manin for most of its length) got its name from the export of plaster taken from Montmartre gypsum quarries to be shipped to places as distant as Louisiana. Reasonable doubt has been cast on this common idea since the work of a historian who established that the striking name given the area referred to a distant, inaccessible place, the "American dream" of many poor people. Nevertheless, according to an 18th-century voyager's diary, precious plaster of Paris was indeed loaded on boats bound for America.
The controversy remains unresolved.
When quarrying stopped in 1872, the unstable subsoil was not considered suitable for the reconstruction of the "America" district. Few people were willing to build on land riddled with holes.
The presence of a few shacks on barren mounds of earth was as far as city planning went in those days. However, it did make an excellent base for dropouts, pickpockets and criminals of all sorts.
When the entrances to the quarries were filled in, housing developments began very gradually to take shape along the main roads of the area, where people risked building small, brick or stone houses, fronted by tiny gardens full of rambling roses and ivy. They provided modest, but convenient, lodgings for factory workers on the east side of Paris. Life was good in the countryside around Paris, not far from Belleville and near Buttes-Chaumont. Today, the resident population of "*Américains*" has changed; most of the locals today quite obviously do not work factory shifts!
Wandering along these side streets produces an indefinable feeling of contentment. The simply built, colorful little houses, tucked away behind fences, are a captivating, cheerful sight, and, in spring, the fruit trees and flowers scent the air everywhere. No longer known as the "Quarries of America", the area gets its name – Mouzaïa – from a locality in Algeria.

SUCH A PRETTY VILLAGE...

RUE ÉMILE-DESVAUX AND RUE PAUL-DE-KOCK / 19th
METRO: TÉLÉGRAPHE

Located between Rue des Bois and Rue de Romainville, a small, attractive group of houses and small apartment buildings in Rue Émile-Desvaux and Rue Paul-de-Kock, dating back to the 1930s and reminiscent of the "Mouzaïa" area nearby [see p. 247], can be seen at the top of a slope.

The roads form a loop and are lined with imaginatively-built houses, which make the area look like a picturesque village in the middle of the 19th arrondissement. It is difficult to say which house is the most beautiful and the most original. An ancient pediment, a mosaic frieze, an attractively-designed window, a sweet-smelling rose tree, or even a roof terrace as in the case of Villa Koutok at 17 Rue Émile-Desvaux – each house has something to enchant visitors coming to this little "village" on the outskirts of the city.

Rue Émile-Desvaux

TELEGRAPH TOWER

THE HIGHEST POINT IN PARIS
40 RUE DU TÉLÉGRAPHE / 20th
METRO: TÉLÉGRAPHE

Situated at 40 Rue du Télégraphe, just beside the Belleville cemetery, is the highest point in Paris, which stands at 144.48 meters (474 ft.). While, today, high-rise buildings block the view from this vantage point, this was not always the case.
Physicist Claude Chappe was looking for land in Paris to verify the results of an initial experiment carried out in the Sarthe.
He also wanted to grab the government's attention. His brother introduced him to Louis Michel Le Peletier de Saint-Fargeau, a big landowner in Belleville. With permission granted, he set up his equipment on the spot of today's cemetery. It was a new invention: the telegraph. The semaphore system involved a set of blinds, which when pivoting vertically or horizontally, produced various figures that could transmit complex messages.
On July 12, 1793, a few sentences were exchanged between Belleville and the town of Saint-Martin-du-Tertre in the Val d'Oise. The experiment marked the advent of the telegraph, a valuable asset in wartime as it enabled the reliable transmission of information on troop movements.
The end of the semaphore line was later moved to the Louvre, with a relay tower on Saint-Pierre church in Montmartre.
But the network's fate fluctuated with political events and individual choices,

such as the time a Belleville inhabitant adamantly refused to trim a poplar tree, thus forcing the removal of the telegraph pole to Notre-Dame-des-Victoires!
As the Belleville telegraph was abandoned and fell into neglect, it was demolished in 1860.

CHARMING COTTAGE

VILLA CASTEL
16 RUE DU TRANSVAAL / 20th
METRO: COURONNES

Protected from the street by an iron gate that is not always padlocked, Villa Castel comprises about ten small, spick-and-span, red-brick houses fitted with old-fashioned awnings. This attractive, though modest group of buildings, erected in the late 19th century, has managed to survive in a part of Belleville where property developers are not in the habit of exercising restraint when putting their excavators to work. Unfortunately, the culs-de-sac along Rue des Envierges or Rue Piat have not been quite so lucky.

Saint-Martin chamber

BELLEVILLE WATER

SAINT-MARTIN WATER INSPECTION CHAMBER
42 RUE DES CASCADES / 20th
METRO: JOURDAIN
Other chambers: La Lanterne (213 Rue de Belleville)
Messiers (17 Rue des Cascades)
Roquette (36-38 Rue de la Mare)

The street names in the 19th and 20th arrondissements – Rue des Rigoles, Rue de la Mare, Rue de la Duée, Rue des Cascades (rivulets, pond, spring, waterfalls) – recall the countless springs that gushed forth in Belleville and its neighboring areas. As early as the 12th century, water "from the North" was collected for religious communities such as the Saint-Lazare Hospitallers and the Saint-Martin-des-Champs Priory on the right bank. Belleville watercourses were easy to drain, and, over the centuries, were exploited to meet the constantly increasing demand for water in Paris.
First of all, the water was directed along open channels, and then collected in dry-stone conduits, covered with slabs of stone and clay, leading to small inspection chambers, some of which can still be seen in the 20th arrondissement.
Near Place des Fêtes, in the 19th arrondissement, stands the handsome Lanterne chamber which used to be connected to a solid-looking aqueduct, of which there are only a very few remains today. This chamber – 4.70 meters wide and 8.80 meters high – is the biggest one of its kind still standing today. It was built between 1583 and 1613, and has an elegant dome with a lantern.
Another two inspection chambers of the Belleville aqueduct are still standing. At 17 Rue des Cascades, there is the Messiers chamber, whose name meaning "official crop watchers" recalls the occupation of rural policemen employed under the Ancien Régime to supervise the harvesting.
The Roquette chamber (38 Rue de la Mare) mainly supplied the Roquette Convent.
A large spring under Rue de Savies used to gush forth on a piece of steeply-sloping land belonging to Saint-Martin-des-Champs Abbey. It was drained, covered, the water collected in the Saint-Martin chamber (at 42 Rue des Cascades). It can be observed from the top of Rue de Savies. Built in 1804, this stone building has two drains for the water still flowing from the embankment behind it. As early as the 13th century, pipes carried water from here to the Temple and Saint-Martin-des-Champs. Saint-Martin water was also supplied to Hôtel Saint-Pol, the residence of the future King Charles V in the heart of the Marais. (For more information on Paris water supplies, see p. 177).

Messiers chamber

BUTTERFLIES IN THE CABBAGE PATCH

THE LEROY SÈME SHARED GARDEN
CITÉ LEROY, 315 RUE DES PYRÉNÉES / 20th
METRO: JOURDAIN
Open Saturdays from 2:30 to 5:30 PM and Sundays from 10 AM to 1 PM

This housing development was created in 1869 by a certain Mr. Leroy, a rubble-remover by trade. The occupants of the few humble homes that he built here shared a well and paid him a fee for use of the latrine ditch. A century later, pioneers of another sort began sharing the space.

Not too many years ago, these two dead-end streets joining in a fork rambled over a desolate, empty lot that was hidden behind a corrugated steel fence along Rue des Pyrénées, portending yet another real-estate development in the capital. In fact, a building permit for an apartment block of 130 units was filed in 1993, despite a 1980 ordinance declaring the zone as unsuitable for construction due to a series of landslides. Local residents banded together in the Cité Leroy to lobby against the development. After several years of endless meetings and discussions, including the presentation of a new construction plan, an agreement was reached in 2005 to turn the plot into a shared garden. It received the status of *espace vert intérieur protégé* (protected green space).

Should you pass by there on a nice day, you just might meet a botanist who will gladly explain the logic behind the shared garden. The garden is maintained year-round by volunteers. And their dedication shows. After the glum of winter, the garden springs back to life and, by May, is in full bloom. It is incredible but true, planting cabbage suffices to attract a whole family of butterflies to the heart of the 20th arrondissement.

AN ORPHANAGE IN PALLADIAN STYLE

PAVILLON CARRÉ DE BAUDOUIN
119-121 RUE DE MÉNILMONTANT / 20th
METRO: GAMBETTA

Recently restored by the City of Paris, the Pavillon Carré de Baudouin opens its doors to the public for special events. The front lawn is greatly appreciated by neighborhood residents. It is a lovely vestige of historic Ménilmontant "country homes," and a pleasant place for those who enjoy strolls through Paris.
In the mid 18th century, Nicolas Carré de Baudoin, a man "active in royal affairs," inherited this estate. Around 1771, he had the "lower" pavilion renovated and embellished by a peristyle with four Ionic columns. Consequently, Pierre-Louis Moreau-Desproux, the architect retained for the works, opted to give the façade a Palladian style, quite in vogue at that time.
After a series of subsequent owners, the property was purchased by the Daughters of Charity of Saint Vincent de Paul in 1857. The sisters founded an orphanage and erected the long edifice perpendicular to the older house.
Unfortunately, a tour of the interior is disappointing as nothing remains of the luxurious decors that graced these walls in the 18th century.

A LIGHT SHINES

MEMORIAL TO THE DEAD
PÈRE-LACHAISE CEMETERY
BOULEVARD DE MÉNILMONTANT / 20th
METRO: PÈRE-LACHAISE

Though much visited, Père-Lachaise cemetery offers an abundance of surprises to all visitors. Facing the main entrance, and at the end of the central drive, stands a monument dedicated to the dead. It is often overlooked by visitors. The nearly forgotten sculptor Gilbert Bartholomé spent eight years of his life completing this masterpiece.

Absorbing the spirit of the moment requires a certain time. Sadness, followed by a strange sensation of plenitude, engulfs the visitor. Ensconced in a hillside, and covered with Egyptian architectural motives, it dissembles the cemetery's ossuary, a vault which contains the remains of Parisians exhumed from their graves after the expiration of the "perpetual" contracts for their final resting place.

Shunning any grandiloquence, Bartholomé deliberately opted for an extremely sober depiction of the passage into the afterlife. On each side, nude women, men and children wait their turn. In the center of the composition is a couple; the woman's hand gently rests on her companion's left shoulder. On the level below them, a slender couple has been claimed by Death. The baby between them, also called away from the land of the living, serves as a reminder of how fragile our existence is. The discreet inscription behind them – *"Sur ceux qui habitaient le pays de l'ombre et de la mort, une lumière resplendit"* (a light shines on those who inhabited the land of shades and death) – hardly reassures the visitor.

In 1888, after the demise of his young wife, Bartholomé decided to create a funerary piece. During a first showing of fragments of his work in 1891, the public was greatly

moved by the simplicity of his pieces. In 1895, the show featured a scale model of the monument. On August 1st of the same year, the State and the City of Paris commissioned Bartholomé's stone monument. Bartholomé threw himself wholeheartedly into the project: "I renounce all other occupations. I see but one thing: my work has an ideal setting, and I accept your offer without any hesitation." Completing the work was a long, arduous task. It took not less than four years of work in an on-site shelter to give shape to the figures. On November 1st, 1899, over one hundred thousand Parisians discovered his chef-d'oeuvre. "People stood there hushed. They said not a word as they approached the monument [...] A staggering reward for my labor and pain, and I could wish for nothing more," Bartholomé stated. The recumbent effigy of the artist, who died in 1928, was chiseled on the right side of the monument by Bouchard, who placed beside the figure of the artist the tools from which these splendid figures were created. A fitting and moving evocation of the inevitable. Touching ordinary mementos and small bouquets are often laid here in memory of a dear one, a salute in their own small way to Bartholomé's secular work universally devoted to the dead.

JUSTICE!

MUR DES FÉDÉRÉS (WALL OF THE FEDERALISTS)
PÈRE-LACHAISE CEMETERY, AVENUE CIRCULAIRE, AND GROUP OF SCULPTURES,
SQUARE SAMUEL-DE-CHAMPLAIN / 20th
METRO: PÈRE-LACHAISE

There's no use examining this Père-Lachaise cemetery wall for bullet impacts. There are none. Yet, these smooth stones nevertheless bear witness to the massacre that occurred here on May 28, 1871 as troops from Versailles, and the two hundred federalists combating for the Commune met face to face in a final battle, dubbed *la semaine sanglante* (the week of bloodshed). The bodies of the last of the communards shot here were tossed in mass graves at the base of the wall. By All Saints' Day that same year, anonymous wreaths were already laid in their memory. Then, in 1880, the socialists called a rally beside the wall to be held on the last Sunday in May. For many years, this workers' demonstration was the only one of its kind permitted in Paris.

In Square Samuel-de-Champlain, is a sculpture near Avenue Gambetta that many people wrongly assume is the *Mur des Fédérés*. The bullet impacts on the stones have fueled popular belief that the stones were taken from the *Mur des Fédérés*. But it is only a legend.

Carved by Paul Paul Moreau-Vauthier, this piece was originally planned for the *Mur des Fédérés*, but the partisans of the Commune opposed the plan and the city of Paris preferred to calm everyone's nerves by erecting it outside the cemetery. Today, the spot is isolated indeed. The piece depicts a woman stretchings her arms wide to protect ghostly figures behind her. Dedicated to "the victims of all revolutions," it is engraved with Victor Hugo's mournful protest, "*Ce que nous demandons à l'avenir, ce que nous voulons de lui, c'est la justice. Ce n'est pas la vengeance.*" (What we ask of the future, what we expect of the future, is justice. Not revenge.)

TADPOLE POND

JARDIN NATUREL (NATURE GARDEN)
100-120 RUE DE LA RÉUNION / 20th
METRO: ALEXANDRE-DUMAS
Open Monday to Friday at 7:30 AM
(9 AM on weekends and holidays)
until sundown (between 5:30 and 10 PM)
For information on the park's many activities, call Paris-Nature at: 01 71 28 50 56

A highly unusual yet refreshing nature garden stretches northward from the end of Rue de la Réunion which ends at the foot of the massive wall of Père-Lachaise cemetery. Beneath the shade of the trees in these thick woods, an entire ecosystem lives and thrives.
The rustling of tree tops is only drowned out by the clamor of schoolchildren at recess from the nearby school. Formerly a wasteland of 6,500 square meters, the City converted into a park in the years 1994 to 1996. Over two hundred species of plants grow according to Nature's plan here – no insecticide, no herbicide, and only the intervention of gardeners attempting to create the illusion of a nature area.
A small pond, graced by reeds and waterlilies, is one of the most pleasant places in this garden. It is swarming with all sorts of life. First, circle the pond and appreciate the diversity of plants, then take the path uphill to reach the park's edge. Stand very still and quiet. Patience. Look down for your reward. Only inches away, the algae is disturbed by pointy, webbed feet. Red dragonflies buzz over the home of spotted newts, fresh-water shell fish (Lymnea), and water-striders (Gerridae), and a host of insects of all types. A shy croak, followed by a bolder croak, then an even louder croak, signal the presence of a frog on a waterlily. The countryside hidden deep inside Paris. Continue your exploring over dry and wet lands where weeds abound, where limestone juts out of the soil (reminders of the area's quarries actively exploited until

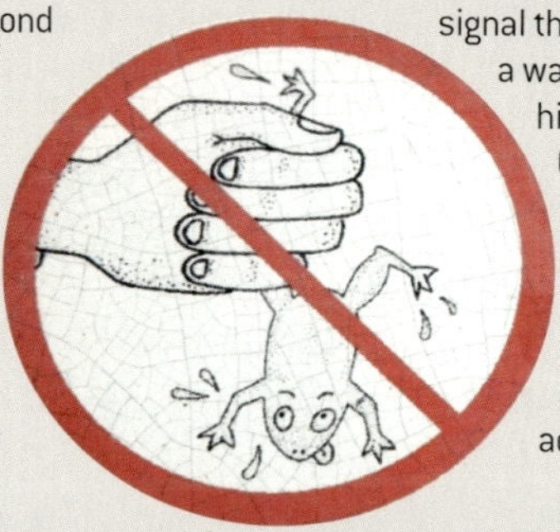

the 18th century). This land is a tribute to the once vast Domaine de Charonne. Metal plaques set into the ground will help you learn the names of the plants composing the undergrowth. In this paradise for birds, you can relax on a bench and enjoy an unending concert of birdsong. A robin or a black redstart may suddenly flutter out of its hiding place to escape the claws of one of the many neighborhood cats. The tabbies here do not only chase mice! Today's garden differs from yesterday's. Tomorrow's will be different still. The constant change is a good reason to return often. Jean-Jacques Rousseau often enjoyed wandering these heights, and wrote: "And from here, over footpaths through the vineyards and the meadows, I would go all the way to Charonne, through the delightful countryside separating the two villages. On my way back, I would cut through those same meadows, but each time chosing another path."

AN IMPOSTOR AND A DRINKER

CHARONNE CEMETERY
111 RUE DE BAGNOLET / 20th
METRO: GAMBETTA

The charming Saint-Germain-de-Charonne Church is the only church in Paris with an adjoining cemetery (except for Calvaire Cemetery in Montmartre: see p. 237). The small, country-like graveyard contains more than 650 tombs. The sons – killed in a car accident – of writer André Malraux are buried here, as is writer Robert Brasillach, sentenced to death and executed at the time of the Liberation in 1945. The latter wrote this about the cemetery: "[I love] this place where only trees and a country church tower are to be seen, and where the huge city with its tall buildings is lost from view."
At the far, left-hand side of the cemetery, a bronze statue of a dignified old man, wearing a cocked hat, stands on top of the tomb of a certain François-Éloy Bègue, known as "old Malgloire", and who liked to pass himself off as secretary to French revolutionary Robespierre. The truth of the matter was less spectacular: he was a house painter (1750-1838), enjoyed life, and drank a good deal. Legend has it that he was buried with a bottle of wine.
The statue has nothing to do with the deceased, since it was Malgloire's friend and landlord, Mr. Herbeaumont, a scrap metal merchant by profession, who unearthed it from some junkyard or other and put it on his tomb.
Once outside the cemetery, you will be able to savor the convivial atmosphere, often reminiscent of life in a village, of the streets in the Saint-Blaise district.

CHÂTEAUX IN THE 20TH ARRONDISSEMENT

PAVILLON DE L'ERMITAGE
148 RUE DE BAGNOLET / 20th
METRO: PORTE DE BAGNOLET

When Belleville was surrounded by countryside, the aristocracy and wealthy Parisians found it most attractive. There were rich country houses everywhere, not to mention sizable estates. However, the end of the 18th century proved fatal to most grand châteaux. Nothing remains of Château de Charonne, where cardinal Richelieu liked to stay, nor of Château de Bruyères, which belonged to Prince de Rohan. The same goes for the biggest château of all, Château de Ménilmontant, which extended over an area whose boundaries would have run along Rue de Romainville, Rue Pelleport, Rue du Surmelin, and out to Boulevard Mortier. Built in 1734, Pavillon de l'Ermitage escaped demolition and is all that remains of Château de Bagnolet, which used to belong to the Duchess of Orleans. The surface area of the estate is difficult to imagine today – eighty hectares comprising trees, thickets, and gardens with long avenues. A path, Allée de Madame, later to become Rue des Orteaux, was laid out in order to avoid the congestion in Rue de Bagnolet when coming to the estate. The splendors of this way of life did not last, and in 1769 the property was parceled out, deforested and sold by lots. In 1787, Baron de Batz-Lomagne bought the Pavillon de l'Ermitage for 36,000 pounds of silver. His residence soon became the headquarters for counter-revolutionaries, who attempted to save Louis XVI from his tragic fate (he was guillotined in 1793). On June 17th, 1794, the fifty-four "Charonne conspirators" were guillotined on Place du Trône. Their leader was nowhere to be found... but was later awarded the Order of Saint Louis in 1823. You will appreciate the subtle quality of rear façade of the pavilion from the Debrousse public garden.

COUNTRYSIDE IN CENTRAL PARIS

RUE JULES-SIEGFRIED, RUE IRÉNÉE-BLANC (AND SURROUNDING AREA) / 20th
METRO: PORTE DE BAGNOLET

Several flights of steps lead up to the attractive housing development, *La Campagne à Paris* (Country in Paris), perched high up, almost a hundred meters, above Porte de Bagnolet metro station nearby.
A leisurely walk down Rue Irénée-Blanc and Rue Jules-Siegfried will give you a chance to examine the 89 two-storied houses lining these twisting, village-like streets. Built in brick or burrstone, the neat little houses, fronted by tiny yards full of greenery and graced with small back gardens, are very much sought after by Parisians. Many of the residents are descendants of the founders of the development. Back in 1906, buying this wasteland, and building a small, low-income housing development on it, must have been a matter of trusting to luck. Some people had such faith in the project that they founded the *Campagne à Paris* company, and bought 15,800 square meters (4 acres) of land that nobody wanted. The substratum was unstable – a former gypsum quarry – and had been hastily filled in with rubble recuperated from the building of Avenues Gambetta and de la République.
Despite this, eight shareholders began building their houses, and, in 1913, thirty-eight others followed suit.
The development was finally inaugurated on June 20th, 1926, and the founders were congratulated for their tenacity.

At left: Rue Irénée-Blanc
Below: Rue Paul-Strauss

BIBLIOGRAPHY

- Benton (Tim), *Les Villas de Le Corbusier,* Paris, Philippe Sers, 1984.
- Braire (Jean), *Sur les traces des communards. Guide de la Commune dans le Paris d'aujourd'hui*, Paris, Les Amis de la Commune, 1989.
- Brassart (Isabelle), Cuvillier (Yvonne), *Le Guide du promeneur, 4ᵉ arrondissement*, Paris, Parigramme, 1993.
- Chadych (Danielle), *Le Guide du promeneur, 12ᵉ arrondissement*, Paris, Parigramme, 1995.
- Chadych (Danielle), Leborgne (Dominique), *Le Guide du promeneur, 18ᵉ arrondissement*, Paris, Parigramme, 1996.
- Châteaureynaud (Georges-Olivier), *Une petite histoire de la Société des Gens de Lettres de France*, Paris, SGDL, 1994.
- Chemetov (Paul), Marrey (Bernard), *Architectures à Paris, 1848-1914*, Paris, Dunod, 1985.
- Claval (Florence), *Le Guide du promeneur, 15ᵉ arrondissement*, Paris, Parigramme, 1994.
- Colin-Bertin (Françoise), *Le Guide du promeneur, 7ᵉ arrondissement*, Paris, Parigramme, 1995.
- Collectif, *Le 20ᵉ arrondissement, la montagne à Paris*, Paris, Action artistique de la Ville de Paris, Archives de Paris, 1999.
- Colson (Jean), Lauroa (Marie-Christine) [dir.], *Dictionnaire des monuments de Paris*, Paris, Hervas, 1992.
- Crosnier Leconte (Marie-Laure), *Le Guide du promeneur, 16ᵉ arrondissement*, Paris, Parigramme, 1995.
- Dansel (Michel), *Paris incroyable*, Paris, Hachette, 1989.
- Delorme (Jean-Claude), *Les Villas d'artistes à Paris*, Paris, Les Éditions de Paris, 1987.
- Dérens (Isabelle), *Le Guide du promeneur, 3ᵉ arrondissement*, Paris, Parigramme, 1994.
- Duclert (Ariane), *Le Guide du promeneur, 10ᵉ arrondissement*, Paris, Parigramme, 1996.
- Dreyfuss (Bertrand), *Le Guide du promeneur, 5ᵉ arrondissement*, Paris, Parigramme, 1996.
- Dreyfuss (Bertrand), *Le Guide du promeneur, 6ᵉ arrondissement*, Paris, Parigramme, 1994.
- Dubois (Anne-Marie), *Le Guide du promeneur, 20ᵉ arrondissement*, Paris, Parigramme, 1993.
- Gady (Alexandre), *Le Marais. Guide historique et architectural*, Paris, Carré, 1994.

- Housieaux (Pierre), Poulle (Yvonne), *À la découverte de la maison du fontainier*, Paris, Association pour la Sauvegarde et la Mise en valeur du Paris historique, Notre-Dame-de-Joye, 1995.
- Joannis (Claudette), *Les Petits Métiers des jardins publics*, Paris, Christine Bonneton, 1977.
- Lambeau (Lucien), *Histoire des communes annexées à Paris en 1859 : Charonne*, 2 tomes, Paris, Ernest Leroux, 1916 et 1921.
- Langlois (Gilles-Antoine), *Le Guide du promeneur, 13e arrondissement*, Paris, Parigramme, 1996.
- Leborgne (Dominique), *Le Guide du promeneur, 2e arrondissement*, Paris, Parigramme, 1995.
- Michel (Denis), Renou (Dominique), *Le Guide du promeneur, 11e arrondissement*, Paris, Parigramme, 1993.
- Minnaert (Jean-Baptiste) [dir.], *Le Faubourg Saint-Antoine, architecture et métiers d'art*, Paris, Action artistique de la Ville de Paris, 1998.
- Moulin (Jacques), Ponsot (Patrick), "La Chapelle de la Vierge à l'abbaye de Saint-Germain-des-Prés", in *Archéologia*, n° 140, mars 1980.
- Philipp (Élisabeth), *Le Guide du promeneur, 19e arrondissement*, Paris, Parigramme, 1994.
- Pouillon (Fernand), *Mémoires d'un architecte*, Paris, Seuil, 1968.
- Procès-verbaux de la Commission municipale du Vieux Paris.
- Pronteau (Jeanne), "Note… sur une borne limite de Paris", in *Procès-verbal de la Commission du vieux Paris*, 14 décembre 1987.
- Sorel (Philippe), *Le Guide du promeneur, 8e arrondissement*, Paris, Parigramme, 1995.
- Trouilleux (Rodolphe), *Le Guide du promeneur, 17e arrondissement*, Paris, Parigramme, 1995.

CONTENTS

1st arrondissement

Telescoping street lights on Pont du Carrousel, **8**
Vestiges of the fleur-de-lis, Comédie-Française, **9**
Bœuf à la mode restaurant, **10**
Double spiral staircase, rue de Valois, **11**
Colonne Médicis, astrologer's tower, **12**
Gargoyles, Saint-Germain-l'Auxerrois Church, **13**
Commemorative Plaque and bust of Molière, **14**
Former Innocents Cemetery, **15**
Signs, rue Montorgueil, **16**

2nd arrondissement

Au Rocher de Cancale restaurant, **17**
Jean sans Peur Tower, **18**
Vidocq staircase in Galerie Vivienne, **19**
Studios of Nadar the photographer, **20**
Bas-reliefs, rue Réaumur, **21**
Passage du Caire, **22**
Ramparts of Charles V, Passage Sainte-Foy, **23**
Hôtel de Saint-Chaumond, **24**

3rd arrondissement

Cariatids, rue Réaumur, **25**
Conservatory of Arts and Crafts, **26**
Cariatid, rue de Turbigo, **27**
Rue de la Corderie, **28**
Théâtre Déjazet, **30**
Saint-Gilles-Grand-Veneur Garden, **31**
Library of the Amis de l'Instruction, **32**
Square Georges-Cain and Carnavalet – History of Paris Museum, **33**
Impasse des Arbalétriers, **34**
Fontaine du Chaume, **35**
Grotesques, rue Rambuteau, **36**
Nicolas Flamel's House, **37**
Doorway to the linen merchants' guild, **38**

4th arrondissement

Saint-Jacques Tower, **39**
Vaults of the Châtelet métro station, **40**
Café de la Gare, **41**
Jacques Cœur's House, **42**
Rue du Trésor, **43**
Vestiges of the Bastille fortress, **44**
Wall of Philip Augustus, **45**
Hôtel de Sens, Forney Library, **46**
Saint-Gervais-Saint-Protais Elm Tree, **47**
House of Héloïse and Abelard, **48**
Mock medieval house, **49**
Rue Chanoinesse, **50**
Zero Kilometer Marker for French highways, **51**

5th arrondissement

Saint-Séverin Charnel House, **52**
Salvador Dalí's Sundial, **53**
Sign, rue Galande, **54**
Old College des Bernardins, **55**
Bièvre river crossing vestiges, Post office, **56**
Lutetia Arenas, **57**
Mosque of Paris, **58**
Rock Garden in Le Jardin des Plantes, **60**
Former Horse Market, **62**
Hôtel Scipion, **63**
Old seminary of the thirty-three, **64**
Saint-Étienne-du-Mont rood screen, **65**
Rue Saint-Jacques (former rue des Marionnettes), **66**

6th arrondissement

School of Mines and Mineralogical Museum, **67**
Carousel, Luxembourg gardens, **68**
Zadkine Museum, **69**
Philippe de Vendôme's Mansion, **70**
Chapel of the Priests of the Lazarist Mission, **71**
Saint-Joseph-des-Carmes, **72**
Saint-Sulpice Church Gnomon, **73**
Saint-Sulpice Church Crypt, **74**

Former brothels, **75**
Revolutionary meter, **76**
Auguste Comte's home, **77**
Refectory of the former Cordelier Convent, **78**
Former School of Medicine, **80**
Cour de Rohan, **81**
Square Laurent-Prache, **82**
École des Beaux-Arts, **83**

7th arrondissement

Chocolaterie Debauve et Gallais, **84**
Former Protestant cemetery, **85**
Glass House, **86**
Square Roger-Stéphane, **87**
Chapelle de la Médaille-Miraculeuse, **88**
Industrial site, rue Oudinot, **89**
Hôtel Desmares and former country home, **90**
Hôtel des Invalides, **91**
Lavirotte architecture, **92**

8th arrondissement

René Lalique's home, **93**
Chapelle Notre-Dame-de-la-Consolation, **94**
Élysées Ceramic Hotel, **95**
Loo's house, **96**
Hôtel Menier, **98**
Monceau Park, **99**
Nissim de Camondo Museum, **100**
Chapel of Atonement, Square Louis XVI, **102**
Poster, rue Royale, **103**
La Madeleine public toilets, **104**

9th arrondissement

Fragonard Perfume Museum and Théâtre des Capucines Museum, **105**
Old steam baths, **106**
Société Générale Bank, **107**
Animal frieze on the old Maison d'Or, **108**
Square d'Orléans, rue Taitbout **109**
Dosne-Thiers Library and Hôtel de la Païva, Place Saint-Georges, **110**
Academy of billiards, **111**
Cité Malesherbes, **112**
Viollet-le-Duc building, **113**
Cité Napoléon, **114**

10th arrondissement

Art nouveau façades, rue d'Abbeville, **115**
The old Saint-Lazare prison, **116**
Tiniest house in Paris, **117**
Hôtel Gouthière, **118**
Hôtel du Nord, **119**
Saint-Louis Hospital, **120**

11th arrondissement

Maison des Métallos, **121**
Clown Bar, **122**
Le Bataclan theater, **124**
Cour du Coq, **125**
Cabinetmaker's shop, **126**
Cour Damoye, **127**
Passage du Cheval-Blanc, **128**
Passage Lhomme, **129**
Bistrot du peintre, **130**
Sainte-Marguerite Church, **131**
Notre-Dame-de-Bon-Secours and La Madeleine de Tresnel Convents, **132**
Site of the guillotine, rue de la Croix-Faubin, **133**
Dr. Belhomme's Home, **134**
Workshops, rue Titon, **135**
Rue des Immeubles-Industriels, **136**

12th arrondissement

Picpus Cemetery, **137**
Culs-de-sac off rue de Reuilly, **138**
Aligre-Beauvau market **139**
Lenoir market wash house, **140**
Cour du Bel-Air, **141**
Rue Crémieux, **142**
Parc de Bercy, **143**
Notre-Dame de Bercy, **144**
Bastion no. 1, Boulevard Poniatowski, **145**
Paris boundary marker, rue de Charenton, **146**
Saint-Esprit Church, **147**
Bois de Vincennes Buddhist Center, **148**
Georges-Ville farm, **149**
Pyramid in the Bois de Vincennes, **150**

13th arrondissement

Villa Planeix, **151**
Pitié-Salpêtrière Hospital, **152**
Temple du Droit Humain, **153**
Orangery, rue des Gobelins, **154**
White Queen's castle, **155**
Vestiges of the Cordelières Convent, **156**
Former Convent of English Nuns, **157**
Square René-Le Gall, **158**
Antoinist Temple, **159**
Square des Peupliers and rue Dieulafoy, **160**
Cité Florale, **161**
Villa and cité Daviel [Little Alsace], **162**

14th arrondissement

Meridian marker in Parc Montsouris, **163**
Cité Universitaire Internationale, **164**
Square de Montsouris, **166**
Villa Seurat, **168**
Villa d'Alésia, **169**
Rue and Villa Hallé, **170**
La Rochefoucauld Hospice, **171**
The last of Paris' old-fashioned public urinals, **172**
Hôtel de Massa, **173**
Celebrated homes on rue Cassini, **174**
Port-Royal cloister, **175**
Turncock's House, **177**
Passage d'Enfer, **178**
Montparnasse artists' studios, **179**
Montparnasse Cemetery, **180**
The Windmill of Charity, Montparnasse Cemetery, **181**
Notre-Dame-du-Travail Church, **182**
Rental property, rue Raymond-Losserand, **183**
Plaisance district, **184**

15th arrondissement

Rue and Villa Santos-Dumont, **185**
La Ruche, **186**
Square Vergennes, **187**
Pasteur Museum, **188**
Art Alley, chemin du Montparnasse, **189**
Le Bal Nègre, **190**
Saint-Séraphin-de-Sarrow Church, **191**
Sainte-Rita Church, **192**
Square Violet, **193**
Saint-Christophe-de-Javel Church, **195**
Le Paquebot, **196**

16th arrondissement

Villa Mulhouse, **197**
Hameau Boileau, **198**
Home of the Goncourt Brothers, **199**
Greenhouses of Auteuil, **200**
Le Corbusier Foundation, **202**
Rue Mallet-Stevens, **203**
Castel Béranger, **204**
Auteuil Foundation, **206**
Villa Beauséjour, **207**
Balzac's House, **208**
Wine Museum, **209**
Clemenceau Museum, **210**
Square Lamartine fountain, **211**
Panthéon bouddhique, **212**
Arc de Triomphe Flame, **213**

17th arrondissement

Château des Ternes, **214**
Notre-Dame-de-la-Compassion Chapel, **215**
Sainte-Odile Church, **216**
Hauts-de-Malesherbes gardens, **217**
Sarah Bernardt's former home, **218**
Hôtel Gaillard, **219**
Cité des Fleurs, **220**
Cour Saint-Pierre, **221**

18th arrondissement

Villa des Arts, **222**
Tomb of Alphonsine Plessis, Montmartre Cemetery, **223**
Cité Véron, **224**
Impasse Marie-Blanche, **225**
Montmartre maquis, **226**
Outdoor staircase, rue Durantin, **227**
Saint-Jean-de-Montmartre Church, **228**
Crypt of the Martyrium, **229**
Chevalier de La Barre statue, **230**
Saint-Pierre-de-Montmartre Church, **231**
Folie Sandrin, **232**
Square Suzanne-Buisson, **233**
Château des Brouillards, **234**
Montmartre Museum, **235**
Saint-Vincent nature garden, **236**
Saint-Vincent Cemetery, **237**
Square Léon-Serpollet, **238**
Montmartre aux Artistes, **239**
Swimming pool, rue des Amiraux, **240**

19th arrondissement

Saint-Serge Church, **241**
Butte Bergeyre, **242**
Buttes-Chaumont Park, **244**
Meccano factory, **245**
Villa de l'Adour, **246**
The Mouzaïa district, **247**
Rue Émile-Desvaux and rue Paul-de-Kock, **248**

20th arrondissement

Highest point in Paris, **249**
Villa Castel, **250**
Saint-Martin water inspection chamber, **251**
Leroy Sème shared garden, **252**
Pavillon Carré de Baudouin, **253**
Memorial to the Dead, Père-Lachaise Cemetery, **254**
Mur des Fédérés, Père-Lachaise Cemetery, group of sculptures in Square Samuel-de-Champlain, **255**
Nature garden, **256**
Charonne Cemetery, **258**
Pavillon de l'Ermitage, **259**
La Campagne à Paris, **261**

Being from Paris does not
necessarily mean having seen
the light of day there
– but seeing each day in
a renewed clear light

SACHA GUITRY

EDITOR : Laurence Solnais

GRAPHIC DESIGN : Isabelle Chemin

LAY-OUT : Nota Bene

COPY EDITING : David Heath

PHOTOGRAPHS : © Jacques Lebar
www.jacqueslebar.com
www.parimages.com

PHOTOENGRAVING : Alésia Studio, Sèvres
Printed by Mame in Tours, April 2009

DÉPÔT LÉGAL : May 2009
ISBN : 978-2-84096-573-2